Asheville-Buncombe
Technical Community College
Learning Resources Center
340 Victoria Road
Asheville, NC 28801

DISCARDED

JUN 2 2025

DISCARDED

Safe As Houses

Also by Sam Jaffa and published by Robson Books

Maxwell Stories

Safe As Houses

*The Schemers and Scams
Behind Some of the World's
Greatest Financial Scandals*

Sam Jaffa

Robson Books

First published in Great Britain in 1997 by Robson Books Ltd, Bolsover House, 5–6 Clipstone Street, London W1P 8LE

Copyright © 1997 Sam Jaffa

The right of Sam Jaffa to be identified as author of this work has been asserted by him in accordance with the Copyright, Designs and Patents Act 1988

British Library Cataloguing in Publication Data
A catalogue record for this title is available from the British Library

ISBN 1 86105 070 4

All rights reserved. No part of this publication may be reproduced, stored in a retrieval system, or transmitted in any form or by any means, electronic, mechanical, photocopying, recording or otherwise, without the prior permission in writing of the publishers.

Typeset in Sabon by Columns Design Ltd., Reading
Printed in Great Britain by St Edmundsbury Press, Bury St Edmunds, Suffolk

To my Aunties Betty and Helen Rakusen, my wife Celia and wonderful children, Lewis, Lucy and Torquil.

Acknowledgements

I would like to thank the following for their help in producing this book: Gill Steene for her support whilst I was in America; Chris Leach, the librarian at the University of Humberside for some extra research he did for me and to my good friend Margaret Cole who glanced at the final manuscript.

Contents

	Introduction	1
1	The South Sea Bubble	5
2	The Reverend Doctor Dodd	21
3	Rothschild to the Rescue	24
4	Overend & Gurney	31
5	The Barings Banking Crisis	38
6	Barings Finally Fails	44
7	Ivar Kreuger	67
8	Horatio Bottomley	81
9	John Poulson	108
10	Banco Ambrosiano, the Vatican Bank	125
11	Savings and Loan	129
12	'Greed Is All Right …'	143
13	Barlow Clowes	168
14	The Hong Kong Stock Exchange	179
15	The Recruit Scandal	182
16	The Guinness Affair	184
17	The Robert Maxwell Affair	207
18	BCCI	235

19	Japan	264
20	Sagawa Kyubin	271
21	Asil Nadir	277
22	The Case of New Era Philanthropy	288
23	Daiwa	296
24	Sumitomo Corporation	307
25	Miscellaneous Mischief	312

Introduction

What is a financial scandal? It is a question that has exercised the minds of many in business ever since the heady days of the 1980s – when a quick buck seemed to be easy to make, and super-rich entrepreneurs flaunted their wealth. In some countries, Britain amongst them, there has always been a feeling that 'new' money was somehow to be disdained. In America, a contrary view seemed to hold sway, namely that what mattered was not so much how wealth was acquired, but that everyone should seem to have an equal chance of making it. But in the late eighties, as the economic climate changed, so too did people's perception of wealth creation. The public seemed to want vengeance against those who had made or were making fortunes, almost as if in some way they blamed them when the bubble burst, when interest rates went up, when borrowing became more expensive – in short, when recession bit. It was against this background that some celebrated trials of fortune-makers took place. The people wanted someone to pay, and to be made to pay in public. So in America Ivan Boesky was prosecuted, in Britain the Serious Fraud Office was set up and the first Guinness trial took place. But in the last weeks of December 1994 questions were being asked about the sentences imposed upon the four men convicted in the first Guinness trial. Though their appeal was later rejected, the fact that it came before the courts was in itself a sign that the pendulum of public opinion was swinging back. Blood was no longer being demanded by those who had not made huge fortunes in the 1980s from those who had, and it appeared that ordinary folk were beginning to consign those days to history. This is partly because the events that led to such court cases have receded into the past and the public outcry at the time is no longer so keenly felt, and partly because of that unresolved question: What is a financial scandal?

The fact is that, in the leading business markets of the world in the late 1990s, questions are being asked about the most effective means with which to deal with fraud, the main manifestation of financial misdeeds. In Britain, until recently, a view strongly held – by many businessmen and women, at least – was that self-regulation, in effect a closed trial by the business community, was the best way of handling such matters. This was a very British response, the view that if a chap does something wrong then the best thing to do is throw him out of the club. In other words, the loss of his contacts, of his ability ever to work in financial circles again, are the most effective sanctions against wrongdoing. Advocates of this view suggest that it is cheaper and more effective than court cases lasting many months and costing taxpayers millions of pounds or tens of millions of dollars. There is something to be said for this view, though opponents counter by asking how then can the public be sure that justice is being done? And why should a very rich businessman be able to swindle millions of pounds, possibly ruin thousands of lives, and yet get away without going to prison, when an ordinary burglar may suffer a custodial sentence simply for breaking and entering with intent to steal? Behind the attitude of many apologists for fraudsters lies the notion that somehow within 'white-collar crime' there exists the victimless crime, a notion quashed by the judge in the first Guinness trial.

There is nothing new about financial scandals. Dickens used contemporary real-life examples as backgrounds for his fictional villains, and the time trail stretches further back than that. But in the computer age, with financial transactions taking place across the globe as quickly as it takes one terminal to 'talk' to another, the dividing line between what is illegal and what is unethical has sometimes been drawn very fine. It is, in any case, the sort of line that many people might be tempted to cross when there are riches beyond the dreams of avarice as a reward for success. And if they were not tempted, and if they did not occasionally cross that line, then there would be no book for me to write!

1

The South Sea Bubble – The first financial scam?

Quite certainly, there have been financial scams ever since money was invented, but the South Sea Bubble is probably the best known example of what can happen when 'investment opportunities' go badly wrong. The scandal took place against the background of the continuing war between England and France in the early 1700s. During the winter of 1710–11, London finance houses began to press the Government for repayment of a £4 million loan to the Navy. The newly appointed Chancellor of the Exchequer, Robert Harley, turned to his own advisers in an attempt to find a way of softening the effect upon the Government of such a massive repayment. One of those men was Sir John Blunt, secretary to the Sword Blade Bank, who, with Sir George Caswall, one of the partners in the bank, and Sir Ambrose Crowley, one of the biggest contractors with the Navy Board, hit upon a plan by which the Government's debts would in effect be cancelled in return for an equivalent amount of stock. The Government's short-term creditors, holding debts of nearly £9 million, were to be incorporated as 'the Governor and Company of Merchants of Great Britain Trading to the South Seas and other parts of America and for encouraging the Fishery'. In reality this meant an exclusive charter to trade with South America – the company was to have a monopoly of trade with the east coast from the River Orinoco to Tierra del Fuego, and of the whole of the west coast. What wasn't quite as clear was how this trade was to be carried out, given Spain's jealous guardianship of her domination of the region; furthermore, Spain was France's ally in the continuing War of the Spanish Succession, as it came to be called.

The idea was at first sold to the public because of the belief in riches beyond the dreams of greed that always accompanied any notion of going to the New World, where, it was thought, any link with commerce was bound to bring rich returns. To add fuel to this idea, the general public were informed that Spain would concede four fortified towns on the American mainland, which could be used by the company as trading bases. When the Government was forced to give up this claim in October 1711, under Franco-Spanish pressure, the company itself formed plans to seize a town or two by force; indeed, it even appointed a date for the departure of the expedition – 26 June 1712. But with the British Government committed to peace, all this talk of violence was just so much hot air. In March 1713 a treaty between Britain and Spain was signed in Madrid which clearly defined the new company's rights. The deal was not a good one. The claim for fortified towns was dropped; in its place the company was to establish unfortified factories. It was also given permission to send a 500-ton ship once a year to trade at the fairs of Cartagena and Veracruz, and ships of 150 tons could be sent to supply the factory sites. The King of Spain was to receive 28 per cent of all trading profits. In addition, the company was assigned for a thirty-year term the rights to supply New Spain with African slaves, delivering 4,800 every year, and paying tax on 4,000 of them, as well as 10 per cent of all profits to the King of Spain. In the final draft agreement, dated November 1713, a clause was included giving the British monarch, Queen Anne, a $22\frac{1}{2}$ per cent share in profits. Under pressure from the company, the Queen ceded this back in June 1714, a month before her death.

The newly crowned King, George I, faced the problems of the huge cost of recent wars. The War of the Spanish Succession had added nearly £35 million to the long-term debts already incurred, and there was a further £11 million in short-term debts to the Bank of England and the South Sea Company. This was almost a third of total Government expenditure. Besides these funded debts there were lesser but still important ones – nearly £5 million in Exchequer bills, arrears of army pay and foreign subsidies. Clearly, something had to be done, and reducing the national debt became a priority. Two succeeding First Lords of the Treasury, the Earl of Halifax and then the Earl of Carlisle, devised and implemented plans which went some way towards rationalizing the debt and paying it back at lower, and therefore more favourable, rates of interest. In June 1715 Carlisle put forward a plan to settle the large arrears of interest due to the South Sea Company. Negotiations continued until August, when an agreed bill was introduced into Parliament (no company in those days was supposed to operate without a Royal Charter). The company's capital was to be increased by a little over £822,000 to a round £10 million. Carlisle had made some headway when he handed over to Robert Walpole in October 1715. The thirty-nine-year-old who succeeded Carlisle as First Lord of the Treasury still faced several important problems. The bulk of the redeemable national debt still carried interest at more than 6 per cent, though the maximum for private individuals was by now only 5 per cent. It looked as though £1 million was payable for army debts, and there was the delicate question of the irredeemable annuities, it being common practice in the eighteenth century for lenders to advance money to the Government in return for a tax-free annuity payable, for example, over the course of their lives.

Fundamental to Walpole's plan was that Government creditors were to be asked to accept the common rate of interest, knowing that their deposits would be even more secure than the alternatives. In the King's Speech on 20 February 1717 a Committee of the whole House of Commons was ordered to consider the problems. Under the chairmanship of William Farer and with Walpole's guidance fourteen resolutions were agreed upon. The redeemable part of the national debt, including debts to the South Sea Company and the Bank of England, were to be repaid or reduced to an interest rate of 5 per cent. Those holding long and short annuities were to be offered the choice of exchanging their terms of years for redeemable stock. There were other measures, but only one of them was ever put into practice, because Walpole resigned in mid-April 1717. However, in June of that year new proposals – largely based on Walpole's ideas – were put to the House, but with one very important change of policy: they dealt only with redeemable debts, and omitted any reference to the annuities. This omission from the legislative process was probably a wise move, given that those holding annuities were reluctant to let the Government off the hook, not least because it gave the rest of the proposals for reducing the national debt a greater chance of success. The problem of the annuities was not to be taken up again until 1719–20.

The measures taken between 1715 and 1719 had therefore solved all the Government's main problems resulting from the war except the most difficult one – the high interest payable to the annuitants for years into the future. Before anything could be done about this, or so the theory was now put forward, those holding annuities had to be persuaded to part with them.

The stimulus for the South Sea Company's scheme to transfer the national debt came from France where, since 1716, the Scottish exile (he had killed a man in a duel, for which he had been sentenced to death) and exponent of monetary reform, John Law, was economic guru in residence; indeed, in that same year, with his brother, he had established the first bank in France, and later he was to be Controller-General of French finance. He hoped to pay off French Government debt by encouraging creditors to exchange their notes for shares in the rapidly appreciating Compagnie des Indes, of which Law was a founder. The plan was launched in October 1719, new shares being created as required. The British Government watched the French scheme closely, but at about that time the fortunes of the South Sea Company were stuck in the doldrums, the renewal of war with Spain in 1718 having cut the company off from its trade with the New World. Nor was the outlook good. The company's trade with Spanish America, of which such high hopes had been entertained, seemed likely to be more of a liability than an asset. There was no rich seam of trade to tap into as there was with the East India Company or John Law's Compagnie des Indes. But perhaps, or so the directors thought, a scheme to ease the national debt might provide the company with a lifeline. So it was that discussions began between the Government and the directors of the South Sea Company. Those most intimately involved included, on the Government side, John Aislabie, the Chancellor of the Exchequer, James Craggs, the Postmaster-General, and William Clayton, one of the Treasury Commissioners. The chief representatives of the South Sea Company were John Blunt; Sir George Caswall, who wasn't a director but was an old friend of Blunt and, as has been said, a director of the Sword Blade Bank, with which the company kept part of its cash; Francis Hawes, another of the company's directors, and the company's cashier (that is, accountant), Robert Knight.

Rumours of these discussions began to leak into the press in early 1720. There was also talk of large investments in the South Seas Company's stock by the Chancellor, Aislabie. We know that through his broker, Mathew Wymonde, Aislabie spent £20,000 on shares in January, a further £10,000 in February, and £20,000 more in March; by the end of June, these purchases totalled £77,000, and all were quickly sold for a profit. At the same time, Aislabie was also buying and selling stock in the Bank of England. Shortly afterwards, the Chancellor was involved in, and benefited from, the massive bribery which helped secure Parliament's approval for the South Sea Company's proposals. Its directors' plans had, therefore, already received important backing before they were first officially clarified on 21 January 1720.

As noted earlier, the Government's chief problem in reducing its debts lay with the long-term annuities. At the time these were yielding holders nearly 7 per cent on the original sums lent, and were due to run out between 1792 and 1807; the short annuities, which yielded 9 per cent, were due to expire in 1742. Both were known as Irredeemables, since the Government could not reduce the levels of interest without the consent of the investors – and let's face it, who would accept a market rate of around 5 per cent at the time if they were locked into 7 or 9 per cent? Under the terms of the new scheme, however, the South Sea Company was to offer the holders of the Irredeemables and Redeemables (the latter including, for instance, government stock at 4 per cent and 5 per cent which could be repaid or redeemed by the Government at a year's notice) South Sea stock in exchange for their securities. For the privilege, the company was to pay the Government £1.5 million, and would in addition purchase for two years all the Irredeemables exchanged. The scheme was attractive to the Government not so much for these payments, however, but for the hope that annuitants would agree to take a lump sum in new South Sea stock in exchange for their annuities. In this way the state would owe the South Sea Company an additional debt equal to the government securities exchanged for new South Sea stock, but it would pay interest on this at a lower rate, and would be able to repay it as and when it had the means to do so.

A bill was introduced in Parliament to facilitate the scheme, and a fierce debate ensued. The South Sea Company's proposals had been made in order to enable it to turn a healthy profit, and that depended on the amount it would have to pay the Government. This in turn was directly affected by the value of the company's shares since the amount payable was not set, but based on a proportion of the subscribable debt converted to new shares. The scheme allowed for the company to increase its capital by the same total of subscribable debt – £31 million. If South Sea shares were trading at 200, then it would be obliged to assign £15.5 million to the public creditors, which would leave it with £15.5 million to sell at the highest possible rates for its own benefit. However, if the shares were trading at 400 the whole of the subscribable debt could be exchanged for only £7.75 million new South Sea stock (half the cost of that at 200 per share). The company would still be able, under the terms of the agreement, to increase its share capital by £31 million – which would leave it the remaining £23.25 million to sell on a rising market.

Many opponents of the scheme noticed that its success depended on the price of South Sea shares, a price which could not be justified by their trading record (how often we have heard that phrase since). Indeed, the newspaper *The Theatre*, in its issue for March–April 1720, calculated that the company's shares were not worth more than 140*s* (£7.00) but were currently trading at 200*s* (£10.00). Critics also pointed out that there would be a temptation for the company to try to boost the share price somehow in order to ensure success. A share support scheme of sorts was in fact introduced, under which prominent people were given shares in exchange for their support, while not actually either paying for or receiving them. Under the scheme, the price of the share was noted at the time of the deal, and then a 'sale' price, projected at some point in the future, was also set down. Since the share prices moved upwards, the company's supporters were actually given the difference in hard cash between what they would have paid for the shares and what the shares would have realized had they then sold them at the hypothetical selling date.

Another group of supporters of the South Sea Company scheme comprised the parliamentarians who had debated its merits. Many took the plunge and bought shares themselves; indeed, ministers appear to have been expected to subscribe – hence Robert Walpole's purchase of a shareholding, despite his opposition to the scheme. Many of the ordinary MPs were, however, to be caught up in the South Sea speculation and lost money as a result – which perhaps accounts for their fury when it all went wrong.

It is, perhaps, difficult nowadays to understand how quite such a massive financial disaster, as it turned out to be, could have been allowed to happen, or indeed how the plan could have been allowed to be put into operation in the first place. According to *The Secret History of the South-Sea Scheme*, written in 1721 by one of the directors who claimed he was innocent of any malpractice, Blunt and his cronies on the board managed to hide the truth from the effective head of the company, the Sub-Governor, Sir John Fellowes, who in any case didn't really understand the scheme in the first place. It would appear that, when it comes to excuses, there really is no new thing under the sun, and certainly this apologia has been used many times since in business scandals. It is true, however, that a look at a list of appointments to six important South Sea Company directors' committees in 1720 shows that eight directors were nominated either five or six times, and nine not at all. The names that occur most frequently are those of Robert Chester and Richard Houlditch, the two Governors, Blunt, Chapman and John Gore. Those not named at all were Sir Lambert Blackwell, Stephen Child, Peter Delaporte, James Edmundson, Sir William Hamond, Arthur Ingram and John Turner. Five of the latter were to be lightly punished – Delaporte, Edmundson, Hamond, Ingram and Turner – something which probably reflects the view of those who had responsibility for clearing up the mess that they had been less active participants in the scam. Four men – Blunt, Gibbon, Chester and Houlditch – had control of the £574,500 in fictitious stock that was used for bribes, but there is no reason to doubt that Blunt (he became Sir John Blunt when a baronetcy was conferred on him in 1720) was the ringleader. A large portion of blame also falls on the shoulders of Robert Knight, although he was not a director but the company secretary. After the collapse, he was lampooned in contemporary cartoons and fled to Holland, where, luckily for him, the authorities refused to send him back to face his accusers. It was alleged that he had had virtually complete control over the loans the company made in 1720, and that directors applied to him if they wanted to borrow either for themselves or their friends. A year later, in 1721, his estate was valued at more than £260,000. It is highly likely that Knight, together with Blunt and the two principal politicians involved, Chancellor

Aislabie and Postmaster-General Craggs, played a highly significant role in devising and operating the South Sea scheme.

The directors of the South Sea Company had started their ill-fated scheme in 1720 by seeking subscriptions for new shares in the company. Logically, they should have started with the exchanges of the Government annuities in return for South Sea stock. They reversed this natural trend, however, because they knew that they could legally increase their capital without any limit, provided they used part of the proceeds to pay off the Government's creditors. They also wanted to make the exchange of stock for annuities in stages, so as not to spoil the healthy market by taking them up all at once. At the forefront of the directors' minds, too, was the desire to cash the cheque which the Government had handed over to them as quickly as possible without waiting to see if there were funds coming in to meet it. During the year there were three subscription dates – in April, July and August – and all three issues proved tremendously popular. In July the company proposed to take in £6 million of the £13.3 million ordinary Government stock which formed the bulk of the redeemable debt. But the value of the shares subscribed turned out to be more than £11 million, nearly twice the amount it had been intended to raise. *The Weekly Journal, or Saturday's Post* reported that: 'On Thursday the South Sea Company opened their Books at their House in Broadstreet to take in Subscriptions ... in the Sum of Six Millions before they closed them. The People came thither in great Numbers, and great Crowding there was to subscribe.' The public creditors of the Government took up the company's offers with an enthusiasm untouched by reason. They had not agreed terms in advance, yet throughout 1720 they had no more than the expectation that they would own South Sea stock. Nor was it just the ordinary investor who was caught – powerful institutions like the Bank of England and the Million Bank made subscriptions running into six figures. As a result, 80 per cent of the long and short annuities, or Irredeemables, and 85 per cent of the Government ordinary stock, the Redeemables, were converted into South Sea shares. The company's nominal capital increased by over £26 million, on which the Government was to pay interest – partly at 4 per cent, partly at 5 per cent. The terms which the public creditors bound themselves to accept showed that the whole exchange of debts was a confidence trick dependent on the continued upward movement of the share price. At the date of the first exchange the price per share was between 370 and 380, but by the second exchange, only three months later, it was around 900.

The rise of the South Sea Company's share price was not only the result of buying by MPs and other socially important people, but was also a consequence of massive purchases from abroad. In the autumn of 1719 business activity in the City of London had begun to accelerate markedly, with money pouring in from other European financial centres. A large proportion of it was from France during the middle and latter part of 1720, where investors were expecting a crash of their own stock exchange, but large sums also came from Amsterdam and Ireland. There were, however, other reasons why the share price continued to climb. In April the company announced that there was to be a midsummer dividend of 10 per cent, which would be paid in stock. Given the rise in the price of the stocks this served to fuel enthusiasm for shares in the South Sea Company. In addition, the company itself began to lend money to holders of South Sea stock, and the prospect of this money finding its way into the Stock Exchange also encouraged share prices across the board to rise. And last, but by no means least, although there is no evidence, it is likely that the company was buying its own shares in order to keep prices high.

When the bubble of speculation burst at last, it did so largely because of actions by the directors of the South Sea Company. They felt that the listing of new companies diverted investors' money that might otherwise have been used to buy their shares, and so they backed Government measures to control the floating of such new ventures. In February 1720 a House of Commons Committee had been appointed to consider 'the several publick and private Subscriptions in and about the Cities of London and Westminster'. As a result, a bill was drafted in May, and received the Royal Assent in June. This statute, which became known to posterity as the Bubble Act, made it an offence to 'presume to act' as a corporate body without the authority of a Royal Charter, or to divert an existing charter to unauthorized ends. At the time, the act was seen as a move by the South Sea Company to put smaller rivals in their place. The *Original Weekly Journal* for 25 June 1720 noted 'that if there was not a stop put to this Affair, it might take off abundance of their Bubbles and by lessening the number of their Buyers, lessen, if not spoil, their market'. At first the legislation appeared to have the desired effect. Most such businesses were put on hold, and contemporary reports speak of Exchange Alley (in the City of London, and the principal haunt of stock-jobbers) being emptied. But soon activity began to pick up again. This prompted the authorities to act under the new legislation, and in mid-August writs were issued against three companies for defying the laws in relation to the buying and selling of unwarrantable stocks. It was from this date that the rise in the value of South Sea Company shares was thrown into reverse. At first the decline was gentle, but soon a momentum built up – fuelled by heavy selling by foreign investors – and by mid-September South Sea stock had fallen 250 points to 520. By 1 October the shares had lost another 230 points, falling to 290. The bubble was bursting. By the time Parliament reassembled in early December 1720 South Sea stock stood at 191, having lost nearly 600 points since September. There was indeed a crisis to be sorted out, although opinion inside Parliament was divided as to the best way out of the mess. Some politicians, both in the Commons and in the Lords, resisted an investigation into the origins of the South Sea scheme. These were led by Aislabie, the Secretary of State, James Craggs, the younger son of the Postmaster-General, and Robert Walpole in the Commons, while in the Lords this view was championed by the most senior members of the Government, the Earls of Stanhope and of Sunderland, respectively the Chief Minister and First Lord of the Treasury. Walpole's view was that, despite what had gone wrong, the company had served its purpose in converting most of the annuities for terms of years into South Sea stock. A second group of parliamentarians, however, wanted an investigation – and revenge. They wanted to get back for the state as much of the money as was owed to it by the South Sea Company. Their leaders included Thomas Brodrick, Archibald Hutcheson and Sir Joseph Jekyll in the Commons, while in the Lords supporters included Lords North and Grey and the Duke of Wharton.

The first task of the Government men was to defeat a call for the whole South Sea scheme to be rescinded. This was achieved on 20 December, when a vote of 232 to 88 confirmed the resolution of the Committee of the whole House that 'all Subscriptions of publick Debts and Incumbrances, Money Subscriptions and other Contracts made with the South Sea Company, by virtue of an Act of the last Session of Parliament, remain in the present State, unless altered ... by a General Court of the South Sea Company or set aside by due Course of Law.' Then, whilst the 'supporters' of the South Sea Company were busy working out a scheme under which South Sea cash would be swapped for Bank of England and East India Company stock, their opponents in the House of Commons scored a notable victory. Parliament called for a series of accounts from the South Sea Company, and appointed a Committee to look at overt and covert company activity as shown by these accounts. The Committee was duly elected by ballot in January 1721, and most of its thirteen members appear to have been antagonistic towards the Government's viewpoint. In seven reports between February and June of that year, much shady dealing was uncovered. Almost at once it found that £574,500 of fictitious South Sea stock had been 'sold' whilst the South Sea Bill had been passing through Parliament early in 1720. Then, on 22 January 1721, Robert Knight, the company cashier, fled abroad, by which time it was clear that company records had been erased or altered. But whatever the transgressions of Knight and his colleagues, the

The South Sea Bubble 17

early reports of the Committee left little doubt that Aislabie and Postmaster-General Craggs had used their official positions to increase their personal wealth, and that they had acted more in the manner of directors of the company than government ministers. Suspicion was also cast on the roles of Lord Sunderland and the Secretary to the Treasury, Charles Stanhope, a kinsman and protégé of the Earl of Stanhope.

Whilst all this was going on behind closed doors Parliament itself delivered more public admonition. On 14 January six South Sea Company directors who also held Crown offices were summarily removed from the latter posts. Less than two weeks later, the four directors who were also MPs were expelled from the House. Then two bills aimed specifically at the directors were rushed through Parliament and became law. Under the first of these acts they were prohibited from leaving the country for one year, and each had to draw up a list of his assets and present it to Parliament. Under the second, they were disqualified from being directors or voters of the Bank of England or the East India Company. Next, the parliamentary attack turned on the current administration, under whose government the South Sea scheme had been permitted to flourish, with disastrous consequences. But by the end of February many of those involved had already fallen victim to a higher power still. Lord Stanhope died of heart failure after defending his Government in the House of Lords. On the same day in March, the 17th, both Secretary of State Craggs and his father, the Postmaster-General, died, the latter, possibly from an overdose of laudanum, at the General Post Office in Lombard Street, and his son from smallpox. Charles Stanhope was cleared of charges of corruption by just three votes, and Sunderland too was saved in a Commons debate which lasted until 8 pm. On the other hand, Aislabie was involved too heavily to be saved, and was in any case too unpopular. On 8 March 1721 the House of Commons passed eleven resolutions accusing him of corruption, with the result that he was expelled from Parliament, and even committed to the Tower of London for a time. He eventually retired to his Yorkshire estates where he died twenty-one years later at the age of seventy-two. However, Aislabie almost didn't have an estate to retire to, for the Government passed a bill confiscating the estates of the directors of the South Sea Company, with a view to distributing the proceeds of the sale of these properties amongst, as the bill describes them, 'the unhappy sufferers in the South Sea Company'. Parliament wanted Aislabie's estate to be forfeited as well, but was persuaded to modify its demands by Robert Walpole.

Fortunately for the country, Walpole had emerged both as Aislabie's successor as Chancellor, and as Lord Stanhope's as leader of the Government, the First Minister.* Known as one of the ablest financiers of his day, he nevertheless needed all of his skill in order to come up with a plan which would enable the South Sea Company to continue in business. This he finally managed to do, the Government deferring debt payments that the company was due to make to it, and the Bank of England buying from the South Sea Company the right to annuities due to it from the Government. Under this scheme the company was able to survive as a going concern, at least for the time being. It ceased trading in 1750, but continued as a business dealing in government securities until 1854, when another Chancellor, Gladstone, finally put an end to it.

If one of the few beneficial effects of the bursting of the South Sea Bubble was the introduction of measures to control speculation and to limit opportunities for fraud, another, even more important, was the appointment of Robert Walpole as

---

*Walpole is taken to be the first Prime Minister, although the office was not officially recognized until 1905. Until then, the nominal head of the government had been the monarch, and his senior politician the First or Chief Minister. George I's lack of English and his boredom with parliamentary procedure led him to attend Parliament less and less frequently, while Walpole's excellent relations with the King's son, the Prince of Wales, later George II, brought greater strength to his position as political head of the Government. From his appointment in 1721, he took to chairing a small group of ministers, the forerunner of the present Cabinet, and hence his being seen as the first Prime Minister.

First Minister. He took a firm grip of the country's finances, establishing public funding in Britain which was to set a - pattern for the future, and which, Britain remaining more honest than her Continental neighbours of the day, were the envy of Europe.

As to the villains in our story, most of them actually suffered but little from their involvement in the South Sea Bubble. A list of them all shows that despite the confiscation of millions of pounds in assets, none of them died paupers, and the taint of their involvement does not seem to have continued for long. For example, though Sir Theodore Janssen, one of the directors involved in the scandal, never recovered all his wealth, and had to give up the seat he held in Parliament, his son, Stephen Theodore Janssen, became Chamberlain of the City of London and Lord Mayor of London. Sir John Lambert's baronetcy descended in the male line into the twentieth century, as did Sir John Blunt's, whose descendants were to become prominent as administrators in Bengal. In his obituary in 1737, Sir William Chapman was described as an eminent City merchant, while Robert Surman, the South Sea Company's deputy cashier, was a prosperous goldsmith and banker through until the 1750s, though his career ended in bankruptcy. And what of the arch-villain, Robert Knight? Well, in August 1742, a few months after Walpole, having fallen from grace, had resigned all his offices, Knight, by then living in France, received a pardon for his offences, paying £10,000 for the privilege. In January 1743 he offered to pay another £10,000 in satisfaction of all demands against him, and to this the courts agreed. He returned to England and died there nearly two years later, in November 1744. His son, also called Robert Knight, despite being less talented and a good deal nastier than his father, made a career in Parliament and business, and rose by ranks through the Irish peerage, finally being created an earl by George III in 1763.

It is interesting to note that nearly three hundred years ago those involved in the South Sea Bubble – which could, I suppose, be described as the ultimate 'white-collar crime' – though they ruined the lives of thousands of their investors, were hardly punished at all. The same criticism can be levelled against those convicted of crimes of fraud and financial mismanagement in the late twentieth century. And the class division, so marked in the eighteenth century, remains scarcely unchanged in matters of criminality – today, a working-class burglar might have to serve a quite lengthy prison sentence for stealing a few pounds, yet someone from a higher social group might only have to face a hefty fine for running off with millions of pounds belonging to his investors, often ruining the lives of many of them. How much greater the contrast must have been in the 1720s, in an age when the sums we have been discussing were wholly beyond the understanding of most ordinary people, and when public hangings for petty theft were not uncommon.

2

The Reverend Doctor Dodd – A cleric and a crook

William Dodd, Canon of Brecon, is today a little-known figure except perhaps, for the notoriety surrounding the final hours of his life, which came to an abrupt end in 1777. He was a clergyman, a popular preacher, and a celebrity of his day. He had been tutor to the fifth Earl of Chesterfield,* and Chaplain to King George III. He managed to maintain an expensive lifestyle – his stylish dress earned him the nickname 'the Macaroni Parson' ('macaroni' then being a popular term for a dandy) – until, finding it had become difficult to keep up, he forged the signature of his former pupil, the fifth Earl, on a bond or 'note of hand' for £4,200, and borrowed heavily against it. He had hoped – vainly, as it turned out – to be able to repay the moneylenders before the fraud was discovered, and had possibly relied on his erstwhile charge's goodwill and likely unease at seeing his old tutor, a clergyman, publicly censured and hanged.

*The successor of the famous fourth Earl, once Dr Johnson's patron, a distinguished diplomat, statesman and writer, and the author of *Letters to His Son*, for which he is now chiefly remembered. When that son died, his cousin and godson took his attention, and succeeded as fifth Earl of Chesterfield; he, too, had a (much less well known) book addressed to him. The Chesterfield family name is Stanhope – they were kinsmen of both those Stanhopes who had been caught up in the South Sea Bubble.

However, Dodd was discovered and arrested. Perhaps he had given the Earl a bad time in the classroom, for it seems to have concerned that fine gentleman not a jot that he was sending this unfortunate if foolish clergyman to an untimely death. Dodd was sent to the infamous Newgate prison in London, from where he appealed to one of the most articulate men of the time, the writer, critic, lexicographer, conversationalist and wit, Dr Samuel Johnson, to plead his case. Dodd and Johnson had never met, and so the wretched prisoner sought the mediation of an acquaintance common to both men, the Countess of Harrington, who was also related by marriage to Lord Chesterfield. She wrote to Johnson setting out the potentially terminal difficulties in which the Reverend found himself, whereupon the good Doctor promised to 'do what I can'. True to his word, he wrote this letter for Dodd to sign and send as his own, in a direct appeal to the King for clemency:

> Sir
>
> May it not offend your Majesty, that the most miserable of men applies himself to your clemency, as his last hope and his last refuge; that your mercy is most earnestly and humbly implored by a clergyman, whom your lay and judges have condemned to the horror and ignominy of a public execution.
>
> I confess the crime, and own the enormity of its consequences, and the danger of its example. Nor have I the confidence to petition for impunity; but humbly hope that public security may be established, without the spectacle of a clergyman dragged through the streets, to a death of infamy, amidst the derision of the profligate and profane; and that justice may be satisfied with irrevocable exile, perpetual disgrace, and hopeless penury.
>
> My life, Sir, has not been useless to mankind. I have benefited many. But my offences against God are numberless, and I have little time for repentance. Preserve me, Sir, by your perogative of mercy, from the necessity of appearing unprepared at that tribunal, before which kings and

subjects must at last stand together. Permit me to hide my guilt in some obscure corner of a foreign country, where, if I can ever attain confidence to hope that my prayers will be heard, they shall be poured with all the fervour of gratitude for the life and happiness of your Majesty.

Johnson told Dodd not to admit that he, Johnson, had written the letter, and also wrote him a sermon to be preached in prison, entitled 'The Convict's Address to his Unhappy Brethren'. A petition for clemency on Dodd's behalf, signed by 20,000 people, was presented by his friends, and Johnson wrote 'Observations' to be printed in newspapers at about the same time. The Hon. Charles Jenkinson, a government official with some influence, was also written to by Johnson, with a further plea about the respect for clergy, and Dodd ('so far as I can recollect, the first clergyman of our church who has suffered public execution for immorality') in particular.

Dodd clearly had many and eloquent supporters, but all was for nothing. His crime of forgery was one to be discouraged in a country that was rapidly expanding commercially and industrially – a crime made that much worse for having been perpetrated against a nobleman. The latter point against him sealed his fate. The Reverend did, however, appreciate all the efforts that had been made to save him, however impotently, and wrote in reply to Johnson's final letter of comfort with his thanks: 'Accept, thou great and good heart, my earnest and fervent thanks and prayers for all thy benevolent and kind efforts on my behalf.'

On 27 June 1777, William Dodd, clergyman and forger, was hanged at Tyburn.

3

Rothschild to the Rescue – The banking crisis of 1825

The events of 1825 were not so much a scandal – though no doubt, in an age of near-hysterical speculation, behind the scenes there were many such scandals – they were more a knee-jerk response to an accumulation of bad news. Following the Battle of Waterloo in June 1815, which brought the final victory over Napoleon and peace to Europe, the City, as might perhaps have been expected, went through boom times. It seemed that investments could only go one way, and that was up. Sooner or later, however, this trend had to suffer a correction, and that duly happened through November and December in 1825. The causes of the corrections proved to be a combination of circumstances. The boom in foreign loans and company promotions suddenly collapsed, and so too did the speculation in imported commodities, while rash investment behaviour on behalf of the country banks did little to help. The by now long-established Bank of England, which had rather distinguished itself by its wise and cautious counsel during the South Sea crisis, no longer seemed to have a proper policy worked out. As was to be seen time and again throughout the nineteenth century, the Bank seemed uncertain as to whether it were a national bank, which should always intervene in a crisis in order to provide support to the other banks, or a private bank which should compete headlong against all other banks.

The signs that a change in the economic climate was about to occur had already been evident in October. Sam Williams, a noted American merchant, stopped paying his bills, and many in the City noted that there was 'universal pressure for money'. Then, in the middle of November, the Norfolk-based banking family of Gurney had noted that all was not well in London, and blamed the Bank of England for restricting the money they lent to the discount houses, whose business was the large-scale discounting of bills of exchange using 'call money' (money loaned by banks and recallable on demand). Though by the start of December the Bank had begun to reverse this policy, it proved to be too little, too late, and a full-blown crisis developed. On Saturday, 1 December, one family bank, Pole, Thornton, Free, Down & Scott, found itself facing the prospect of having insufficient funds to pay out its depositors. The panic had by now gripped everyone, and one steady customer of the bank, who always kept £30,000 in his account, withdrew it in one lump and without giving any warning. Young Henry Thornton – who had by then only been with the family bank for a few months – was left to try to solve the crisis. He had to borrow money from somewhere, but where? Everyone else seemed to be having the same problem. He went to the firm's arch-rivals, the finance house of Smith, Payne & Smiths, run by John Smith. Swallowing his pride, Henry Thornton called on them and explained that according to his calculations his bank had to pay out £33,000 and would only have takings of £12,000 to cover it. Could Smith help? The latter said that his company was also pressed, but having extracted a solemn promise from Thornton that Pole, Thornton, Free, Down & Scott was basically sound, he agreed that he would do what he could, and the two men returned to Thornton's offices to see if what could be done was enough.

Henry Thornton now feared that the extra money Smith had lent him would still be insufficient, but this time luck was on his side. Whilst he had been absent from the office two deposits had been lodged with the bank, so that, with the extra money from Smith, the books exactly balanced. The two men waited anxiously for the clock to tick round to five o'clock and the end of the trading day, desperately hoping that in the time remaining no one else would want to withdraw their money. For now, the bank had been saved.

Young Henry Thornton's heroics had only delayed the inevitable, however, for the next day dawned even darker. There was no hope of further support, and Thornton realized that they would have to declare the firm bankrupt on Monday morning. The Bank of England had told him that it could provide no support, and he calculated that thirty-eight country banks would come down with his house. However, on Sunday the directors of the Bank of England met and appeared to have a change of heart. The Governor, Cornelian Buller, was connected by marriage to Henry's senior partner, Peter Pole, and the Bank agreed to lend £400,000 – on condition that one partner, Free, leave the business. He had committed the bank to some poor investments, which had created a situation whereby too much of its money was tied up. In the event, though, even this support wasn't enough. Rumours had swept the City that Pole's, with its extensive county bank network, had had to be bailed out, and on Thursday, 8 December, the leading Yorkshire bank, Wentworth and Co., went under. This began a run on the county banks, and the fragile Pole's couldn't weather this storm since, not knowing the losses the county banks might sustain, the bank was unwilling to borrow more money. That Sunday the inevitable happened and Pole's stopped trading. On Monday morning, 12 December, the City was greeted, along with the fog, with the news that three dozen county banks had failed, pulled down by the sinking of Pole, Thornton, Free, Down & Scott. To say that the mood in the City was gloomy would be understating the emotional turmoil which followed these events. The *Morning Chronicle* reported that: '... on no former occasion have we witnessed so decided a run on the different banking houses, and especially on those connected with provincial establishments.' The next day was no better and, with rumours sweeping the narrow lanes of the City, a crowd gathered outside the offices of another bank, Williams & Co. of Birchin Lane. Customers clearly believed that if they didn't get their money out first they wouldn't be able to get it out at all. Meanwhile, throughout these anxious days the banking area became so clogged with pedestrians standing fearfully outside the finance houses that it was difficult for traffic to navigate a way through.

And that was exactly what the Bank of England had been frantically trying to do – to find its way through the crisis. The Bank's efforts were given a boost when the Government allowed it to issue £1 notes for the first time since the resumption of gold payments over four years earlier. This was, however, to be only a temporary measure, rather as was originally the case with income tax. That was on Thursday, 15 December, yet the next day the situation appeared to be as grave as ever. That morning Mrs George Arbuthnot and her husband (Joint Secretary of the Treasury and regarded as an expert on currency) were put in the picture by J.C. Herries, MP, the Financial Secretary to the Treasury (and later a Chancellor of the Exchequer), and the member of the Government closest to the City.

> Mr Herries told us that such had been the extraordinary demand for gold to supply the country bankers and to meet the general run upon them that the Bank of England was completely drained of its specie and was reduced to 100,000 sovereigns ... The Bank expects to be obliged to suspend cash payments tomorrow, and they want the Government to step forward to their assistance and order the suspension. Lord Liverpool [the Prime Minister] is unwilling to do this & wishes the Bank to do it upon their own responsibility. By Mr Herries' account there seems to be considerable irritation between the Government and the Governors of the Bank ... Such is the detestation in which Mr [William] Huskisson [President of the Board of Trade and Treasurer of the Navy] is held in the City* that

---

*A committed free-trader, Huskisson had passed measures allowing the colonies to trade with foreign countries, rather than solely with Britain and other colonies, and he had greatly reduced import duties on foreign goods coming into Britain. In September he became the first person in this country to die in a railway accident when he was run over by Stephenson's locomotive, the Rocket, at the opening of the Liverpool and Manchester Railway.

> Ld L & Mr [George] Canning [the Foreign Secretary] did not think it prudent to summon him to London till all the cabinet were sent for & in the discussions with the Bank, he is kept out of sight ... Rothschild has made most gigantic efforts to assist the Bank & he told Mr Herries that, if he had been applied to sooner, he wd have prevented all the difficulty. As it is if they can hold out till Monday, or Tuesday, he will have enormous sums over in sovereigns from Paris, & the pressure will entirely be relieved ...

In the crisis, the great and the good had been forced to turn to an outsider, a Jew, to help them. Nathan Rothschild was, however, one of the greatest financiers not only of that age, but of any other. He was the third son of a Frankfurt financier, all of whose five sons had been dispersed to countries which, their father thought, suited their characters. Nathan had been in London since 1808, and had already made a huge fortune by running bullion operations for the British Government during the Napoleonic Wars; now he saw another chance to save the nation – and protect the financial structure which had already served him so well – as well as to make some more money. Within a few days he managed to organize a massive injection of cash for the Bank of England, employing a sophisticated and well-tested system of communications which used private couriers and homing pigeons. It is worth remembering that these were the days before the telegraph, yet with this system in place Nathan could communicate with his financier brothers in Paris, Frankfurt, Vienna and Naples, and they with him. Indeed, it was said that Nathan Rothschild, using his own communications, had learned the outcome of the Battle of Waterloo before the British Government had been officially informed!

Of Rothschild's intervention, the *Morning Chronicle* reported that the House of Rothschild had put into the Bank of England's coffers 150,000 sovereigns, whilst fifty years later Canning's private secretary remembered that the figure was

£300,000 in coin. Whatever the true figure, the loan gave the Bank of England some breathing space. The Cabinet met to hammer out a way forward for the Government and decided to back the Bank of England's strategy. And fortune was about to smile on the Old Lady of Threadneedle Street. Over the weekend the Bank did run out of £5 and £10 notes, but then in the nick of time a fresh supply arrived, hot off the plates, from the printers. By Tuesday, thanks to the Rothschilds, golden reinforcements came pouring across the Channel – the promised gold from Paris. A mild run on the Bank's reserves continued until just before Christmas, but by then confidence had been restored.

The confidence of the public was even more important back in the early nineteenth century because the capital reserves of most banks – and this applied equally to the Bank of England – were inadequate, and there was no one to police the finance houses, either; indeed, financial regulation was still in its infancy. The world was using London as a financing centre for projects throughout the world. Quite often these were high-risk, high-return ventures, such as the grossly overpriced loans to the newly liberated countries of Latin America. Sometimes the countries were so new they only existed in the imaginations of those seeking finance – in 1825 bonds were successfully issued for 'Poyais', a country supposed to be situated somewhere in Central America, in what is now Belize, but largely the product of a scam run by a Scottish adventurer named MacGregor. Two-thirds of those who settled in what proved to be an inhospitable and all but deserted region, devoid of the many facilities promised by the scheme's promoter, died, mostly from disease.

Following the crisis of 1825, therefore, it was clear that there had to be change, and change did indeed come, eventually leading to the establishment of the framework for the modern banking system that we know today. There was a series of inquiries, the inadequately financed country banks seeming to take much of the blame for what had happened. Legislation was passed which permitted joint-stock banks (that is, banks of which the ownership is shared between shareholders, whose liability is limited) outside a radius of 65 miles from London. Within a few years these houses were permitted to open inside London – the first of them was the London and Westminster Bank (now the National Westminster or NatWest), which opened for business in Throgmorton Street in 1834. The other direct result of the crisis was that the Bank of England decided to keep tighter control of its currency, setting up eleven regional branches in the late 1820s in order to promote a wider use of its banknotes.

After the crisis, Thomas Love Peacock, poet, novelist and an official with the East India Company, put down his thoughts in verse. They seemed to sum up what had happened.

> Oh! where are the riches that bubbled like fountains,
> In places we neither could utter nor spell,
> A thousand miles inland 'mid untrodden mountains,
> Where silver and gold grew like heath and blue-bell?
> Now curst be the projects, and curst the projectors,
> And curst be the bubbles before us that rolled,
> Which, bursting, have left us like desolate spectres,
> Bewailing our bodies of paper and gold.

4

Overend & Gurney – Or it doesn't pay to cross your friends

In Britain during the nineteenth century there were a great many new developments, mainly technological, on which a person might speculate. After all, there were all the myriad manifestations of the railway age – the railway companies themselves, their suppliers, manufacturers of locomotives and rolling stock, land speculators – the list is endless. And the sources of capital with which to speculate were almost unlimited, too. Banks were still very much local establishments, many of which had begun by supplying capital to leading landowners or industrialists in their area. Some of these banks themselves had undergone rapid development and had diversified away from their traditional services, venturing into any number of new businesses. Quite often, however, the financial foundations of these concerns were built on shifting sands, and cyclical downturns in economic activity often made them vulnerable. In a country where rumour was, and still is, a legitimate currency amongst financial traders, a little bad news was often sufficient to push a company out of business.

The firm of Richardson, Overend & Company began life at the beginning of the nineteenth century. By 1807 it had four partners, including Samuel Gurney of Norfolk, all of them Quakers. The company now began to acquire a positive reputation – it lent heavily to the pioneering Stockton and

Darlington Railway in the 1820s, for example. And in the 1830s, following the banking crisis a few years earlier, the company began taking in larger and larger sums on deposit and lending them out again on short loans, in addition to providing country banks with cash. This short-loan lending was discounted by the Bank of England, which effectively acted as lender of last resort, and Richardson, Overend & Gurney – or Overend & Gurney, as it was called from 1827, following the death of Thomas Richardson – became one of the four discounters sanctioned by the Bank of England. Indeed, the company became the leading discount house in England, and from 1833 was based at the corner of Lombard Street and Birchin Lane, or the 'Corner House', as it was known in the City. Overend & Gurney had a reputation for honesty and fairness, though tempered by a certain inconsistency – at times the partners could be tough, at other times merciful. In 1828 they refused to help Fry & Company, tea merchants, despite the latter concern being run by fellow Quakers, some of them relations. Fry's went bankrupt. On the other hand, Samuel Gurney, discovering a large forgery perpetrated against the firm, told the culprit that by law he should hang but that they would let him escape to the Continent, on the condition that he never came back.

There is no doubt that Samuel Gurney was one of the century's most interesting and effective financial players. The portrait painter, George Richmond, said his face held a mixture of shrewdness and benevolence, and it was with this character mixture that Gurney steered his company from success to success. Perhaps he played too great a part, for his death in 1856 was to deal the firm a blow from which it never recovered.

The blow proved fatal to Overend & Gurney partly because of its timing, and partly because of the characters of those who took over from Samuel Gurney. In 1857 the City was bracing itself for another crisis, and although the cause was ostensibly far away, the repercussions were to be strongly felt at home. Put simply, a number of banks and railroads in America had collapsed, something which the Bank of England realized would put pressure on the resources of discount houses like Overend & Gurney. Samuel Gurney's successor, David Barclay Chapman, was by nature particularly aggressive, at every opportunity putting pressure on the Bank of England to stand behind the discounters whatever the circumstances, whatever the liability. Needless to say this was an assurance the Bank was unwilling to give; indeed, it could not do so, being prevented by the terms of the Bank Charter Act of 1844, with which the government of Sir Robert Peel had severely limited the Bank's scope. The act laid down the separation of the Bank's note-issuing arm from its business operations; it placed restrictions on other banks issuing notes, and provided for a fixed ratio between notes and bullion; and it also provided for a fixed fiduciary issue of £14 million (i.e. the total amount that could be issued against securities).

Time and again at times of crisis the City's other bankers would ask for these terms to be eased so that the Bank of England could lend them more money to ensure their survival during runs against them. However, it is salutary to consider how many more of them would have gone to the wall, recklessly, if the Act had not been in place, knowing that the Bank would have been standing behind whatever foolishness they got up to with a blank cheque in its hand. Even so, during the 1857 crisis Chapman is said to have told his friends that he had threatened that he would bring the Bank of England to a standstill unless its directors obtained from the Government a suspension of the Act! We shall see, in the Bank's later conduct towards Overend & Gurney, just how costly this bad feeling between the two banks was to prove. In the end the 1857 crisis passed, just as many have both before and since, with the introduction of simple measures designed to improve confidence. What happened was that those pressing for the repayment of all that was owing to them settled for a portion of the money. Confidence restores credit, and business thus continues to be done. David Barclay Chapman, however, retired at the end of 1857, having become known as 'Gurney's Liar' following attacks upon his conduct during the crisis. Control passed to the younger generation – to the over-ambitious Henry Edmund Gurney and the extravagant David Ward Chapman. The solid Quaker virtues upon which the house had been founded were being left to the past.

It was, without a doubt, with Overend & Gurney in mind that the Bank of England made it clear in March of the following year that it would no longer offer discount facilities to the City's bill-brokers – a policy designed to make the discount houses more self-reliant. The Bank immediately came under pressure to reverse the ruling, but held firm. In early 1860 one of the Gurney family made a further appeal to the Governor, Bonamy Dobrée, but to no avail. By the beginning of April of that year, with interest rates up to $4\frac{1}{2}$ per cent, money was starting to become tight, and the discount houses began to feel the squeeze. *The Economist* called for a truce, saying that there was no doubt that under the old system the bill-brokers, who were always competing for business with the Bank of England, had an advantage because they could afford to take more risks than the Bank, knowing that if anything went wrong they might be able to call for help from the Bank. Now, though, the view was that the credit of the bill-brokers was being affected, and that this could be damaging during a crisis. Far from there being a truce, however, war broke out. During three days in mid-April Overend & Gurney mobilized its Quaker allies and withdrew £1,600,000 in £1,000 notes from the Bank of England, the aim being to reduce the Bank's reserves to the lowest ebb possible. On the following Monday the Governor of the Bank of England was informed that if the Bank's rule over the discount houses should be modified, then the money would be returned immediately. The Bank's directors didn't much take to what amounted to blackmail, and refused to entertain such a notion. Their stand had the desired effect, for on the next day the money was returned when Overend & Gurney got wind that a question was about to be asked in Parliament about the Bank of England's disappearing reserves.

Over the next few years Overend & Gurney continued to be in the hands of Henry Edmund Gurney and David Ward

Chapman. In July 1865 the company went public, encouraged by the success of the Morrison textile business, which had transformed itself into the Fore Street Warehouse Company. The new company was to pay £500,000 in goodwill, the capital was to be £5 million, and Chapman was to retire. The prospectus assured potential shareholders that the directors were only interested in business of a first-class nature, but reaction in the City was mixed. Many welcomed the retirement of Chapman, but thought that prospects for the company were uncertain, following large losses only a few years earlier. However, the Overend & Gurney name still carried a good deal of weight, and the shares went quickly to a premium when trading in them began. During the winter of 1865 Gurney proposed to borrow money from Glyn's Bank at a special rate, but on some securities which to the bank seemed of doubtful value. By early 1866 many in the City had become worried not only by Overend & Gurney but by the large numbers of finance companies created during a boom period around 1863. Several of these were closely linked to Overend & Gurney, including one called the Contract Corporation, which went into liquidation at the end of March. There was at the time a threat of war in Europe, and by mid-April everyone seemed to want to be a seller of stock. During the afternoon of 10 April the bombshell burst – the rumours that Overend & Gurney had failed were later confirmed after the Stock Exchange had closed for the day. Naturally, there were fears that the company's failure would bring others down, but the reasons for the collapse did not immediately become apparent. It was only three years later, when the directors stood trial for having published a false prospectus, that it emerged that the firm had been bankrupt before it had gone public. The problem was an age-old (and continuing) one – too rapid expansion too far from the core business which the company knew so well. During 1859 the new generation at Overend & Gurney had transformed the business, effectively becoming shipbuilders, shipowners, grain traders, ironmasters and railway backers. Many of these investments were long-term, and difficult to move out of without incurring heavy losses; often, too, the investments were poorly judged. By 1861 the firm was in deep trouble. Perhaps the Bank of England's new restrictive practices had in some measure played a part, and encouraged the company to look to new, more profitable ventures than its established business as a discount house. The problems were, however, compounded by an over-zealous commitment to lending to the new finance houses. The company's conversion to a limited liability company in 1865 was a last honest, though desperate, attempt to keep going, following the failure of merger talks with the National Discount Company. In 1869, at the end of the trial, the jury recognized that what Gurney and his fellow directors had done was no more than make a last desperate throw of the dice, and acquitted them.

However honest the directors of Overend & Gurney had been, it is likely that officials at the Bank of England were less than honest with themselves when it came to explaining why the company had been allowed to fail. Once it became apparent that Overend & Gurney were going to require assistance to survive, the Bank appointed a committee of three to look at the books and determine whether or not there was anything that could be done. The three committee members reported back that the business was rotten to the core, and no helping hand was offered. But remembering the strained relationship between the Bank and the company as personified by David Barclay Chapman, and then the £1.6 million blackmail attempt, it is, perhaps, little wonder that there was no support from inside the Bank of England over any plans to save Overend & Gurney. Of course, in Samuel Gurney's day that support would have been there in abundance, for he had been a member of the inner circle, 'the club', as it might be called, and was in any case a highly respected figure in the City. But then, it is almost unthinkable that such a cautious man of business would have been caught out in the way that his successors had been.

The demise of Overend & Gurney led to the usual panic, and the usual call for the suspension of the 1844 Bank Charter

Act. Gladstone was the Chancellor of the Exchequer at the time, nearing the end of a seven-year stint in that post (which he had also held in the 1850s), and he refused to bow to pressure. The City thought of nothing else but the demise of Overend & Gurney, and the banking houses were besieged. Several companies failed, but the Bank of England did lend £4 million to other banks, discount houses and merchants. Moreover, the Government stood behind the Bank and allowed it the flexibility to weather yet another crisis of confidence, and the fury of the storm raised by the collapse of Overend & Gurney was soon spent.

There were important lessons to be learned from the crisis. Though no one seemed to mind that the directors had gone public despite the fact that Overend & Gurney was at the time bankrupt, they did mind that the company, to use a schoolroom analogy, had cheeked the head boy. The Bank of England, though, was so pleased with its handling of the aftermath of the crisis that in a speech to the Bank's proprietors, the Governor, Lancelot Holland, said that he and his colleagues would not flinch from what they conceived to be the duty imposed upon them of supporting the banking community. He added that he was not aware that they had refused any legitimate application for assistance. In an article in *The Economist*, the editor, Walter Bagehot, wrote that this was a welcome acceptance of the doctrine of lender of last resort. It was in a sense ironic that in the demise of Overend & Gurney its directors, for so long critics of the 1844 Act, had finally managed to drive a coach and horses through it. There had simply been too many banking crises within too short a space of time for the Bank of England to stick rigidly to the Act, nor could its banking department simply act like that of any other bank. However, as has sometimes been shown by examples from our own century, there are still occasions when it does so act. The Bank does not offer universal succour, but hands out aid subjectively, sometimes to the needy, sometimes to its friends – but rarely to those who don't play the game.

5

The Barings Banking Crisis – 1890

If history did not repeat itself, then historians would have nothing to study. Which is not to say that the crisis at Baring Brothers and Company – Britain's oldest merchant bank – back in 1890 was anything like the one that eventually brought the bank down in 1995. But one of the precipitating agents, to use a chemical analogy, in all financial crises, particularly frauds, is certainly a lack of control. This can be a lack of supervision of subordinates by management boards which have lost touch, or it can be blind insistence on investing in high-risk strategies, when emerging facts suggest this is no longer a good idea.

So it was that in 1890 Edward Charles Baring, first Baron Revelstoke, had committed his company to backing investment in Argentina to a dangerous extent. It was a decision probably in keeping with Lord Revelstoke's character, for he has been described as somewhat overbearing, accustomed to his own authority, impatient of fools though not always able to recognize them. The seeds of the crisis that would hit Baring Brothers were discovered in 1888 when a magazine called the *Statist* (a new rival to *The Economist*) published an article critical of Messrs Baring Brothers' issues. It itemized the company's thirty-one principal issues since 1882 – all, apart from Guinness and the Manchester Ship Canal, had been foreign.

The article also pointed up the rapid growth of business from £6.5 million in 1884, suggesting that 'in the present year, up to date, they have offered somewhat more than 28 millions sterling, irrespective of the Buenos Ayres Drainage, &c, Loan, which we are glad they did not succeed in placing with the public.' Here we have the nub of the problem. The flotation of Guinness had been phenomenally successful, and there was a feeling in some quarters that just to have the Barings name attached to that of a company going to the Stock Exchange (that is, being floated as a public company) was sufficient in itself. Perhaps Lord Revelstoke had begun to believe his own publicity. In any event, from the mid-1880s onwards the company had begun to devote more and more of its resources to Argentina, though Barings was not alone in mounting huge investments there – by the end of the decade these had reached some £150 million (over £7 billion at present-day values). But the Buenos Ayres Drainage, &c, Loan was a deal too much – as the *Statist* had reported, it was a huge flop. Barings had on their hands a vast number of unmarketable shares and was committed to finding further capital for the massively expensive project, as well as to paying off the Argentine government. Political turmoil in Argentina didn't help matters, and towards the end of July 1890 Barings had managed to find buyers for less than a tenth of the £2 million of the ordinary shares of the company. The work of the Buenos Ayres Water Supply and Drainage Company (as it was properly called) had ground to a halt, and with large holdings in other South American securities, Baring Brothers' capital was well and truly tied up.

The company now began to borrow from friends in order to keep operating. During September Martin's Bank lent Barings £500,000, and in October Glyn Mills advanced them a total of £750,000. The problems were compounded by some of the depositors who had accounts with Barings and who, the bank felt, perhaps rather unreasonably, wanted some of their money! The Russian government was steadily withdrawing its large-scale deposits from the finance house, and was due to remove another £1.5 million in the middle of November.

Matters came to a head in the week before when Lord Revelstoke's close friend, Everard Hambro, called and was told by Revelstoke that by the following Monday the latter would know whether or not Barings could survive. Hambro, himself a director of the bank, told Revelstoke that the only man who could save him was William Lidderdale, the Governor of the Bank of England.

Lidderdale came to see Revelstoke at the offices of Hambros Bank in order to keep the meeting as low-profile as possible. He was probably shocked to hear just how bad matters were, for he was briefed about the situation and told that it was not certain that the firm would have any surplus after payment of its liabilities. Lidderdale realized that should Barings fail there would be far-reaching consequences – the collapse of the City's leading flotation house would bring down with it a whole host of other companies. Moreover, the pre-eminence of the City as a financial centre would also be tarnished amidst a fear that credit notes in London might not be honoured.

Barings was fortunate in having Lidderdale as Governor of the Bank of England. He had all the qualities necessary to steer a course through the crisis – although the waters would be choppy for a while. Lidderdale realized that the Bank on its own could do nothing; its own reserves amounted to roughly half of Barings' liabilities. So the first port of call was to the Government, to discuss the possibility of its standing behind any rescue plan. Unfortunately, however, the Government still clung to a Gladstonian belief in the concept of *laissez-faire* in trade, and felt that it was up to the City to rally round. The Chancellor of the Exchequer, George (later Viscount) Goschen, was approached, but although he made sympathetic noises, he declined to pledge Parliament to helping a private company. The impasse between the Government and the Governor of the Bank of England continued, with the latter continuing to assert that the Bank could do nothing without a Government safety net, and the Government insisting that no tangible Government aid could be offered. However, the Bank of England did manage to persuade the Russian government not to make its

£1.5 million withdrawal from Barings. Sir Nathan Rothschild, grandson of the Rothschild who had done so much to end the banking crisis of 1825, then did his bit, persuading the Bank of France to lend £3 million in gold to bolster the Bank of England's reserves, and applying discreet pressure upon his friend, the Prime Minister, Lord Salisbury, to adopt a more interventionist line. Rothschild backed up Lidderdale in his fear that, if Barings were allowed to go under, then the collapse would bring to an end the commercial habit of transacting all the business of the world by means of bills drawn on London. Finally, Lidderdale appointed Bertram Currie of Glyn Mills – the closest of Lord Revelstoke's friends – and Benjamin Buck Greene to determine the future of Barings should the rescue money be forthcoming. On Friday, 14 November 1890, Currie and Greene reported back that in their view Baring Brothers' assets outweighed their current liabilities – despite the firm's pressing need for a £9 million cash advance to tide it over.

Whilst all this was going on, however, rumours in the City were running rife. Some action was now needed, and so at around two o'clock that afternoon the Governor of the Bank of England slipped quietly out of Theadneedle Street and took a cab to Downing Street. There he was greeted by the Prime Minister and, in Goschen's absence, by William Henry Smith,* the First Lord of the Treasury and Leader of the House of Commons. The three men conferred for around an hour. At first neither side would budge from the positions they had taken earlier in the week. Then Lidderdale told the other two that the Bank of England had been taking in Barings' bills all week, but that without the Government's support this could not continue. He added that unless the Government agreed to relieve the Bank of some of the losses, then he would return to Threadneedle Street and throw out all acceptances (that is, bills of exchange or drafts drawn on and endorsed by a bank) of

---

*Smith had developed his father's news agency business into the forerunner of today's giant concern, which still bears his name and initials. On his death in 1891, his widow was created Viscountess Hambleden, and the viscountcy also still survives.

Baring Brothers. The threat worked. The Government gave the Governor twenty-four hours in which to save Barings, and promised that it would bear half the loss resulting from taking in Barings' bills until early Saturday afternoon. By five o'clock that day Lidderdale was back in his office at Threadneedle Street. Currie was waiting for him, and to him the Governor announced that he was setting up a guarantee fund for Barings, with the Bank of England putting up the first £500,000. Currie at once declared that Glyn Mills would also stump up £500,000 on the condition that Rothschilds did the same. Moments later Natty Rothschild arrived at the meeting, and agreed. Over the next half-hour the City's most powerful companies rushed to contribute. That evening Lidderdale met representatives of the joint-stock banks (the forerunners of our high-street banks), and they too joined in the guarantee fund, pledging an impressive £3.25 million between the five of them. Effectively the fund guaranteed the Bank of England against any losses arising out of advances made to Barings to enable it to discharge its obligations. Though the fund was kept secret, it grew steadily, so that it had reached £17 million by the following week. The net result was that Barings was saved. This fact was duly noted in the *Financial Times* on Monday, 17 November, the paper, for once abandoning its usual verbosity, simply headlining the story, 'Saved'. The account went on to say that if Barings had gone under, 'what might have happened on the Stock Exchange is a prospect too fearful to contemplate'.

In what was to prove to be a prophetic insight into what happened David Kynaston, in the first volume of his excellent book, *The City of London*, quotes a City insider of the day, Edward Hamilton:

> Nobody talks of anything else but of the Barings ... There is a strong feeling of sympathy for them. This is not unnatural for more reasons than one: everyone is relieved that the catastrophe has been averted, there is no suspicion of fraudulent intent, the House has always been popular and greatly respected, poor Revelstoke

himself is known to have been the most generous & large hearted man, there is the feeling ingrained in John Bull [i.e. the British public] for the fallen ...

At Barings, though the crisis had been averted, the consequences of the rescue could not be. One partner famously described the humiliation with the remark: 'A great Nemesis overtook Croesus', and added that 'the line has never been out of my head since the Guinness success'. Under the terms of the rescue, the company had to be reorganized. The old partnership was wound up and replaced by a new company, to be called Baring Brothers & Company Limited, with capital of £1 million subscribed by many leading City institutions as well as by members of the Baring family. However, over the next few years the winding-up of the old firm involved the selling off of its assets, and these included the private property of the partners, whose liability was, in the tradition of the City, unlimited. For Revelstoke, it was a bitter and humiliating addition. He lost his beloved country estate and his collection of French pictures and furniture. Gone, too, was his position in the City, and much of his self-esteem. He never recovered and died in 1897, two years after the loan to the Bank of England was paid off. To mark the occasion of that final repayment, the then Chancellor of the Exchequer, Sir William Harcourt, wrote to the by now ex-Governor of the Bank of England, William Lidderdale: 'The Baring Guarantee was a bold and probably necessary stroke. It has ended well. May it never be repeated. Such turns of luck do not often occur in the nature of things.' A celebrated *Punch* cartoon of November 1890 noted the role of the Bank of England – known universally as 'the Old Lady of Threadneedle Street' – in Barings' rescue. The drawing showed a stern-looking Old Lady scolding a group of naughty schoolboys standing with heads bowed and holding playing cards behind their backs. The caption read: 'You've got yourselves into a nice mess with your precious "speculation"! Well – I'll help you out of it, – for this once!' The cartoon was entitled, perhaps prophetically, 'Same Old Game'.

6

Barings Finally Fails – Or how one rogue dealer lost his bearings

The crisis that Barings faced and fought through in the 1890s, when its reserves were inadequate to cover loans to Argentina, was not the only one of its history. The bank – which was founded in 1762 – had almost come unstuck supporting America's Louisiana Purchase in 1803.* But the house which had helped finance the armies that defeated Napoleon finally met its Waterloo when one trader gambled £500 million in Singapore, and lost.

At the end of February 1995 Nick Leeson left his rented flat in one of Singapore's upmarket neighbourhoods, threw some clothes in a suitcase and headed for the airport. The twenty-eight-year-old trader, who had failed his Maths exams at school, had only recently been praised for the impressive profits figures his operations had generated – more than $30 million in a seven-month period. Even at that time, however, it seems that his riskier trading was showing a loss of more than £50 million, although this rather negative aspect was hidden from public scrutiny in an account simply known as Error Account No. 88888. Leeson had joined Barings just three years before, rapidly entering the bank's fast stream because of the

---

*The largest land sale in history, when the USA effectively doubled its size by buying from France, which then occupied the territory, 828,000 square miles for a price of $15 million.

skill he displayed in juggling the most complex share deals. Within the bank itself it seemed he could do no wrong, and he was known to be the protégé of Ron Baker, the forty-three-year-old head of Baring Brothers' financial products group. Leeson's differential calculus may not have been entirely accurate, but he embodied all the characteristics needed to shine on the trading-room floor: a 'pocket calculator mind', a ruthless gambling instinct, and an ice-cool ability to handle risk. His speciality was trading in derivatives, volatile financial instruments the dealing in which amounts to taking bets against changes in the market. The value of derivatives is derived from an underlying asset – it can be cocoa or shares or currencies or bonds, or anything with two basic characteristics: it has a value, and its price fluctuates. They were actually invented as a tool for reducing risk. Futures are simply agreements to buy or sell a quantity of an asset at a certain price at a future date. A cocoa producer who wants to guarantee the price of his crop against market fluctuations will enter into a 'sell' contract to ensure he knows what price he will get. A chocolate maker wanting to make sure he doesn't have to pay a sharply higher price, will enter into a 'buy' contract. Big companies use derivatives to protect themselves against unforeseen fluctuations in the price of raw materials like crude oil, sugar or currencies. Used properly, they are useful insurance policies. But Nick Leeson was said to have treated the derivatives market like a poker game. Futures, in which he dealt heavily in Singapore, are a simple type of derivative. So, too, are the other instruments he used, options. Like futures, options are a way of grudging, or hedging, against price movements. The difference is that, while futures are a firm commitment to buy or sell on a given date in the future, options merely give the right to do so. If, when the time comes, it is not advantageous to exercise the option, it can be allowed to lapse. Very good returns can be made by, in effect, betting on what a certain asset will be worth at some future point. Most professional dealers – unless they are very certain of a particular outcome – will hedge their bets by making trades in other commodities. It is then unlikely that all their 'bets' will come up losers. What Nick Leeson effectively did was to put all his eggs in one basket. He became obsessed by the idea that the Japanese stock market was undervalued and would recover. He bought futures on the Nikkei – the average which measures the Japanese Stock Exchange performance – on the assumption that it would recover to about the 19,000 level by 10 March, the expiry date for the contracts. He added to his bet so that by 24 February his exposure was $7 billion (£4.4 billion) and his loss was standing at about £500 million, all resting on a Japanese stock market recovery that wasn't happening, not least because financial confidence had been dealt a severe blow by the earthquake in Kobe on 17 January.

In Singapore he was known as a lone wolf, making little attempt to join in office socializing, although he was a well-known figure on the island state's party circuit. Managers allowed him to operate independently from the trading team, and this willingness of Barings to give him an increasingly free hand helps to explain how it was that he began building up unauthorized trading positions. The countdown to crisis began just before Christmas 1994, when Nick Leeson returned from a business trip to Osaka and Tokyo. He told his bosses that he had finalized a brilliant new strategy based on exploiting the differences between contracts in the Nikkei 225 stock market index traded on both the Osaka and Singapore stock exchanges. According to bank sources the profits were tiny – three or four 'ticks' (hundredths of a per cent), but, Leeson explained to his superiors, by building up these trades first millions, and then billions, of times, he could accumulate huge profits. The entire strategy was founded on the assumption that the Nikkei 225 index of leading companies in Osaka would sustain a tiny premium over its counterpart on the Singapore Stock Exchange. But, as an insurance policy, Leeson is believed to have set in place a corresponding line of trades to hedge Barings against the risk that Singapore would swing up against Osaka. As events would later prove, these contracts proved to be entirely fictitious. Barings had no counters trade to insure against losses that began to snowball in Osaka. His assurances, contained in faxes to the bank's London headquarters, that the deals had actually been placed, were a 'stream of unadulterated falsehoods', according to a bank insider. These losses mounted so catastrophically that within a few short months Britain's most blue-blooded merchant bank had been brought to its knees.

All manner of investigations followed, but it is still not clear why this had been allowed to happen, or what had motivated Nick Leeson. Particularly puzzling is why he continued to build up his positions in a flurry of share deals after the Kobe earthquake in mid-January 1995 sent shares in Japan tumbling. Leeson would have been aware that he faced heavy losses, as soon as the markets reacted to the earthquake. Was he trying to keep cool and trade himself out of his problems, in the belief that when the markets bounced back he would make profits that would cover his huge losses before they had been noticed? If that is the case, then it was a last desperate gamble, for the exposure (the amount of potential losses to which the company was exposed) on the trades he built up around 26 January 1995 has been estimated at nearly £2 billion. The then Chairman of Barings, Sir Peter Baring, believes Leeson was attempting to 'sabotage' the bank, perhaps with the help of an outside party. Even the Governor of the Bank of England, Eddie George, said that it would have been impossible for the trader to hoodwink the whole of the Barings establishment without some inside help in short-circuiting the bank's share-trading controls, whereby every share transaction would have been supported by documentation lodged in the Singapore office and forwarded to London on a regular basis. There is evidence that Barings discovered that share transaction documents were missing, and there is also evidence that large sums of money could have been siphoned off from clients' profits into 'phantom' bank accounts. There is a finger of suspicion pointing at other employees. The scale of the irregularities uncovered went beyond the Nikkei 225 dealings and would appear to go back over the previous couple of years. Peter Baring told the Bank of

England that it was only on the night before the collapse that the board of directors had any inkling of the scale of the losses incurred by Leeson. There is, however, evidence from inside Barings and elsewhere that some advance warning of the huge derivatives losses was given. Were staff in London involved in a cover-up? Someone must have known something, because it appears that London ordered a discreet inquiry into Leeson's personal finances. Rumours had been flying around the Far East's financial community since mid-January that a trader was in serious trouble with his exposure on the region's derivatives market. There were even rumours that a British-owned bank could be on the brink of collapse. Market insiders found it difficult to believe that no one at Barings was aware of Nick Leeson's activities. Whatever the truth, however, senior executives in London did authorize the advances of large sums of money to the 'rogue trader' at the end of January, to support his activities. It is, furthermore, a matter of record that Barings deposited £500 million pounds with the Osaka and Singapore futures exchanges at this time to cover margin calls on its outstanding futures contracts. The size of these payments indicates that enormous positions had been taken, because the margin calls are just the interim payments required to cover falls in the value of futures contracts. So even if Nick Leeson's superiors had been hoodwinked about the exact nature of his dealings, the scale of the business being run by him in Singapore could not have eluded them. Throughout February he requested more cash as the bank's position became more precarious and the margin calls mounted. When approached by Far East staff in the middle of February about the size of the firm's exposure, officials in London insisted that there was no problem. But within a fortnight complacency turned to panic as the London office realized the extent of Leeson's trading activities, but the discovery that something was wrong in Singapore seems to have been made by accident. It is believed that Peter Norris, the head of investment banking at Barings and the man who finally stumbled across the problem, had gone to Singapore to congratulate Leeson on his contribution to Barings' 1994 profits;

there was even talk of a seven-figure bonus. Once there, however, Norris decided to inquire into the trader's methods, and by Thursday, 23 February he had been told that something was wrong.

Realizing the extent of the problem, Norris was left only one option. At 7.15 am on 24 February the phone rang at the home of Peter Baring, Chairman of Barings. Within the hour he had gathered the board together at the company's Bishopsgate headquarters. It was not as if the bank had not been warned before about the 'success' of its trading operations in Singapore. The increase in profits generated by Nick Leeson meant that he had to be using large sums to generate such business. This alerted head office and eventually an auditor was sent to the island. The ensuing report was enough to worry anyone but the most optimistic banker. In particular, the audit drew attention to the blurring of lines of responsibility for trading operations and 'back office' settlement – a crucial distinction in a modern investment bank. The back office is more than a clearing house for all the paper (receipts, transaction notes and share certificates) produced by dealers in the 'front office'. It is also the first line of defence against possible fraud or over exposure by the dealers. The audit found that controls over Leeson were minimal. 'The general manager [Leeson] likes to be involved in the back office and does not regard it as a burden,' the audit found. There was a 'significant general risk that the controls could be overridden by the general manager'; and his involvement in front and back offices represented an 'excessive concentration of powers'. In other words, Leeson was watchdog for his own deals.

The audit report was taken seriously enough in London to warrant the attention of the main Barings board, headed by Peter Baring, the Chairman, and Andrew Tuckey, his deputy. In September 1995 it was the main subject of a boardroom debate on the operation. That in itself was unusual. But Leeson had on his side his mentor, Ron Baker. A domineering figure, Baker had joined the bank at the same time as Leeson and had built up a 180 strong team. According to sources close to the events, he persuaded the board effectively to ignore the auditor's report. One insider said: 'He took the view that Singapore was too good a business to let them meddle with it.' Baker won the backing of Peter Norris, who was, at the time, a rising star. His group was producing high profits and he was on the fast track to promotion to the main board. But that ambition was never to be realized as the drama of the next few hours unfolded. Suddenly those who did sit on the board were informed that there was a potential loss of £400 million in its Singapore operations – and that it could be much bigger than that. The details were sketchy, but it was agreed that the Bank of England had to be informed. A meeting was set up for noon with the Bank of England's Deputy Governor, Rupert Pennant-Rea, and Brian Quinn, head of banking supervision. Meanwhile, with the crisis about to break, Nick Leeson and his wife, Lisa, had already left their plush flat in the exclusive Orchard Road area of Singapore – their maid, Christine Sampang, saw them leave in a taxi, carrying two suitcases. They crossed the Johore Bahru causeway, which links Singapore with the Malaysian mainland, and travelled 190 miles north to the Malaysian capital, Kuala Lumpur. Just before midnight, Leeson checked in to the Regent Hotel – the most expensive in the city. He was in his shirtsleeves and had just one suitcase with him. He asked for a corporate rate and was ushered to a room on the VIP floor. Lisa was no longer with him, and although she had booked a single seat on a flight to the Thai holiday island of Phuket, she never took up the reservation. Just before noon the next day Leeson used his American Express card to pay his bill. He booked a seat on a Malaysian Airlines flight to the Philippine capital, Manila, but failed to show up. Instead, both he and his wife made a forty-five-minute taxi ride to Subang International Airport, where they caught a flight to Kota Kinabula, in the Malaysian state of Sabah on the island of Borneo.

While the Leesons were checking in to the bougainvillea-covered Hotel Shangri-La, set on an island off the coast, the Governor of the Bank of England and his family were arriving at a ski chalet in the French resort of Avoriaz. Eddie George never had a chance to test the snow conditions because he was almost immediately telephoned by his deputy, Pennant-Rea. George took a taxi to Geneva and bought a standby ticket on a flight to London. By the time he was dropped by a taxi outside his home at 10.30 pm, discussions had already been held with the British banking establishment. Over the weekend the bankers tried to put together a rescue package. Five of the Bank's six executive directors – George, Pennant-Rea, Quinn, Ian Plenderleith, the markets guru, and Professor Mervyn King, head of the economics department – moved between meetings on the ground and first floors of Threadneedle Street. There was no sense of panic – after all, Barings was only a medium-sized bank. Officials were also confident that there was no risk to the banking system itself, but they tried to put together a rescue package before the Far East markets opened on Sunday night (i.e. Monday morning in Singapore) – as Eddie George said: 'What motivated me was trying to protect something that was valuable in itself and very valuable to the City.' Some of the City elite – Andrew Buxton, Chairman of Barclays and Lord Alexander, Chairman of NatWest – were in favour of a bail-out. It was clear that Barings needed recapitalizing, and a 'lifeboat' (a fund set up by dealers in a market to rescue a member who may become insolvent through operations in that market) with all the institutions chipping in was seen as the best solution. After all, the Bank of England had organized such a deal for Barings back in 1890, during the Argentine débâcle. But this time around the situation was much worse. What confronted the bankers here was a potentially unlimited loss. Its positions in Japan made it a hostage to any downward move in share prices. Each time there was a 1 per cent movement of the main indices it would add another £100 million to the cost of saving Barings. The City normally closes ranks to protect its own, and initial meetings suggested that that was what would happen this time. But on Saturday, 27 February the debt had already grown to £585 million. Outside the Bank of England two limousines were parked.

With their distinctive number plates – BRU1 and BRU2 – they belonged to the only man in the world with pockets deep enough to reach in and bail Barings out. Through the Brunei Investment Authority, with $40 billion at its disposal, the world's richest man, the Sultan of Brunei, was considering stepping in for England and saving the day. For a time there was indeed hope. After all, the Sultan would be saving a bank that up until then had had an enviable reputation, particularly in the Far East. In any case, he was a customer, and there is such a thing as customer loyalty. But eventually the concern over unlimited losses proved too worrying even for him. And Barings was fast becoming history. No one could afford to write a blank cheque for Barings.

Other options were also explored. The Bank tried to see if it could persuade the Japanese securities firms to put a cap on the Barings liabilities to prevent another fall in shares in Japan, but that plan fell through. George and his team were only too well aware that Sunday night was the deadline for a rescue plan. By now it was almost 9 pm and the lifeboat was still on the shore. A rescue simply wasn't possible. In the Far East the markets were about to open. Rumours had begun to circulate. Barings had no option but to close. At midnight, three administrators from the accountants Ernst & Young were formally appointed to oversee the stricken bank's affairs. As Governor of the Bank of England, Eddie George went to Downing Street, where he informed the Chancellor, Kenneth Clarke, that Barings was done for. There had never been any possibility of the company being bailed out by the taxpayer, since there was no danger to the banking system as a whole if it failed. All Eddie George was left to do was to try to minimize the fall-out on the markets that might result when the collapse of the merchant bank became known, and when he appeared at a press conference late on Monday afternoon this had by and large been successfully achieved. Media attention was focused on the man who broke the bank, Nick Leeson, and his whereabouts.

Mr and Mrs Leeson, of course, could have watched the media circus on cable television in their room at the Shangri-La. The couple stayed there for four nights, obviously unsure of their next step. Again they booked flights, this time back to Peninsular Malaysia, but again they never showed up. Eventually they booked out of the Shangri-La and moved from the island resort to Kota Kinabula city centre. There Leeson and his twenty-three-year-old wife walked into a Royal Brunei Airlines office at around 11 am the next morning. Both were in T-shirts and shorts. They inquired about flights to Europe, but left without buying a ticket. Two hours later they were back, and Leeson paid cash for two tickets to Frankfurt. He corrected the desk clerk when she spelt his name 'Lesson', and she added to the tickets, 'Should be read as Leeson'. The couple spent another night at a hotel in the city. On that evening a member of staff at the Shangri-La contacted Sabah police and told them two people had stayed there under the name Leeson. This information was disregarded, and the couple left the island on a Royal Brunei flight early on Wednesday morning. Later that day, Janice Loh, a bookings officer at the airline office, realized that the two people who had bought tickets to Frankfurt the previous day were the couple who had featured on the television news. 'I called the police but they didn't seem to be very clear about what I was talking about, so I called the local newspaper.' By then the Leesons were airborne, on their way to Frankfurt.

The day before the couple arrived in Germany, it was announced in London that one of Barings' best-known customers, Queen Elizabeth II, faced a personal loss of some half a million pounds; the bank's total losses were by then estimated at £700 million. The pound had plunged to a record low against the Deutschmark during the crisis, and the Chancellor announced an inquiry into the collapse by the Board of Banking Supervision. When Nick Leeson touched down at Frankfurt airport on 2 March he cannot have known the trail of financial devastation his actions had sparked off. After all, the Dutch bank, ING, was about to buy Barings for a nominal £1 coin! Clutching a paperback thriller, Leeson left the plane, calmly went up to a policeman, and announced: 'I'm the man you want.' He was taken into custody, and, once various formalities had been completed, was then taken to Hoechst prison in the suburbs of Frankfurt, where his accommodation was described as a single room 9 square metres in area, in which there was a bed with blue-and-white check sheets, a table, a chair and a cupboard. The man who was rumoured to have been in line for a $2 million bonus from Barings before its collapse, was now only capable of earning the equivalent of £4 a day in the prison workshops, making wooden toys and pottery, or sealing army envelopes. He began reading voraciously, though he had to have official permission for every newspaper or prison library book he wanted to borrow. He could not communicate with the outside world except through his lawyers. Stephen Pollard, Leeson's English solicitor, from the well-known City firm of Kingsley Napley, said: 'He is fine; he has not lost his sense of humour, but he misses the emotional support of his wife' (Mrs Leeson was staying with relatives in England). Leeson himself was the only Briton among 160 inmates at Hoechst prison, 70 per cent of whom are foreign, and most of them, like Leeson, awaiting deportation.

By now, the authorities in Singapore had already filed specimen charges against Leeson, and wanted him to go back to the island to stand trial. Leeson himself made it clear that he would rather go back to Britain, but the British authorities did not appear at all anxious to have him, though the Serious Fraud Office did state that it wished to interview him. Eleven charges were submitted by Singapore to the authorities in Germany. According to German extradition laws, those offences also had to be punishable under German law for extradition to take place. A Frankfurt court upheld an earlier ruling that the extradition papers met German legal requirements, so Leeson eventually returned to Singapore to stand trial on twelve charges alleging cheating. One of the charges related to forgery, alleging that Leeson had forged two documents which purported to show that Barings had been credited with about £50 million from Spear, Leeds and Kellogg, a Wall Street firm, and that he used the documents as collateral with which to obtain money from Citibank in Singapore in order to continue trading. That charge alone carried a maximum sentence of seven years in gaol. He felt all along that he would perhaps be better treated by courts in Britain, and there was undoubtedly strong resentment of him and his activities in Singapore – when news of his arrest was heard on the Singapore trading floor where he used to work, there were loud cheers from other traders. The Singapore International Monetary Exchange (Simex) and the Monetary Authority of Singapore (MAS), together with the accountancy firm Price Waterhouse which is now managing and investigating Barings Futures Singapore, allege that the bank's top management in London knew three years before Leeson's arrest that their Singapore operation could well lead to crippling losses. Before the world's press, Simex revealed a letter it claimed was a copy of one dated 25 March 1992, and sent by James Bax, head of Barings Futures, to Andrew Fraser, head of equities in London. In part, the letter read: 'My concern is that once again we are in danger of setting up a structure which will subsequently prove disastrous and with which we will succeed in losing either a lot of money or client goodwill or both. In my view it is critical we should keep clear reporting lines and if this office is involved with Simex at all then Nick [Leeson] should report to Simon [Jones, a Barings' director] and then be ultimately responsible for the operations side.' But despite this letter, it appears that Leeson was indeed in charge of both the trading and settlement parts of Barings' Simex operation. It also emerged that on 8 February 1995 a director from Barings in London, Anthony Hawes, the group treasurer, flew to Singapore to reassure Simex that the bank could cope with the huge positions run up by Leeson. Simex said that its internal controls had picked up Leeson's large positions in 'early January'; alarmed, it had queried what was happening with Barings in London throughout that month, and also in February. Further, Simex said that as the positions grew larger it had asked for explanations, and assurances were received, including from Barings in London, that the Barings group position was sound. Price Waterhouse revealed that Barings sent Singapore $1.3 billion (£570 million) to its Singapore arm in January and February to meet its margin calls. Some Singapore $286 million was sent in the seven days, 17 February to 24 February, the week before Barings crashed.

On 18 June 1995, with Nick Leeson still sitting in his jail cell in Germany, the British Chancellor, Kenneth Clarke, stood up in Parliament to give elected members a report on the findings of the investigation (which ran to 500 pages) he had authorized into the collapse of Barings. He blamed the collapse of the 223-year-old bank on a litany of errors by managers, who had signally failed to spot massive unauthorized dealing by Leeson. He also criticized the bank regulatory body, the Bank of England, for errors of judgement, though he added that he did not believe there was any need for sweeping changes in the way the central bank supervised commercial banks. 'It's a picture of the total collapse of management control … It is incredible that such a system of control should exist in a bank like this [Barings],' he continued. By the time the bank went under, Leeson had chalked up losses of £827 million ($1.32 billion) by making a wild $27 billion bet on Japanese stocks and bonds. Nor had the Chancellor finished his catalogue of failures, sins, and crimes. 'Leeson successfully sought to conceal those huge losses by a complex and systematic process of deception and false reporting,' he said, though he added: 'Such a massive unauthorized position could not have been established if there had been an effective system of management, financial and operating controls within Barings.' Barings advanced huge sums to Singapore to fund Leeson's trading without making independent checks: 'If management in London had sought to examine the information from Singapore to support the requests for funds they should have discovered that the information was meaningless.' Managers thought they were transferring money to bankroll clients' trading, but failed to run credit checks. Nor did they question Leeson's 'extraordinarily high' profits. Despite the rogue trader's efforts at concealing his losses, some information was available, but management never analysed it. 'No one within Barings accepted responsibility for Leeson's activities for the whole of 1994,' Clarke told Parliament. Moreover, he said, there were serious shortcomings in Barings' regular reports to the Bank of England and to the Securities and Futures Authority, which helped to keep the problem hidden from view. Turning to external regulatory controls, Clarke said that the central bank had made 'an error of judgement' and displayed 'a lack of rigour' in overseeing Barings. But he added that although improvements were needed to existing procedures, the Bank of England's Board of Banking Supervision, which carried out the inquiry, did not consider Barings' collapse pointed to the need for fundamental changes to the framework of regulation. The Bank of England itself had come to a similar conclusion: 'There is no evidence that on the information available to it the Bank could have prevented the Barings collapse,' it said. Clarke raised questions about the effectiveness of Barings' auditors in Singapore, Coopers & Lybrand, and also expressed regret that the inquiry had, for legal reasons, been unable to obtain all the information it needed from the Singapore authorities. But the Chancellor concluded: 'No regulatory system can provide a 100 per cent guarantee against a bank failure, especially where there is a deliberate intention on the part of individual traders to conceal and to deceive, combined with inadequate management controls.' Nick Leeson's wife, Lisa, broke down and wept when she heard that her husband had been blamed in Parliament for the collapse of Britain's oldest merchant bank.

Of course, censure in Parliament wasn't the end of the drama either for Leeson, his wife or the other key players within Barings. In some financial circles there was a feeling that Leeson's come-uppance justified old-school snobbery – after all, the trader was said to be the 'first oik' hired by Barings. One view was that he had brought down his aristocratic masters because they were too blue-bloodedly silly to notice what he was up to. It is true that Leeson had come a long way from his humble origins. A plasterer's son from a council estate in Watford, in Hertfordshire, he had not distinguished himself academically at the comprehensive school he attended, an offshoot of the now defunct Parmiter's Grammar School in Bethnal Green, East London, founded in 1681 (school motto: 'No man lives for himself alone'). He passed six GCE O levels and two A levels – English and History – but failed Maths. In other days he would probably have drifted into an apprenticeship with a large local employer like Rolls-Royce, but that factory had closed before Nick Leeson left school. So he opted for a career in finance because the school had long-standing links with the City, and went to work in menial posts for the royal bankers, Coutts, and then the merchant bank Morgan Stanley. He kept up links with his old school, becoming captain of the Old Parmiterians football club. There was, perhaps, one portent of things to come – he left debts when he shook off his Hertfordshire roots. In February 1991 Watford County Court made a judgment of £639 against him on behalf of Hitachi, and although he paid that off there was a second judgment for £2,426 owed to the NatWest Bank in May 1992. But Leeson was able to put all this behind him when he made good and joined Barings, getting a post in its Indonesia operation and moving on to Singapore in April 1992. There he was promoted to dealer and was quickly marked out as a ruthlessly aggressive trader with seemingly sound instincts. He had moved to one of the most dynamic business regions of the world, and when he arrived with Lisa, his bride of one month, it became obvious that here was a twenty-five-year-old working-class lad in a hurry. Nick Leeson was an A-level boy who'd joined a bank and blossomed, and while some bank trainees had settled for the goal of managing a branch in the provinces, he had flourished at the sharp end of modern banking – making millions for his bosses by trading in the financial securities markets.

Singapore offered sunshine, glamour and a hectic social life for the expatriate community. It was the new Hong Kong, well run, well ordered, stringently regulated, a place where the streets were free from both litter and beggars. Instead of being jostled by rush-hour commuters in London, his daily routine began with a short drive to work from a £4,000-a-month furnished flat in one of Singapore's most fashionable suburbs. He spent evenings in Harry's Bar, a favourite dealers' haunt, and weekends at the exclusive Charge Alley Sports Club or playing soccer with the Admiralty Football Club. He drove a Porsche and a Mercedes, even moored a yacht off the Malaysian coast. In the evenings the Leesons dined out in Chinatown or in one of the many outdoor restaurants on the Boat Quay alongside the Singapore River. 'Tell me your definition of heaven. For me, this is it,' he once confided to a colleague. At first Lisa was homesick, but the feeling didn't last long. Within two years of arriving her husband was earning nearly £200,000 a year in basic salary, as well as generous bonuses, and this helped make the upheaval bearable. He and his wife were popular on the expatriate cocktail circuit, hosting parties at his company flat and whooping it up in local bars (Leeson was even fined for indecent exposure after dropping his trousers in front of a group of women). He also put on weight, and took to disguising a growing paunch with double-breasted suits. Some colleagues even claimed he'd had plastic surgery to enhance his jawline and remove a double chin. In most ways, Nick Leeson was typical of the new breed of colonials who had rushed into the so-called 'tiger economies' of South-East Asia. They were little different from the British traders who had flocked to that area in past centuries – lured by greed, a love of adventure, and social ambition. The Far East markets demanded a swashbuckling spirit and it seemed that anyone with a bright idea could rise to the top. A former Barings staffer said: 'It was like London in the mid-1980s. There was a constant turnover of staff because people were always being head-hunted. All you had to do was stand on the escalator and ride to the top ... Overnight you could become an expert in some new financial product. It was really just a new way of chopping or dicing a loan or guarantee, but if you knew the jargon you could bamboozle people that you had just invented something that would defy gravity.' Leeson was largely free to do what he wanted. 'We admired Nick because he had almost no fear,' said one Singapore dealer. 'It was like watching someone juggling hand grenades, but we always thought if he dropped one he would blow just himself up.'

When news of what had happened first emerged, his father-in-law, Alex Sims, from West Kingsdown, Kent, said: 'I can't believe this. Nick is such a quiet lad. He has been painted as a council-house yuppie but that's not really him. Dealers generally are loud, brash and flash but Nick was none of these things. He is a genuinely nice guy and I'm proud to call him son-in-law. I don't believe for a moment he is the only one involved in this. It seems he is being made a scapegoat. He is not the sort who would be into fraud or con the bank in any way. If he is responsible for what happened it must have been a genuine mistake.'

Not everyone was to be as charitable – not the Baring family, nor the Singapore authorities, nor those who lost money, nor those who continued to do so even after the bank had been sold. After all, even the Queen's accounts suffered when the bank collapsed. And this was no ordinary bank, but the oldest, most blue-blooded finance house in Britain. Founded 223 years before Leeson's catastrophic dealings came to light, it had grown to such stature that Cardinal Richelieu named it as the sixth great power of Europe after England, France, Austria, Prussia and Russia. Though no longer family-owned, the bank still retained close ties with the Barings, and Sir Peter Baring was the current Chairman. In the immediate aftermath of the Leeson débâcle, he was to say that Leeson's actions must have been part of a conspiracy to topple the bank. Such a view was no doubt part arrogance, part incredulity; after all, the Baring name and fortune had been founded on solidity, not risk-taking. In the 1890s John Revelstoke, the second baron, told a friend considering sending his son into the City: 'It is almost a platitude to say that I consider that character and power of application count for more in the City than brains or brilliant abilities.' Indeed, for a rich and titled family, the Barings have made few waves, hardly rippling the gossip columns, for example, though there was the occasional exception. The third Lord Revelstoke was forced to retire from the bank after a scandal broke when he married a divorcee. The fourth, Rupert Baring, who died in 1994 leaving £787,000, bought Lambay Island, Co. Dublin, in 1934 and lived the rest of his life there as a recluse. The Baring clan extends far and wide – the Princess of Wales is the great-granddaughter of a Baring – and though few of its members are short of money, their fortunes vary widely. The third Earl of Cromer died in 1991 leaving just over £3 million, while the fifth Lord Northbrook left more than £30 million the following year.

But though, by the early 1990s, the bank was still being run by bankers of the old school, its competitors were making more money with new kinds of bankers and new methods. So it was that Barings was forced to look favourably on people like Nick Leeson. In his early trading days in Singapore he revolutionized their operations. In the year to September 1992, Barings Futures in Singapore made £1.18 million. By the end of Leeson's first full year in 1993 the company's net profits from that market had risen eightfold to £8.83 million – and he was winning success in an area that most of the established bankers at Barings knew little about, derivatives. Furthermore, his seniors at head office in London believed that all they had to do to ensure that he made even more money was to give him more leeway. They therefore allowed a young, inexperienced dealer, several thousand miles from head office with no one to report to locally, even more power to decide which deals to make and how much of the company's money to invest. It was a recipe for disaster. So how did Nick Leeson hoodwink his colleagues and his superiors? The answer is that he used a variety of techniques. Alongside his Barings business, he was carrying out a separate, more sinister type of trade from the middle of 1994. Using fictitious client names and the hidden computer account (Error Account No. 88888), which did not show up on monitoring reports in London or to -

outside auditors, he was conducting substantial extra business. By the beginning of 1995 he'd notched up losses of more than £50 million.

As his losses mounted, the trader compounded the problem by purchasing more contracts through the hidden account. Calls for a proportion of the price of these future contracts, the margin calls, were paid for by making other transactions and chalking up further losses. At his trial in Singapore, Lawrence Ang, who led the prosecution, described in some detail the ingenious ways in which Leeson had hidden the mounting losses and tricked Barings' auditors into believing that they did not exist. At the end of January 1995, Leeson was having trouble explaining the loss of 7.8 billion yen (£50 million), which he had tried to disguise by alleging that an American customer would be paying this sum back to Barings. However, there was no customer and there was no more cash (although Leeson forged a letter from the customer stating that the cash would eventually be paid). As the accountants closed in, he devised a plan to transfer an equivalent amount of money to the losses from one Barings bank account to another, before swiftly moving it back to the account to which it belonged before anyone noticed it had gone. He did this to obtain documentary evidence that the alleged debt had been repaid. However, the bank statement which showed the payment also showed the transfer, so Leeson set about altering the statement to remove references to the transfer. The cut and pasted statement was then photocopied and passed on to the auditors. At Coopers & Lybrand no one questioned it, nor a confirmation he faxed on paper headed 'From Nick and Lisa'; the original collage was found in his desk. Meanwhile, he had identified a weak link in the Singapore International Monetary Exchange (Simex), which required futures traders to maintain a reserve account with the exchange to protect it against non payment. Leeson saw that it was possible to key a false trade into the exchange's computer, which had no means of knowing whether that deal had actually been made or not. Once this was done, the false Barings client's account making the loss could be shown to be in balance, therefore allowing Barings to recover almost £75 million of its money held as security at Simex, at a time when it was actually falling deeper and deeper into debt.

When the Singapore authorities applied for Leeson to be extradited from Germany they cited eleven offences. In the end, however, he faced only two of them when he came to trial in December 1995. The first, amended to a minor offence of cheating, carried a maximum penalty of one year's imprisonment instead of the maximum seven years for the original charge. The second charge – related to the more serious matter of messing with the Simex computer accounts – still carried a maximum seven-year term. Once Leeson realized that his campaign to be prosecuted by the Serious Fraud Office and tried in London had failed and that he would have to stand trial in Singapore, his team of lawyers and public-relations advisers then went to great trouble to try to counter some of their client's excessive language about the brutal prison regime in Singapore, and his doubts about receiving a fair trial there. This second campaign appeared to work, following a series of meetings between Leeson's lawyer, John Koh, and the prosecutor, Lawrence Ang. At that meeting the authorities agreed to the charges being reduced to two – effectively meaning that Leeson would face a maximum of eight years in prison, and not fourteen. Even in court both sides seemed anxious to present as favourable a picture of Leeson as they could. Koh described Leeson as a 'dynamic, but in the final analysis, insufficiently experienced trader', struggling against ruthless free-market forces to salvage the fortunes of his bank, misguided, but not motivated by greed or criminal intent. 'What do the facts show?' Koh asked. 'Recklessness. Our client is not a crook.' Lawrence Ang, who was Director of Singapore's Criminal Affairs Department (CAD) as well as prosecuting counsel, did not concentrate on the intensive police investigation, or the story of how Leeson lied to auditors Coopers & Lybrand when they turned up a $78.6 million discrepancy in his by now infamous 'five eights' account. He left heads gently nodding as he painstakingly traced Leeson's ingenious methods, telling the court how the trader had tried to cover up the growing hole in the accounts by suggesting that a vast amount of it was owed to Barings by a New York brokerage firm. He said Leeson had explained to CAD investigators that he had shown the auditors a receipt for the sum, taking the chance that they weren't very good at their jobs. All it needed was a little cut-and-paste work.

Even the prosecution, it appeared, wanted to offer mitigating circumstances – ways to suggest that the court should be lenient. Ang pointed out that Nick Leeson had already spent many miserable months in a German jail. Leeson's lawyers pointed out that their client shouldn't be punished for bringing Barings down but only for the offences laid against him. Koh added that Leeson, having discovered he just couldn't deal his way out of these losses, had panicked. He 'would have welcomed discovery'. In the end, the defence said, he had fled the predicament, the pressure, not the law.

John Koh then began to lay it on more thickly. He said that after his mother's death, Leeson had helped his father raise his siblings (a particularly effective argument in strongly familial Singapore). And whilst there was a financial nightmare looming at work, he and his wife had also suffered the emotional trauma of her miscarriage at the end of January. Leeson's lawyers were also anxious to dispel any idea that their client was going to profit in any way from what had happened. The suggestion that he would be made rich by publishing and newspaper deals, and possibly a film, were dismissed: the proceeds of his autobiography, which was sold to an English publisher for £500,000, 'will go to the agent, the ghost-writer, English and German lawyers and Singapore counsel'. It was pointed out that he had sold property to pay towards his own legal fees, and had even lost a £450,000 bonus by resigning the week before it was due to be paid.

Though the case had not stirred much interest in Singapore, it was still possible to buy 'Barings learns a Leeson' T-shirts there, as well as a new board game called 'In the Nick of

Time'. Local lawyers, however, believed that the Singapore authorities would be concerned – as are most financial centres today – that their markets should be seen to be fair, and that wrongdoing would be severely punished. Those who supported such views were fortunate in the choice of trial judge. There was no need to push Richard Magnus towards a harsh sentence. Nicknamed 'Maximum Magnus' for his tendency to hand down heavy prison terms, he'd set a record only the week before the Leeson trial by jailing a civil servant for fourteen years for corruption. In the event, it did indeed prove that Magnus was determined to make an example of Leeson, and thus maintain the island state's reputation for dealing firmly with criminals, especially those that prey on its institutions. Instead of a few months in prison, which had been suggested as a serious possibility by legal experts, Nick Leeson was instead condemned to six and a half years in gaol. Even with remission for good behaviour, he would serve at least three and a half years.

It is possible that the judge, in handing down his sentence, had in mind what many commentators seem to have overlooked – the victims of Leeson's crime. The concentration on the large sums involved, or on the celebrities like the Queen – those who lost money but can afford to do so – obscures the real losers. These were principally bond-holders. Late in 1993 Barings had raised £100 million by issuing a perpetual loan at $9\frac{1}{4}$ per cent. Normally, perpetual loans of this kind are taken by insurance companies and pension funds, but with interest rates beginning to fall, the Barings bond offered an unusually attractive return to private investors. Brokers bought chunks of the loan and divided it up, selling it on to individual clients. So the creditors – the losers – included small-time investors like a South London doctor, a vicar in North Wales, a retired army officer. Many had invested part of their retirement savings. The new owner, the Dutch bank ING, offered to pay only 5p in the pound, with the possibility of another 20p at some future date.

Apart from the victims outside, there were some on the inside who suffered as well. The proud Baring family was, not surprisingly, humbled, and lost its bank and its place in history. Twenty-one men and women who were judged to have been responsible in some measure for Leeson's fraud were dismissed in July. For one senior manager it was all too much – when he received the hand-delivered dismissal letter from ING he locked himself in the toilet and wept bitterly. There is no evidence that Nick Leeson ever did that. His only apology was the note he left for his colleagues on his desk the day he disappeared. All it said was 'Sorry'.

7

Ivar Kreuger – The Match King

Ivar Kreuger was born in Sweden in 1880, the eldest son of the joint owner of two small match factories in Kalmar and Monsteras. He had an ordinary school career, though he seems to have been involved in organized 'cribbing' and the obtaining of final term marks before they were announced, which he then sold to his schoolmates – a taste, perhaps, of things to come. This was followed by a mechanical engineering course at the Royal Technical University in Stockholm, from which he graduated without any particular distinction; indeed, he appears to have cheated to some extent here, too. He then held an engineering job in hydro-electric power for a year before travelling to the United States in 1900. Here he worked at a variety of jobs in New York, Colorado, Illinois and Louisiana, and then went to Mexico to work on a bridge in Veracruz, where he contracted yellow fever, after which he returned to Sweden.

In 1901 he returned to New York City, where he got a job with a construction company, and was employed as an engineer on the building of office blocks and hotels. It was during this time that he began to notice the financial goings-on that were associated with the construction industry in New York, and which included political payoffs as well as more general bribery. In 1903 he went to Germany, becoming involved in construction contracts near Saarbrucken for some months, moving on to South Africa to install some steel girders from a German plant in the Carlton Hotel, Johannesburg. Three years later he was in Toronto, again in construction contracting. He briefly tried to widen his business activities by opening a restaurant in Philadelphia, but this soon failed, and he returned to New York to work for the Consolidated Engineering Company, where he swiftly rose to become a vice-president. In this post he supervised the construction of the Archbold Stadium at Syracuse University, a project which involved the use of reinforced concrete, at that time a new technique. It was now that he met Julius Kahn, the inventor and patentee of the special iron needed in reinforced concrete, who suggested that Kreuger might like to introduce the new methods into Europe. The engineer knew a good business opportunity when he saw one, and returned to Sweden to try it out.

In 1908, the twenty-seven-year-old Kreuger met Paul Toll, a Swedish engineer who had some experience of working in concrete. They formed the company of Kreuger & Toll in May of that year, for which Kreuger put up Kr 10,000 which he had borrowed from his father, though Toll contributed nothing financially. Their enterprise began to flourish, for the new building technique rapidly became popular, and in late 1908 they were contracted to build a large department store in Stockholm. Kreuger exhibited his novel approach to business in this first contract, which had penalty clauses attached, but which provided for a bonus if the work was completed early. Kreuger managed to complete ahead of schedule, even in the Swedish winter, by means of erecting heavy tarpaulins, arranging for heating and lighting, and making sure the work on the building continued twenty-four hours a day; the company collected a bonus equivalent to $70,000. It was activities of this kind that led to Kreuger & Toll becoming a highly regarded building company in Sweden, and in 1911 the firm incorporated with a capital of Kr 1,000,000. Now, the charter of incorporation stated that the company was to engage in the construction of buildings and similar activities, but was NOT to trade in securities on a regular basis. Kreuger's attitude to making money, however, meant that this proviso was effectively ignored; securities trading by Kreuger & Toll, through various dummy companies, was soon to run into hundreds of millions of kroner.

Kreuger's burgeoning ambition in business was not to remain in construction for long. He was, it will be remembered, the son of a match manufacturer, and it is into the match industry that he moved next. It was his activities in this field that were eventually to raise him to the status of international financier, and, by extension, to lead to his downfall when his international trading ambitions spectacularly outstripped his ability to meet his commitments, leading to fraud, and even outright forgery. The match industry, rather like the construction industry, had recently introduced new methods of manufacture. Several small factories had set up in Sweden using this new process in the last years of the nineteenth century, and by 1903 six of them had amalgamated into a single combine, the Jönköping-Vulcan Trust. This left about a dozen small factories in the country which were not included, but two of those were owned by Kreuger's father and his Uncle Fredrik. Ivar Kreuger's younger brother Torsten was managing the Kalmar factory, and owned one of the two Swedish plants which built match-making machinery. Torsten had been approached by the Swedish Credit Bank to form a rival match combine, using the bank's money and the Kreuger factories as the kernel of the new business. Torsten had rejected this offer, but his brother Ivar agreed. Kreuger had already mentioned to a banker called Oscar Rydbeck, of the Swedish Credit Bank, that something ought to be done about the squeeze that Jönköping-Vulcan were putting on the smaller match concerns.

In 1913 Kreuger formed United Match Factories, also known as the Kalmar Trust, supported by three banks including the Swedish Credit Bank, with a capital of Kr 4,000,000. He began to build his vision of a worldwide match empire. The Kalmar Trust, which although only one-third the size of the rival combine to begin with, grew to command an almost equal share of the market within three years. Kreuger began by buying the only other match-making machinery company, and also acquired other match factories not in the Jönköping-Vulcan Trust. He then lowered costs and improved the quality of his company's matches, not least by producing his own raw materials. The setting up of an effective foreign sales organization followed, though the Swedish match industry's foreign markets suffered severely during the First World War. By the end of 1917 Jönköping-Vulcan were beginning to lose out, and Kreuger was able to negotiate a merger of Jönköping-Vulcan with his own Kalmar Trust into the Swedish Match Company, with himself as President. This transaction was one of the first in which he showed the trend of his future trading activities, managing to overvalue the shares of Kalmar so that, although still not as large as Jönköping-Vulcan, the smaller absorbed the larger.

Meanwhile, Kreuger & Toll was still doing well, having by now a total of six subsidiary companies. Kreuger split the building firm into two companies in January 1917, one of which was the Kreuger & Toll Building Company, run by Paul Toll. This company continued as a respectable and prosperous company, and was not directly involved in any of the subsequent activities of Ivar Kreuger. The other company, Kreuger & Toll, Inc., was a financial holding company for Kreuger's expanding personal pecuniary ambition. New stock issues meant that by 1918 the authorized shares of Kreuger & Toll were Kr 16,000,000, with even greater reserves. Shortly afterwards, Kreuger's other business activities began to get involved with this new company; 120,000 Swedish Match Company shares (about 25 per cent of all issued) were transferred to Kreuger and Toll for $2,000,000.

The match empire, however, continued to expand, and Swedish Match managed to capture most of the Asian, British and German markets with the help of Swedish banks. Kreuger began to buy European match factories from their war-impoverished owners, until he controlled virtually the whole

European match industry, realizing that near-monopoly would negate the undercutting he was facing from match concerns in Germany, Poland and Belgium; it was not for nothing that he became known as 'The Match King'. He also began to speculate on the foreign exchange markets (by buying property with shaky European currency in war-affected Europe and reselling it to US investors for solid dollars), and invested in the giant I.G. Farben Trust of chemical companies in Germany. Kreuger now began his international financial dealing, and his fraudulent activities, in earnest, though what exactly prompted him to do so is still to some extent a matter for conjecture. He had been manipulating the books of his companies since 1917 in order to siphon off money for his personal accounts, and to inflate the value of his match companies. He kept his staff generally unaware of the state of the companies by keeping their activities carefully separated from each other; no one had a true overall picture but himself. However, he now formed a holding company in the US called American Kreuger & Toll, capitalized at $6,000,000, and also began acquiring stock in American match and other companies, including Diamond Match. In this way he managed to accumulate some $400,000,000, which he transferred to Europe through a series of banks, both real and dummy ones of his own creation, whilst continuing to issue stock and borrow heavily for both Swedish Match and Kreuger & Toll in Europe.

Kreuger approached the reputable private banking firm of Lee, Higginson & Company in the US to handle his interests in America, and arranged for their British associates in London, Higginson & Company, to represent him there. Several new companies were created to channel the American proceeds to Europe, including Industrie AG and the Continental Investment Corporation, both in Liechtenstein, and Finanz Gesellschaft in Zurich. His match empire continued to grow, forming in Delaware the International Match Company in 1923 with the help of Lee, Higginson, initially capitalized at $30,000,000 and later issuing gold debentures of a further $15,000,000. As with Diamond Match, Kreuger transferred most of this to Liechtenstein. Nine years later, International Match had sold securities to a value of $148,500,000 in America, of which all but $4,500,000 had been transferred to Kreuger's companies in Europe and was never seen again.

The financial world had not ignored the activities of Ivar Kreuger; indeed, International Match had been audited by the firm of Ernst & Ernst, but most of the company's apparent assets were in the European subsidiaries, whose books Kreuger did not permit the auditors to examine. Nothing seemed to be suspected, and Kreuger now began to think bigger, dealing not only with large sums in match company deals, but also for deals involving government-controlled match monopolies in other countries. Examples of the latter deals included the match industries of France, Estonia, Latvia, Yugoslavia, Romania and Ecuador, but the first 'government' deal was in fact nothing of the kind. This was the 'Garanta' company. In July 1923, Kreuger announced that he had agreed secretly with the Polish government that a Dutch company, NV Financeaelle Maatschappij Garanta, whose stock was supposed to be held by Polish citizens, would have the monopoly of match sales in Poland. The agreement was, in fact, wholly spurious, but Lee, Higginson managed to issue 450,000 International Match shares on the grounds that it did actually exist. Of the $20,000,000 received in this way, $17,000,000 was sent to the Swedish Match Company, on the apparent grounds that Swedish Match had advanced this sum to Garanta, which, unsurprisingly, it had not. In effect, this was a transfer of funds from International Match to Swedish Match. Garanta was, of course, yet another of Kreuger's dummy companies, staffed by a sole employee in Amsterdam, one Karl Lange, who had been fired from a Stockholm bank for dishonesty.

Kreuger now had a continuing need for funds to bribe officials and make loans to governments, and matters began to snowball. In 1927, France needed external loans in order to stabilize her economy. American financiers refused to help, but Kreuger agreed to loan the French government $75,000,000 for 20 years at 5 per cent interest. This was in return for the right to import matches into France in unlimited quantities. A grateful France awarded him the Grand Cross of the Légion d'honneur. This type of loan-for-monopoly deal was repeated in the other countries already mentioned when the US would not make loans to them, so that American investors were, in effect, actually supporting countries which their government or financial organizations thought were not suitable for such loans. Kreuger also began to buy into interests other than matches, such as iron ore in Sweden, Africa and Latin America, Swedish pulp, paper and telephone concerns, and even the Swedish Boliden Mining Company, a gold-mining operation. It is ironic that it was a telephone company deal in America that triggered his eventual downfall, but in the meantime his activities spread. He continued to buy stocks and bonds in sound companies like General Electric and I.G. Farben (in which he had had an interest since the war), and invested in good French government bonds; however, he also continued to exaggerate the number he held in order to ensure that his Kreuger & Toll stocks kept selling – and they did indeed become the world's widest-selling securities.

In October 1929 there occurred an event that should have shaken, if not toppled, the whole teetering edifice of dummy companies and inflated stock holdings: the Wall Street Crash. It did not, chiefly because by keeping all the details of his activities in his head, Kreuger was able to meet his commitments by borrowing or obtaining money on the apparent strength of his empire, and by switching funds from one company to another. In fact, two days after the crash he was able to announce that he was going to lend the German government $125,000,000 at 6 per cent, once more in return for a match monopoly. This deal, however, shows another and even less attractive side to Kreuger, for it transpired he was a supporter of Hitler and the Nazis, and wanted to bolster Germany against the Soviet Union, whose match industry he had been unable to penetrate. He obtained $50,000,000 of the total German loan, from US banks and the rest, ironically enough, from France, who thereby paid him back a part of her earlier loan.

But the Depression began to bite even the Match King. He began to find it more difficult to borrow, and Kreuger & Toll shares started to slide. Most US investors had bought Kreuger & Toll on margins, and as the brokers collected, shareholders sold. The quoted price began to slip, and he had to throw in more of his reserves to bolster the price, transferring money from legitimate banks to his dummy or non-existent ones, thus propping up his stock by reporting large 'reserves', which simply did not exist in genuine banks. By 1930 he was beginning to feel embattled, and found himself compelled to resort to yet another form of fraud to bolster his 'reserves': forgery. He had had some correspondence with the Italian government concerning yet another match monopoly. The deal came to nothing, but as a result of his attempts he had obtained, on letters to him, the signatures of both Signor Mosconi, the Minister of Finance under Mussolini, and Signor Giovanni Bocelli, the Director-General of State Monopolies. He arranged for lithographs to be made of imitation Italian government bonds with a face value of £500,000 each, together with promissory notes for interest of £1,500,000 each. Then he patiently forged the names of Mosconi and Bocelli on the fake Italian treasury bonds, to the eventual 'value' of £29,000,000.

Kreuger now headed a match empire which operated in 43 countries and had 250 factories, effectively producing and selling 75 per cent of the world's matches, as well as all his interests in iron ore, chemicals and telephones; to all appearances he was a highly successful financier, the pride of Swedish business. In May 1931 he visited President Hoover in Washington, then went on to New York to negotiate the merger of L.M. Ericsson Telephone in Sweden, one of the concerns that he had bought, with the International Telephone & Telegraph Company in the US. IT&T signed an agreement under which 600,000 Ericsson shares would be deposited by Kreuger in a Swedish bank in exchange for $11,000,000. In addition, the American telephone company would acquire a further 410,000 shares within 12 months of Ericsson's 1931 accounts being audited by the British accountants Price Waterhouse.

However, Kreuger had made enemies. Some critics had begun to question how, in a recession, his seemingly huge profits could be maintained at a level to pay the dividends on such a vastly expanded capital. His time was nearly up. Some of his enemies in France organized raids on his companies, thus driving Kreuger & Toll share prices down still further (in a raid, a group of people or companies sells shares in a business at the same time, in order to lower the price of the shares, which can then be bought back at a lower price; raids are often the opening moves in hostile takeover bids). He needed further reserves to bolster the stock price, and turned to the Swedish Riksbank for a $10,000,000 loan, supported by his shares in Swedish Boliden Mining. In January 1932 he went back to the United States and tried to borrow from the Bank of America, and even to gain control of the bank through Transamerica, a holding company of the bank's stock. These attempts failed, and Kreuger now had several major payments due which he was in no real position to make. The Swedish Match Company was due $2,000,000 in New York, and International Match was owed $4,000,000. Kreuger & Toll needed $1,250,000 to meet dividends, and Turkey and Lithuania were owed over $3,000,000 between them for payments on loans they had made for match factories Kreuger had established there.

Meanwhile, Price Waterhouse, as auditors, and Edwin Chinlund, the controller of IT&T, had arrived in Sweden to look at the L.M. Ericsson accounts. Awkward questions were asked, and eventually Kreuger's men admitted that the balance sheets were false. These showed, among other irregularities, that Ericsson had a large balance in cash and on deposit, but $6,000,000 of this was actually an inter-company balance with Kreuger & Toll. Chinlund returned to New York, and IT&T decided to pull out of the merger with Ericsson, demanding that the $11,000,000 paid to Kreuger be returned. With all his other commitments, the Match King was completely unable to repay it. His health began to suffer, and he became deeply depressed. In February 1932, the Swedish Prime Minister, Karl Ekman, agreed that the Riksbank and two private banks should provide Kreuger with the $2,000,000 he needed for the Swedish Match Company payment and the $1,250,000 for the Kreuger & Toll dividend; Ekman paid for this error of judgement by losing office shortly afterwards. The problem of the International Match payment was solved by persuading four US banks to make it, partly on the apparent strength of Kreuger's assets. Some of these assets were German government bonds to the value of $50,000,000, held for International Match at the Deutsche Union Bank in Berlin (another Kreuger-owned bank). Kreuger had, however, transferred them as a pledge for his large private debt to the Scandanivska Bank in Copenhagen. He realized that he would have to replace these bonds before the Ernst & Ernst auditors discovered they were missing. He therefore persuaded the executive committee of International Match to authorize the replacement of the German bonds with Italian government bonds. So far, so good; the Italian bonds were, of course, the ones forged by Kreuger. The auditors, naturally, questioned this transaction, and Kreuger promised that it would be reversed immediately. Unsurprisingly, it was not.

On 4 March 1932, Ivar Kreuger signed the document in New York rescinding the merger of Ericsson and IT&T, agreeing to the repayment of the $11,000,000. He sailed for France the same evening. The Ernst & Ernst auditor, A.D. Berning, contacted Berlin and checked with an auditor there to see if the German bonds had been replaced. They had not, and Berning set off for Europe to get an explanation from Kreuger in person. By now, the embattled Match King had arrived in France, and went to his Paris apartment. Arrangements were made to meet Berning in Berlin and sort out the bonds; Kreuger even told his staff that he would go to Rome and get the Italian government to buy back their bonds, which, since they were fakes, was clearly not possible. Kreuger & Toll share and debenture prices went on falling, New York brokers continuing to issue margin calls.

Kreuger had at last realized that the game was up. On 11 March 1932 he asked one of his many mistresses, a young

Finnish girl, to spend the night with him. She left him early on the morning of the 12th, shortly after which Kreuger went into the bedroom, lay on the bed, and shot himself in the chest just under the heart. When he did not keep an appointment he had for 11 am, Littorin, a director of Swedish Match, and Kreuger's secretary, Miss Bokman, called at his apartment and found him dead.

The full truth about Kreuger's activities only emerged gradually. News of his death was kept from Wall Street until it closed at noon (12 March was a Saturday), to keep the sale of Kreuger & Toll shares going. At $5 a share, they were still regarded by the US investors as a good buy, having traded at $27 in early 1932, and as high as $49 in 1929. Despite this, 165,000 shares of Kreuger & Toll were traded that morning in New York. The fact that most of the selling orders came from France is a demonstration of the fact that he had made many enemies there, and though it was never discovered who exactly had flooded the New York market, one of the French speculators was later arrested and sentenced to five years for illegal stock trading.

In Sweden, the Riksdag (parliament) had declared a moratorium on all payments to Kreuger & Toll; the Match King was, then, still a national hero, and 13 March was declared a day of mourning, with flags flown at half-mast. Ivar Kreuger was cremated in Stockholm on 22 March, with all honours and great numbers of wreaths, including one from IT&T. On 15 March, however, the Swedish government had arranged for Price Waterhouse to investigate all the Kreuger enterprises. The British accountants' report was delivered on 6 April, and proved to be something of a bombshell. In it, the auditors stated that the position of Kreuger & Toll had been seriously misrepresented; the 1930 balance sheets gave a 'false impression', and it was clear that Kreuger had been falsifying accounts. When a Stockholm printer admitted printing the fake Italian bonds, it was clear that the late industrialist and financier had forged them. The investigation proceeded, and the full scale of the whole tottering edifice of dummy holding companies and false banks, and the pillaging of cash, began to emerge. Price Waterhouse reported that Kreuger's accounting had been 'so childish that anybody with a rudimentary knowledge of bookkeeping could see that the books were being falsified'. Entries for amounts totalling nearly $700,000,000 in the books of Kreuger & Toll, Swedish Match, the Garanta Company, and the Continental Investment Company did not tie up with the corresponding entries in the books of other companies; for example, Kreuger & Toll had only 16 entries in its books for Continental Investment, but Continental Investment had 117 for Kreuger & Toll. In the end, Kreuger & Toll was found to be, in UK terms, about £40,000,000 deficient, while Kreuger personally owed £17,000,000 to the Kalmar Trust, and £30,000,000 to Swedish Match. The assets of International Match were non-existent, whilst its liabilities approached £20,000,000. There followed years of patient tracking down of all the widely scattered investments and accounts. Kreuger & Toll and International Match were declared bankrupt. The people who suffered most were the American investors, who only received, for example, 20c on the dollar for the $150,000,000 they had put into International Match, and the smaller European investors, many of whom were ruined.

Surprisingly, there were no criminal prosecutions in the US. Lee, Higginson & Company is estimated to have lost $9,000,000, and was closed down. Swedish Match was able to carry on as a separate organization, because Kreuger had kept it comparatively free of false dealings. In Sweden, a long stream of shady accountants and other Kreuger placemen was dealt with, including Lange of the Garanta Company, and men such as Bredberg and Holm, who had run some of the dummy Liechtenstein, Dutch and Swiss holding companies, and Huldt, who had run one of the fake banks. Eventually, about twenty people were imprisoned, their sentences ranging from only a few months to three years. These included Oscar Rydbeck of the Skandinavska Bank, who still believed Kreuger to have been misrepresented, despite himself having to serve ten months for his part in the frauds, and Kreuger's brother

Torsten, who was gaoled for eighteen months for some minor irregularity over bonds for a Swedish pulp mill sold on the basis of bogus earnings statements. In prison, Torsten became increasingly bitter, but he continued to insist that his brother's enemies in France had engineered the run on his stocks in March 1932, and even that they had had him murdered. He spent most of the rest of his life trying to prove these things, publishing propaganda through two Swedish newspapers which he owned. Inevitably, perhaps, such rumours gained a hold, not least because they concerned a man who had been the confidant of statesmen, and a powerful and outwardly colourful figure (though privately Ivar Kreuger was somewhat secretive and remote).

Who was Ivar Kreuger, and why did his business empire mushroom from a comparatively stable and sound base in construction and match manufacture to a gigantic balloon of fictitious companies and investments notionally worth hundreds of millions? Much of the money remained undiscovered – where did it all go? And how had he gone undetected for so long?

Kreuger's practice of keeping all his dealings to himself, apart from those activities he had of necessity to entrust to his confederates, meant that until his fall, no one had even imagined the scale of his dealings. His unofficial motto had been 'silence, more silence, and still more silence'. He had never been close to anyone, except, perhaps, to the Norwegian girlfriend of his youth who had died very young. In short, the private man appeared remote and disinterested. To the financial world, however, he was a very different animal – a flamboyant entrepreneur whose schemes worked, while his outward activities, such as supporting the share prices of his companies, were not unusual practice for the time. It may be that, other than those whom he had bested in deals, like his French enemies, there was no one with a particular reason to suspect him of major fraud.

Kreuger had something of a reputation for high living, maintaining flats in Stockholm, Paris, Berlin and New York, as well as a home on his 'island retreat' of Angsholmen in the Stockholm archipelago. He also had many mistresses, whom he maintained in some style. He must, too, have needed to keep his shady financial confederates well paid. But the cost of these things can only have accounted for a small proportion of the fortune he came to control. The rest disappeared in gigantic stock-market flotations, in supporting his companies' share prices by buying up his own stock, and in loans to governments in difficulties. Furthermore, it appears that some of the money never existed in the first place, except in Kreuger's 'childish' accounts, or in his head.

The motivation behind it all is more difficult to pin down. Was Ivar Kreuger just by nature a deceiver, as some aspects of his school and university careers might suggest? Was he seduced by the prospect of the power he had been able to generate for himself? Did he actually believe he was, as he once suggested in a lecture in Chicago, acting out of 'enlightened self-interest' in his dealings with governments and in other philanthropic acts? Or was it simply that, once he had started along the road of inflating the value of his companies he found it difficult to stop? It is probable that his financial activities would not have succeeded, or at least would have been discovered far sooner, in a world that was financially more stable than that war-dislocated one of the 1920s. Whatever his motives, it is certain that his downfall made the Great Depression deeper, and resulted in wide-ranging reform in accounting practice both in the US and, particularly, in Sweden, where lax accounting had contributed to his 'success'. But in spite of the financial world's experiences with Mr Kreuger, the Match King was not to be the last swindler to take its members in.

8

Horatio Bottomley – The People's Tribune

It was said that Horatio William Bottomley, who was born in Bethnal Green in 1860, was actually the son of Charles Bradlaugh, sometime MP for Northampton, and a comparison of photographs of the two men when in their fifties certainly shows a remarkable facial likeness (though Bradlaugh was described as a 'giant of a man', physically large and powerful, while Bottomley was only 5 foot 5 inches, and tended to corpulence). Horatio did not resemble the man whose name appears on his birth certificate as father, one William Bottomley, a tailor's foreman. His mother, Elizabeth Holyoake, was a sister of George and Austin Holyoake, great friends and supporters of Bradlaugh in his work for the 'freethinkers', a group of people who were against organized religion, and involved in the early Co-operative movement in the North and Midlands. She had married William Bottomley, apparently without any particular affection being involved. This was not, perhaps, surprising – he was subject to bouts of 'madness' and spent at least two periods in the Bethlehem Asylum. There has been some speculation that he was suffering from tuberculosis rather than insanity; but whatever the malady, after yet another relapse he died, aged thirty-six, in 1863.

Elizabeth was left with young Horatio and his elder sister Florence to provide for, and the Holyoakes, though themselves not well off, helped to support her. However, Elizabeth denied herself sufficient food in order to ensure her children did not go without, something which merely hastened her death in 1865 from cancer. Florence and Horatio were left orphans at the respective ages of seven and four. Their Holyoake uncles were unable to care for them, having large families themselves. Florence was boarded out with a City chop-house owner and his wife in Cheapside, who had a daughter of her age. She was happy with them, and they eventually adopted her; later she married Charles Dollman, of whom more later. Horatio was boarded with a Mrs Wormley, a rather dreary widow woman who looked after him well enough, but did not apparently give him much affection. The Holyoakes eventually decided that they could no longer support both orphans, given their other family commitments, and chose to support Florence rather than Horatio. The young Bottomley was sent to Mason's Orphanage in Erdington, Birmingham, which had been started by the industrial magnate and philanthropist Josiah Mason, an old friend of George Holyoake.

Horatio was educated at Mason's Orphanage, where life was hard and restricted, and on leaving at the age of fourteen started his working life in Birmingham, as office boy to a builder. He longed to return to London, and was soon able to do so when George Holyoake sent for him at the request of his aunt, Caroline Praill, with whom he had been staying in Birmingham. He worked first at a haberdashers, then as a clerk to a firm of solicitors. He left for a firm of shorthand-writers, and soon became a first-class legal reporter. No doubt he learned much from this work about the law and court procedures, as well as about arguing cases, knowledge that was to stand him in good stead later in life. He married, at the age of twenty, Eliza Norton, who worked in a dressmaker's shop and lived not far from him in Battersea. She wasn't an ambitious woman, remaining content never to rise above her humble origins. Bottomley evidently did not take her feelings into account, with the result that she played little part in his subsequent life, living for long periods in the south of France for reasons of health, though remaining on good terms with her husband throughout. She even came to terms with his philandering. Not long after marrying they had a daughter, also named Florence, and the three of them then went to live with Bottomley's sister, Florence Dollman, and her husband.

In the 1880s Bottomley, who had risen to become a partner in the law reporting firm, began his career in 'business' by starting a small newspaper, the *Hackney Hansard*, which reported the debates of the Hackney 'local parliament', one of the many local political debating societies, organized along parliamentary lines, that were popular at that time. Over a period of two years he acquired a string of other small newspapers, such as the *Draper's Record*, the *Baby, or the Mother's Magazine*, and the *Municipal Review*, a weekly periodical popular with two councils and local boards. He also started the *Financial Times* (not, in fact, the one still published today), in competition with the then widely read *Financial News*, and in 1885 founded the Catherine Street Publishing Association as a parent company for this newspaper chain. He soon needed capital for this concern, and approached the financier Osborne O'Hagan who, though taken with the young man, turned him down because the operation was too small for him. Bottomley returned a few weeks later with Douglas MacCrae, a printer who had spare capacity at his works, and thus was able to put up to O'Hagan a bigger deal, involving a merger between MacCrae & Co., Catherine Street Publishing, and Curtice & Co., a small newspaper publisher and advertising agent. This time the financier was interested, and floated the operation with a capital of £100,000. Bottomley became Chairman, and promptly paid a dividend of 12 per cent, which convinced everyone that the company was off to a good start. After a year or so, however, Bottomley and MacCrae fell out, and the former therefore suggested that one of them should run the newspapers, and the other the printing. MacCrae was not best pleased, according to Bottomley, but chose the newspapers, becoming proprietor of the *Draper's Record* and the *Financial Times*. Bottomley, meanwhile, prepared to launch an organization – larger and more ambitious than Catherine Street Publishing – which in due course was to bring him into the public eye in a way that he might not have entirely anticipated. It was to be the first of many such schemes.

This was the Hansard Publishing and Printing Union, a name that was to become famous, if not actually notorious. The scheme merged MacCrae, Curtice & Co. with four leading companies from the newspaper world of the time: Wyman & Co. (printers), Clement Smith & Co. (publishers of pictorial posters), Henry Vickers (newspaper publishers), and Vacone & Co. (which produced newspaper illustrations). Bottomley announced that his company had obtained a new government contract for the publication of the debates in Parliament, which, as Hansard had had the monopoly for years, was a great coup (hence also the significant name of his new scheme). He now had to persuade people to back this venture. This he did by dint of, firstly, approaching the famous journalist, writer, editor, and adventurer, Frank Harris, whom he had met before and who had been impressed by the young journalistic entrepreneur. Bottomley asked Harris to try to secure Viscount Folkestone and Coleridge Kennard, respectively proprietor of, and a major shareholder in, the *Evening News*, as directors of the Hansard Union, offering Harris £10,000 if he were successful. Kennard agreed, but Folkestone declined. However, Bottomley managed to recruit Sir Henry Isaacs, the Lord Mayor of London, as Chairman (though it was not known at the time that Bottomley had paid Joseph, Sir Henry's brother, £2,000 to persuade him to agree). Also attracted were C. Kegan Paul, the publisher, and Sir Roper Lethbridge, the Press Commissioner to the Government of India. The managing director of this highly respectable organization was to be Horatio Bottomley himself.

Hansard Union was quoted on the Stock Exchange in April 1889, capitalized at £500,000. The four concerns mentioned earlier were sold to the new company for £325,000 by a certain John Phillips who, it later transpired, was one of Bottomley's clerks. The latter also appointed Henry Burt, a well-known and respected figure in the trade, as general manager, to give the impression that the business would be soundly run. His brother-in-law, Charles Dollman, now offered to sell to Hansard, for £105,000, paper mills in Devon and a printing works at Redhill, which Bottomley accepted on the board's behalf, a deal received by the other Hansard directors without any apparent realization of the links between Bottomley and Dollman. There was now little change left out of the original £500,000, and Bottomley next applied his considerable persuasive powers to increasing the company's capital to £1 million. All seemed well to the shareholders, and when their managing director planned that Hansard should merge printing and publishing concerns in Europe, the board authorized him to go to Vienna as a representative of the Anglo-Austrian Printing and Publishing Union, which he had formed for the purpose. His visit to Vienna was accompanied by all the Ruritanian pomp and circumstance of a comic opera, thanks to the preparatory work of his only agent in that country, and he was treated as an immensely rich financier, the personal representative of the Lord Mayor of London (Isaacs). The negotations were conducted by Dr Ludwig Krunwald, a lawyer who spoke excellent English (Bottomley, needless to say, spoke not a word of German), who arranged for him to meet Count Eduard von Taaffe, the Austrian Prime Minister, to ensure the success of the deal.

Bottomley signed 'binding contracts' with thirteen Austrian printing firms, and returned to Britain. At the end of the year, however, the Anglo-Austrian Union asked for a £75,000 advance on the amount agreed for the takeover. Bottomley called an Extraordinary General Meeting in March 1890, at which he persuaded Kennard to advance the money. Everything still seemed to be going well; a profit was announced, and a dividend of 8 per cent paid, though in actuality £250,000 of debentures had been issued to support this, and Bottomley had also arranged to borrow a further £50,000 from the Debenture Corporation. In truth, the Hansard Union was near to insolvency. Its dubious financial shenanigans could not go on. In

December the interest on the £50,000 fell due, but the company had no funds with which to pay. Debenture holders demanded their money, Burt resigned, and nasty rumours began to circulate in the City. The company's premises were seized, and in March 1891 the Anglo-Austrian shareholders held an investigation, the report of which showed the parlous state of things in its true light. Bottomley had obtained £100,000 from the two companies, but there was no sign of it. He filed for bankruptcy, and was examined in detail by the Official Receiver. It was decided to prosecute Bottomley, Dollman and Sir Henry and Joseph Isaacs for the firm's collapse, and they were charged with conspiring to obtain money from the shareholders of Hansard and Anglo-Austrian. It looked as though Bottomley was finished, but this was only the beginning of a colourful (and highly public) career in high living, dubious finance, fraud, populist politics and sheer self-promotion.

The Hansard trial began in January 1893, before Mr Justice Hawkins, regarded as a 'hanging judge'. Bottomley chose to defend himself, and his wide knowledge of legal matters from his days as court reporter, coupled with his persuasive and dramatic oratorical style, stood him in good stead. He managed to cast the Official Receiver as having been, unwisely, the real authority behind the decision to bring the prosecution. His masterly performance, helped by the evident sympathy of the jury and the praise of the judge for the way he conducted his case, led to his acquittal, and that of his co-defendants. (The admiring Mr Justice Hawkins later sent round his notes of the case, and the legal wig he had been wearing during the trial, as a memento for the victorious Bottomley, who kept them as a kind of museum exhibit on permanent display in his country house.) Horatio Bottomley emerged from the trial a hero to many and, in the public mind, a financial genius. The fact that Hansard and Anglo-Austrian had collapsed in two years under his stewardship was temporarily forgotten, with unfortunate consequences for some of the people who were to have dealings with him in the future. Bottomley might well have proved a highly successful barrister, had he chosen that route (indeed Mr

Justice Hawkins strongly urged him to take that course after the Hansard trial), but he saw his fortune being made much more quickly in business. He also had political ambitions. First, however, he had to clear his name by having the winding-up order against his companies rescinded, which he achieved in August 1893 by means of revisiting Austria (staying in a small hotel this time) on the pretext of collecting the assets of Anglo-Austrian. The fact that he returned from Vienna without any assets does not seem to have been a difficulty.

Bottomley's extravagant lifestyle meant that he was in need of a constant flow of funds to support his habits. These were not all selfish or destructive, and he was fond of philanthropic acts, such as throwing parties for poor children, or giving a job to any local unemployed man at the country home, which he called 'The Dicker', he had bought in the village of Upper Dicker, near Eastbourne. However, he did have many extremely expensive personal habits and hobbies. He was a great consumer of champagne, for which he appears to have acquired a taste early on in his career, even during his struggling days as a legal reporter. He was such an enthusiast that he got through a bottle a day, and refrained from smoking so as not to dull his taste buds. Throughout his life he regularly breakfasted on kippers and champagne, or at least for as long as he was able to pay for them. He also spent gigantic sums on his other enthusiasms. He was always extending The Dicker, often in unplanned and vulgar ways. He kept a racing stable and a string of horses, which he never failed to bet on extravagantly, though his knowledge of racing and form bordered on ignorance. He also had a weakness for young women, usually from the lower social classes (which, apparently in the 1890s, included barmaids, waitresses and 'women journalists'!), and he maintained several simultaneously at a variety of addresses in the West End. Bottomley was also what, in theatre parlance, was and still is called an 'angel', a financial backer of shows and productions. In most of these he seems to have exhibited the same skill at picking winners as accompanied his racing ventures, and needless to say he lost large sums of money. But though this hobby might have been damaging to his bank balance, it enhanced his social life. Amongst the theatrical acquaintances he had made was a pretty actress, albeit of little talent, who went by her stage name of Peggy Primrose. She eventually became the love of his life, and he began to spend both a great deal of time and money on her. He also realized that a new source of funding would have to be found.

In late-Victorian and early-Edwardian times, Britain's colonies still retained in the public mind the image of faraway places where men of action were making huge fortunes out of mining one rare mineral or another. Consequently investment in such mines was a perennial favourite of the speculator, and because communications with the colonies were still slow, it was also a favourite of the fly-by-night City operator. These unscrupulous promoters were able to float a company, sell shares and disappear before investors discovered that the mine in which they had bought shares was not a success, and never would be. Horatio Bottomley was a man of just that kind, even though his investors sometimes saw through him. In the 1890s, huge quantities of gold were discovered in Western Australia, around Kalgoorlie: 'Westralian' mining shares were booming. Bottomley decided that he too could cash in.

He applied again to Osborne O'Hagan, the financier who had earlier supported his Catherine Street Publishing Association. He obtained £2,000, which he used to set himself up as a promoter of mining company shares. The companies Bottomley dealt with would pay a dividend in the first year, to show all was 'well'. He would pay himself huge expenses, and then proceed to reinvent the company under a new name. In this way he got through twenty-three companies in one year. Out of fifty companies floated, twenty went into voluntary liquidation and twenty-four were 'reconstructed' under new names. It was surprising that investors came his way, given that he was still being pilloried in some sections of the press after the Hansard affair. But then, Bottomley was a convincing con man.

By now, of course, he had collected a group of men around

him who would be happy to do his bidding, usually with no questions asked. These he called his 'bodyguard' or, more often, and probably out of his passion for racing, his 'stable'. One was his brother-in-law, Charles Dollman, and Saul Cooper, an Austrian furrier, was another, as was Dalton Easum, a 'tame' accountant, as well as a collection of ex-boxers and ex-policemen who came in very handy on occasion. There was also Tommy Cox, whom Bottomley had met when he had been a struggling legal reporter and Cox a medical student. Cox never qualified, however, and spent his days working on Bottomley's behalf; he also arranged Bottomley's harem for him. There were several others, such as Ernest Hooley and Henry Houston, associates who came into their own when the inevitable happened and Bottomley's activities fell under scrutiny, as, for instance, when irregularities were discovered in connection with the Westralian Market Trust, one of his endlessly reconstructed mining companies. At a meeting of shareholders, Bottomley made a very clever speech which allayed the worries of most, in which he was helped a great deal by the applause and cheering of those of his 'stable' who were planted in the audience. Bottomley's outrageous progress continued.

He now felt he was in a position to begin a serious assault on his remaining ambition – a career in Parliament. Bottomley, whether he was the natural son of Charles Bradlaugh or not, seems to have been influenced by the latter's political energy, and his championship of the ordinary citizen; he seems, too, to have decided to try his hand at public speaking in imitation of Bradlaugh. He discovered his 'gift of the gab', as he called it, and the results were plain to see. He also saw plenty of opportunity for personal fame and glory as the 'People's Tribune'. In fact, he had already made one tilt at the Palace of Westminster, when he stood at the invitation of the Liberals (Bradlaugh was an Independent Liberal) at Hornsey in 1887. Hornsey was a Tory stronghold, but Bottomley applied himself with enthusiasm, and spoke at every meeting he could, wherever and whenever possible. He worked hard to gain the good opinion of the constituency, and in the end only lost by a small margin.

This performance had so impressed the Liberals, then in opposition, that he was presented with a silver tea service, and received the congratulations of the party's leader, William Gladstone himself. He was subsequently asked to represent the Liberals at the next election (which was due in 1892), standing at North Islington, where there was another large Tory majority. He applied himself vigorously again, and made a strong impression on the voters over a two-year period. Unhappily for him, however, his bankruptcy over the Hansard affair forced his resignation as a candidate.

But once the Hansard problems were out of the way his City activities in the 1890s continued to keep him in the public eye, and the Liberals invited him to stand for their largely working-class South Hackney, a more winnable seat. Bottomley soon made himself very popular, answering every begging letter, sending money to deserving causes, and throwing big Christmas parties every year for the constituents. Tommy Cox made sure his activities were well publicized. His first try for the seat, in the general election of 1900, resulted, nevertheless, in defeat, albeit by only 280 votes. Placed against the wider background of that 'Khaki Election' of 1900 during the Boer War, which the Tories won by a landslide, his success was actually quite remarkable. It is also quite possible that an attack on him as a dodgy promoter, made in the *Critic* newspaper by Henry Hess, an Austrian, may have made the difference between victory and defeat. Hess was, unsurprisingly, sued for libel by Bottomley in 1902, the latter once again conducting his own defence in his dramatic style. Hess had backed a loser, and was unable to substantiate any of the claims he made. Bottomley was awarded £1,000 in damages.

By 1906 the electorate had begun to tire of the lengthy Conservative tenure of office, and Sir Henry Campbell-Bannerman, leader of the Liberals since 1899, was in a strong position to bring his party back to power. Was this to be Bottomley's big chance? He was again asked to stand in South Hackney. Tommy Cox and the 'stable' worked tirelessly once more, and big crowds were attracted to Bottomley's meetings.

They loved his down-to-earth cockney style and ready wit. When he was asked: 'Is the candidate in favour of mixed bathing for the unemployed?' Bottomley replied, 'I am quite unable to consider the possibility of their being unemployed under such conditions.' He was elected with a large majority, as were the Liberals in the country as a whole.

His maiden speech in the House that year was heard in deathly silence, partly because he was regarded as a lightweight politician, and partly because of his still shady reputation, but he laid low and bided his time. He spoke more often during the next session, in 1907. The House began to appreciate his ready wit, and he attacked a series of circumstances which he held to be unjust or inequitable, including the Government's foot-dragging over the establishment of old-age pensions (ironically enough, he was eventually to need – and to be denied – one himself). Over the latter issue he questioned the figures put out by the Government – which, it should be remembered, was formed from his own party – and suggested ways in which money could be raised to pay for the measure, including an employer's tax of a penny in the pound, super tax on investments, stamp duty on share certificates, and a tax on betting. All of these were subsequently to be adopted, and in some form or other, still exist today.

However, Bottomley's lifestyle and hunger for publicity (albeit disguised, and, to some extent, excused in the stance of a fighter for the man in the street) were hardly satisfied by an MP's salary or speeches in the House. He was active on several business fronts whilst sitting in Parliament. The first was a continuation of his mining promotions, which had kept him busy in appearances at bankruptcy hearings (twenty-four in 1904, and sixteen in 1906, the year he was elected!). In 1908 he was tried again for fraud, after coming up against an incorruptible solicitor, Edward Bell, who had accurately summed up Bottomley and his activities. The case concerned the Joint Stock Trust, one of his mining finance groups, but after a trial in which his inimitable style stood him in good stead once more, he was acquitted yet again.

He also entered on a new, and rather more cynical, phase in

his dealings with the public. Whilst setting up and reconstructing dubious companies, his victims had been drawn in partly as a result of their own greed for a quick profit; often they had little knowledge of business. In 1905 he began targeting old men of large fortune and failing faculties, or young men of fortune and no experience. This confidence trickery was based on the printing of false and duplicate share certificates, which he sold with the help of another member of the 'stable', Ernest Hooley. Hooley was tall and dark, a successful entrepreneur of the 1890s who had introduced to the market some famous names, such as Dunlop Tyres, Bovril and Schweppes. He became Squire of Risley, in Nottinghamshire, was accepted in 'society', and at one time bought the Prince of Wales's yacht. However, his companies went into liquidation in 1898, and he filed for bankruptcy, after which irregularities in his company dealings came to light. Tried for fraud, he was found guilty and received a sentence of twelve months in gaol.

Shortly after being released Hooley came up with the idea of selling dud stock to 'victims'. Bottomley was introduced to him in 1905, and found that he and Hooley had a lot in common. The two formed an effective team for extending the number of victims, people Bottomley secretly described as 'lambs to the slaughter'. Examples of his 'lambs' are many. Vincent and Reginald Eyre were sold worthless shares in the London and South Western Canal, which, although it actually existed, had been dry for many years. Eventually they sued, but were not successful. James Platt was a retired wool merchant, aged seventy-eight, who had invested in the Joint Stock Trust, and thereby lost £20,000. Platt was one of the witnesses at the Joint Stock fraud trial, and had once called at Bottomley's flat, threatening to shoot him. The MP invited him in, plied him liberally with champagne, and finished by selling him £4,000-worth of shares in yet another bogus company – such was Bottomley's persuasive power. Platt eventually received justice, after he had brought a case against Bottomley's stockbroker for the selling of bogus shares. Judgment was given for Platt, and the stockbroker repaid him. Another victim, Robert

Masters, was a retired member of the Indian Civil Service, in his eighties and with a poor memory, to boot. Bottomley and Hooley swindled him out of £90,000. Masters's daughter sued; the jury awarded her £50,000, but she never received a penny. Other people who had fallen foul of Bottomley's schemes continued to sue him, and by now a momentum had built up. Eventually his past was to catch up with him. By 1912 his financial position was becoming hopeless, and a serious blow was dealt by Mr Justice Swinfen-Eady, who ruled that despite his acquittal in the Joint Stock Trust trial, Bottomley was liable for damages for 'fraudulent breach of trust and misfeasance'. He was duly declared bankrupt and this time, despite being returned for South Hackney again in the election of 1910, it proved too much for the House of Commons; he was forced to resign his seat and leave Parliament. It was a sad blow to him, but it left him freer to be the 'People's Tribune' in the pages of *John Bull*, a newspaper he had founded only two months after being returned at South Hackney in 1906.

Bottomley had, of course, started out as a legal journalist, and his first group of companies had been involved in newspaper publishing. He had never lost his interest in journalism, especially when it gave him opportunity to promote himself and his schemes. He had planned to start a weekly newspaper that would expose all the evils and injustices of the day, supporting the common man. But he needed backing, and had gone to Odhams Press, then only a small company, to discuss the matter with Julius Elias, its managing director. Elias was destined to have a long and relatively successful, albeit a somewhat uneasy, association with Bottomley. He was also aware of the reputations of both Bottomley and Hooley, but decided to take a gamble. As it turned out, *John Bull* appealed to a certain class of reader, and became a successful publication from the moment of its launch in 1906. Bottomley's brand of popular journalism proved to be very similar in style, if cruder, to that of some modern tabloids, combining sensationalist reporting of such things as murders with a chauvinistic patriotism that was, frankly, a string of insults against foreigners. It should perhaps be remembered that fervent patriotism was the order of the day in Edwardian England; however, printing such lines as 'The Foul French ... it will be well to remember that the French are corrupt, tyrannical, bloodthirsty, sycophantic, unmannerly, treacherous and lecherous' was somewhat strong even for those times. There were similar entries about Germans in another issue.

The style, like Bottomley's oratory, was fearless and lively, with coverage of subjects dear to his heart such as Parliament, the courts, the City, and even racing tips; the first issue was sold out within hours, and the weekly became very popular indeed. The public showed their support of the publication by subscribing for shares to the value of £100,000 in the John Bull Investment Trust – Bottomley was up to his tricks again. The paper ran a series of articles debunking popular figures; Rudyard Kipling and the Liberal politician Joseph Chamberlain being among the targets. As a result, the paper was served with a stream of writs, and Elias and Odhams became most concerned. Not so Bottomley, who could not have cared less and delighted in the prospect of defending each suit personally. In the autumn of 1912 *John Bull*'s circulation had reached 1.5 million.

That year, a horse of Bottomley's won one of racing's most prestigious races, the Cesarewitch, and its owner landed a gambling bet worth £70,000 on the day. However, this was a sum which only just balanced his gambling losses, and he needed another 'earner', even though he was by now in great demand as a speaker and lecturer. In Lucerne, on his way home from his annual 'cure' at the spa in Carlsbad, he was approached with a proposition by a hitherto unknown admirer, a Birmingham printer and professional 'punter' called Reuben Bigland. Bigland suggested that *John Bull* should run a sweepstake on the Derby. Bottomley had heard of the big profits being made by Swiss lottery organizers (lotteries were at that time illegal in Britain) and had stopped in Lucerne to study their operations. However, he felt that the Derby sweep was not for him, but asked Bigland whether he could introduce him to some Swiss bookmakers, which the other man duly did. After they had both returned to Britain, Bigland received a letter from Bottomley asking him to call. They had a disagreement at that meeting, but later in the year Bigland was approached again, Bottomley having apparently changed his mind about racing sweepstakes, which he felt could be run via Swiss operators in order to get around the Lottery Act. Bigland was cross-examined eagerly by Bottomley, who promised to give him an order, as he was a printer, for a million books of tickets. This order was never forthcoming; the People's Tribune had just been picking Bigland's brains, regarding the printer as a small-time operator. However, Bigland was eventually to have a dramatic effect on Bottomley's activities.

The sweepstakes, run through Swiss bookies and promoted in *John Bull*, got off to a good start, the 1913 Derby sweep receiving £270,000 in ticket money. Another sweep was held on the 1914 Grand National, with a first prize of £5,000. Bottomley's 'stable' held all the tickets for the fancied horses, but his plans were foiled when an outsider called Sunloch won the race, which meant that the sweep was won by a Welshman called Tibbs, who turned up at *John Bull*'s offices with his solicitor the next day demanding his £5,000 in cash. All Bottomley's persuasive powers could not induce him to take half his winnings in shares, and he left with his money. Tibbs did not live long to enjoy it, however; he bought an expensive car and drank himself to death within two years. The 1914 Derby sweep was won by a woman whom *John Bull* called 'Madam Glukad, the blind lady of Toulouse'. This woman was indeed blind, but did not live in Toulouse; she was actually Helen Gluckman, a sister of Saul Cooper, one of Bottomley's 'stable'. The prize money all went to Bottomley, apart from £250 to the lady and a cut for Cooper. *John Bull* went on to run a wide variety of sweeps, not only on horse races but also on such events as the FA Cup, all bringing in lots of income for Bottomley, who was still officially a bankrupt. He had, however, treated both Bigland and Henry Houston, his accomplice in the Swiss-based sweepstakes, very contemptuously. It was a mistake which was to cost him dear.

In August of the same year, a momentous event occurred which was to launch Bottomley on his penultimate major activity; the First World War began. For Bottomley the war was, at first, an inconvenience, as it resulted in the cancellation of all horse racing, and clearly restricted his travel opportunities. It was also an embarrassment, for the war had been entered into by Britain ostensibly to defend Belgium and on behalf of Serbia, which had been annexed by Austria-Hungary. Certain elements in Serbia objected to this, and in July Gavrilo Princip assassinated the Archduke Franz Ferdinand, heir to the throne of Austria-Hungary. Austria, provoked, declared war on Serbia, and the whole deadly business snowballed as Europe's alliances found themselves drawn deeper and deeper into a war which few of them wanted. By 4 August, when Britain declared war, she found herself ranged with France and Russia against Germany and Austria-Hungary, with smaller nations also joining one side or the other. Unfortunately for Bottomley, the current issue of *John Bull* had carried the headline 'To hell with Serbia! Why should Britain shed her blood to save a nation of assassins?' He cursed his luck, and decided that the weekly should immediately launch wholeheartedly upon a policy of jingoistic patriotism. By 15 August the headlines ran, 'The dawn of England's greatest glory. The day has come. The golden eventide.' He was fifty-four years old, and could see some great opportunities with the coming of war. He told Houston: 'I am going to draw a line at 4 August 1914, and start afresh. I shall play the game, cut all my old associates, and wipe out everything pre-1914.'

Bottomley was already, as has been said, a popular speaker and lecturer. Seymour Hicks, an actor-manager, invited him to make a recruiting speech on 14 September at the London Opera House. It was billed as '*John Bull*'s Great Patriotic Rally for Recruiting', and brought in an audience of over 6,000 people, more than had been attracted to a meeting just before at which two Cabinet ministers had spoken. He spoke about

Germany in abusive language, having had plenty of practice in the pages of *John Bull*. The next rally, the first of many, was at the Albert Hall on 15 January 1915. It was a very successful meeting, with thousands waiting outside on the off chance of a seat. He had become, in his own words, 'unofficial recruiting agent of the British Empire', using all the jingoistic artifice common at the time, but infusing his speeches with his own, very effective, brand of persuasion. His fame spread throughout Britain, and he was in great demand to hold meetings all over the country. From the winter of 1915 onwards he gave 340 patriotic lectures, for which he received fees, generally taking between 65 and 85 per cent of each event's gross takings; he was making a lot of money whilst doing his patriotic duty. However, he only held twenty recruiting meetings, for which he took no fee, because he hated the idea of sending young men to their deaths. He visited the Grand Fleet at sea, and the trenches in France, and became extremely popular with the men of the armed services. It was a punishing effort for a man who now weighed eighteen stone, and who by now not only produced frantic copy for *John Bull*, but also contributed articles to the *Sunday Pictorial*. No one could doubt that he worked hard for the war effort, but through it he was making money again.

By late 1916 the Asquith coalition government's handling of the war was proving unpopular, for hundreds of thousands of men had been lost in battles like that on the Somme for little apparent gain, and Lord Northcliffe, the proprietor of the then influential *Daily Mail*, among other papers, started a movement to replace Asquith with Lloyd George, then the Minister of Munitions, in which he was eventually successful. Bottomley was also keen to help in any way he could in the new administration, and started to put himself forward to the Government, applying to the Ministry of Information and Propaganda. He was, however, still too disreputable for the Establishment, and was turned down. In fact, certain sections of the press were keen to see someone like Bottomley in the Government, and he came close to being summoned to Downing Street, but his hour never actually arrived.

Despite all his popularity during the war, Bottomley's enemies were now preparing a vigorous attack on him, and one that was eventually to prove his downfall. Prominent amongst these enemies were Reuben Bigland, whom he had treated with such contempt, and the former racing correspondent for *John Bull*, with whom he had fallen out over £4,200 in worthless shares in the weekly, William Lotinga. All through the period of his patriotic lectures, pamphlets by Bigland and Lotinga would appear wherever he was speaking, detailing his disreputable past, and denouncing him as a fraudster. These pamphlets were accurate and reasonably well-written, and Bottomley started to worry about their effect. They began to undermine the reputation of England's most popular 'patriot', and Bottomley eventually had to pay off Lotinga by giving him his £4,200, and come to an accommodation with Bigland, who later came to work in the 'stable'. But the rot had set in.

By 1918 Bottomley was still doing his bit for Britain, despite the occasional surfacing of a series of pamphlets attacking him and his shady past. He also continued to harbour dreams of taking up his political career again (though he was still an undischarged bankrupt), of being called to the Cabinet, even of being the next Prime Minister; hopes that he thought were realized when he was summoned to Downing Street by Lloyd George. Alas, the Prime Minister's purpose was only to ensure the accuracy of reporting in *John Bull*. None of his ambitions were to come to pass, not least because the war was by now approaching its end. He managed to console himself with thoughts of the success of yet another money-making scheme, which was also tied to the unusual circumstances brought about by the war. The purchase of War Bonds was considered a patriotic duty; it was also an opportunity Bottomley was unable to resist. He announced his 'War Stock Combination' in *John Bull* soon after the issue by the Government of the new War Savings Certificates, which were available at 15s 6d each, and would be worth £1 after five years. Bottomley decided he would have £77,500 subscribed by readers, and would buy the Savings Certificates with it, netting, he hoped, £100,000.

Readers rose to the bait, subscribing over £80,000. However, it was only possible to buy the certificates to a maximum value of £500 in a single name, and he therefore used the money to buy War Stock, a holding that was to cause him trouble later. The first prize in the scheme was drawn shortly afterwards. Those who were 'unlucky' – that is, virtually everyone – were then given the chance to subscribe to Bottomley's 'War Stock Consolation' scheme, from which he obtained over £90,000. Prizes for both the schemes were eventually drawn in 1918, and the winning numbers – but not the names – were published in *John Bull*. These War Stock schemes were, in fact, exactly the same racket as his pre-war racing and other sweepstakes.

With the war at an end, he busied himself with having his bankruptcy discharged, so that he could stand in South Hackney once more at the elections that would follow the dissolution of the wartime coalition government. This he managed to achieve by setting up a collection of dummy companies to purchase some of his debts, an old ploy of his. The director of most of these companies was Tommy Cox. His political friends settled more debts, and the remainder he cleared by using money subscribed to the War Stock Combination. When examined by the Official Receiver, his complicated explanations of his companies were accepted without deep questioning, though it is possible that a certain leniency was shown because of his valuable war work. Having cleared himself, however shabbily, he was free to stand again, and was duly re-elected with a huge majority. His campaign, though, was a shadow of its former vigour, mainly because he was exhausted from the effort of the war years, and was feeling the effects of the excessive champagne drinking with which he had kept himself going. Fortunately the 'stable' managed the campaign for him, and his victory was a walkover.

In 1919, in order to aid reconstruction, the Government issued its Victory Bonds which, priced at £5 each, were too expensive for most people. Bottomley saw another scheme. *John Bull* announced a Victory Bond Club, where people could buy one-fifth of a Victory Bond, and with it the chance to enter a £20,000 draw. This time, he stated that the bonds would be handed over to trustees and that subscribers could have their money back at any time; he also allowed no expenses for himself. Henry Houston, one of his long-time associates, thought Bottomley was losing his touch, and was horrified at the slipshod set-up of the scheme, which permitted so many loopholes for subscribers. However, the money flooded in and it proved the most popular scam yet run by Bottomley, bringing in – at its height – £100,000 a day! But he made an ill-judged decision not to buy the bonds immediately, as he was sure they would go down in price on the open market, and that he would be able to buy them cheaper.

Difficulties soon arose. The vast success of the scheme caused its own problems, and Bottomley, no office administrator, was unable to help his small group of untrained clerks cope with the huge influx of applications. The mess simply grew bigger and bigger. He made the Victory Bond Club certificates simpler, to help with the applications; they were now so simple that they were easy to forge, and hundreds of spurious certificates began to be sold in London pubs, many of which were paid for with dud cheques. The clerks simply could not cope, and one or two even helped themselves to some of the cash. Soon thousands of subscribers started writing in demanding their money back, as *John Bull* had made it clear they were entitled to do. Some £50,000 was paid out in the first month of the scheme, and £150,000 by the end of 1919. Many people were overpaid in the incredible muddle, and some even applied successfully several times for their entitlement. Nevertheless, Bottomly duly bought £500,000 of Victory Bonds. He then decided, on a whim, to expand his newspaper empire, and bought the *National News* and the *Sunday Evening Telegraph*, using a bank loan scured by some of the bonds he had bought for the Victory Bond Club. This deal cost £41,500, and both papers were losing money.

The Victory Bond Club continued to collapse, and by now the public were beginning to realize that it was a huge swindle. People continued to apply in droves for their money back.

Bigland urged Bottomley to publish the names of the draw winners, but he could not do so because of the administrative mess, and because there simply wasn't enough money. He could not hope to sort out the chaos, and called in Henry Houston to help. Houston realized the mess was almost impossible to put right, but took on the task simply to stop it from getting worse.

Meanwhile, Bottomley's relations with Bigland had continued on a downward spiral. The two had quarrelled over a scheme Bigland had been taken in by – unbelievably, it claimed to use chemicals to make petrol out of ordinary water. Bottomley had spotted it as a fraud – he knew one when he saw one – and was not inclined to be sympathetic. But Bigland was incensed by Bottomley's superior attitude and high-handed manner, and exclaimed 'From this moment I shall be your enemy!' The great swindler had simply laughed at the man he regarded as little more than a buffoon. Had he known it, however, he was finally on the road to ruin.

Now a sworn enemy, Bigland's problem was how finally to expose Bottomley. The legal profession had, after all these years, a healthy respect for Bottomley's prowess in court, and the Government ignored all Bigland's letters. But Bottomley was busy contributing to his own downfall. He had finally grasped the nettle, and admitted the Victory Bond Club chaos to the subscribers. He proposed a new scheme, where the subscribers would buy French Crédit National Bonds instead. Victory Bond subscribers could exchange £10 worth of their certificates for French bonds of £15 denomination in this new 'Thrift Prize Bond Club', on payment of the £5 difference. Amazingly, 50,000 did, worried about the status of their Victory Bonds investment. What Bottomley had not revealed to them, however, was that the French bonds could be bought for £9, thus guaranteeing him a large profit. The magazine *Truth*, an old adversary of his, pointed this out, and tried to warn people off. Bottomley sued them for libel several times, but they simply ignored his writs and continued to attack him. The 'swindling bonds club' became a subject of ugly rumour, and Bottomley was forced to abandon the 1920 Derby sweepstake;

it became impossible, under the attacks of *Truth*, to keep up his one-man control of the bond clubs. Meanwhile, Bigland had re-entered the battle against him after some unsatisfactory first attempts, and had realized that the only way to trap Bottomley was to get him into the witness box. This he would accomplish by getting himself arrested, and forcing Bottomley into court at a disadvantage. His first attempt at this also failed, however; he seemed to be losing his battle, but he did not give up.

Bigland next decided to print and distribute a scurrilous pamphlet about Bottomley. He and several friends contrived to sell them in the large towns and cities of the West Country, the North and Midlands; they sold so well that he printed 250,000 for London. This was too much for Bottomley, who, against the advice of his solicitor and barrister friends, sued for criminal libel and blackmail, and applied for Reuben Bigland's arrest. The latter was only too pleased to give himself up, and was brought to a committal hearing at Bow Street before Sir Chartres Biron. He was defended by Arthur Comyns Carr, a tenacious junior counsel whose skilful cross-examining style Bottomley was to experience, to his detriment. The prosecution, led by Sir Ernest Wild, tried to play on the supposed blackmail which had been threatened by Bigland, who was alleged by Bottomley to have threatened to print and distribute the libellous pamphlets unless he was paid £60,000 towards what he had lost in the petrol hoax. Wild, on Bottomley's behalf, denied that there was ever any irregularity in the bond clubs, stating that his client was actually out of pocket as a result of the schemes. Bottomley was then called to the witness box.

Once there, he found in Sir Chartres Biron a magistrate who, unlike the previous justices he had encountered, was not prepared either to be lenient or to let him twist the court to his advantage. This seems to have thrown him, especially when Biron continued to ask awkward questions about the clubs. Then Comyns Carr was given his chance. His thorough and aggressive cross-examination of Bottomley took four days, and needled counsel for the prosecution, so that Wild was soon at loggerheads with the magistrate, who was not predisposed towards Bottomley in the first place. Other witnesses were called, all of them friends or employees of Bottomley, and all of whom supported the blackmail theory; all, that is, except Houston who, under cross-examination by Comyns Carr, was forced to admit that he thought that Bigland was unlikely to have contemplated blackmail. There was in any case little or no documentary evidence of intended blackmail, and in the end Biron decided, after castigating most of the prosecution witnesses including Bottomley, to dismiss the blackmail charge, but commit Bigland to the Shropshire Assizes (the blackmail attempt had allegedly taken place during the by-election for the Wrekin, when Bottomley had been there supporting one of the candidates) on a charge of inciting others to distribute a common libel with a view to extortion. The libel trial would take place later, at the Old Bailey. Bigland replied that he looked forward to substantiating in court every one of the statements in the pamphlet.

Bigland's trial for criminal libel began on 23 January 1922. His solicitor, the incorruptible Edward Bell, and his defence counsel, the capable Comyns Carr, had worked feverishly to obtain evidence to support him, in the face of the stonewalling and obstruction of Bottomley's solicitors, and even the unhelpfulness of *Truth* magazine, which was reluctant to get involved in a criminal trial. Bell had finally obtained sight of the bond club bank records, and the defence had been able to reconstruct the gross manipulation which Bottomley had carried out. Bigland and his legal team had assembled seventy-eight witnesses and filed a plea of justification of the libel containing fifty-seven allegations of fact. It was a formidable defence. Bottomley and his representatives desperately tried to have the trial adjourned for as long as possible, on the grounds that the receivers were waiting for all claims to come in and had all the accounts relating to the clubs, and that the prosecution was waiting for copies of the latter in order to refute the libels. Comyns Carr would have none of this, and pressed for the continuation. As to the prosecution's case being held up by the non-appearance of the accounts, he pointed out that Bottomley had had a great deal of time in which to prepare a case, and if he was waiting for the club members to present their claims, then this was simply proof that the administration of the clubs had been so bad that the records could hardly help the prosecution anyway. In the end, the prosecution decided to offer no evidence, and Bigland was found not guilty. Bottomley was attacked next day in *The Times*, and attempted to defend himself in the *Sunday Illustrated*. This article was ruled in contempt of court, and he and the paper were fined £1,000 each. He was now regarded by the public with a good deal less admiration and a good deal more concern. The Shropshire Assizes would be Bottomley's last chance.

Comyns Carr was again in action for Bigland. Although he gave the three prosecution witnesses, all Bottomley's men, a hard time, they all had their stories well learned, and the prosecution declined to bring any more witnesses. It looked as though Bottomley was going to avoid the witness box. Bigland was concerned about the progress of the case, and decided that he must submit himself to cross-examination. Comyns Carr reluctantly agreed, realizing that his client would have a hard time at the hands of the prosecution counsel. Bigland duly appeared in the witness box, and detailed a whole string of activities in which he and Bottomley had been involved, including the War Stock Combination scheme and the Victory Bond Club. He was quite prepared, he said, to admit to his shameful involvement in order to expose Bottomley, and to clear his conscience. The evidence was damning, and made doubly so when the other witnesses for the defence, who now included Henry Houston, backed up Bigland's evidence. Bottomley had been making remarks to the prosecution and the jury throughout the trial, to the irritation of the judge, who was not well disposed to him in his summing up. The jury retired for just three minutes, finding Bigland not guilty. Public opinion was now firmly against Bottomley, and the end would not be long in coming.

He was duly summoned to appear at Bow Street by the Director of Public Prosecutions, on a charge of fraudulently converting £5,000 of the Victory Bond Club money to his own use. It was not surprising that he was committed for trial at the Old Bailey. He was sixty-two, and in rapidly failing health. He relied more and more on quantities of champagne (which he referred to as his 'medicine') to keep him going, and ate very little; he was probably close to alcoholism. Mentally, he was a shadow of his former alert and crafty self. His creditors had sold his possessions from under him, and he was living in his flat with just a bed, a borrowed card table and two wooden chairs. How had the mighty fallen.

Bottomley's trial started in May 1922, and, naturally, he chose to defend himself. Unfortunately, the judge was Mr Justice Salter, a man of meticulous habits who refused to be hurried or bamboozled, while counsel for the prosecution was Travers Humphreys, noted for his fairness and excellent grasp of figures, and who had already had triumphs in several notable trials, including those of Dr Crippen and Sir Roger Casement. They were the worst possible combination for Bottomley. Suffice it to say that Bottomley's defence was weak, depending as it did on his assertions that he had repaid the Bond Club moneys, and that he had advanced the club his own money to begin with, and so had simply been paying himself back. Humphreys's cross-examination was devastating, not only debunking these assertions, but also exposing the defendant's money-making during his patriotic war work. All Bottomley's attempts to persuade the jury were unsuccessful, though some were moved by his final impassioned speech, a return to his old form and delivered in his old declamatory style. Mr Justice Salter's summing up went against him, and the jury took just twenty-eight minutes to find him guilty on all counts except one. He received a sentence of seven years' imprisonment, which, for a man of sixty-two in poor health, was not a pleasant prospect.

Bottomley was taken to Wormwood Scrubs to begin his sentence, where his health deteriorated still further; he was effectively 'drying out'. He appealed against his conviction, of course, but the appeal was rejected, and, because he was still an

MP, he was obliged to resign from Parliament. By March 1923 he was declared bankrupt for the third time, as a result of which he lost The Dicker to his son-in-law, Jefferson Cohn, though his wife and daughter still lived there (though the latter was by then divorced from Cohn). In July 1923 he was moved to Maidstone Gaol, where the regime was even harder, and where he was recognized by the other inmates after his life story was published in a Sunday paper. He became a favourite of his fellow convicts and as his health slowly improved, he established himself as 'king' of the prisoners, though later that year a new governor swiftly tightened up on the prison's discipline. In 1927 a new Home Secretary, Sir William Joynson-Hicks, decided to release Bottomley two years early for good behaviour. The latter was overjoyed at the prospect and saw it as an opportunity for 'putting the record straight'. On 28 July 1927, at the age of sixty-seven but looking much older, Bottomley was released. During his years in prison he'd lost a great deal of weight, especially whilst he was ill. He returned to his family at The Dicker, where in his absence life had continued in reduced circumstances. The *Weekly Dispatch* had signed him up to write a series of articles, but what he produced was poor stuff; and the series ended after two months. Ever the optimist, he tried to start a new newspaper, called *John Blunt* in imitation of his old mouthpiece, which had passed into reputable ownership while he had been in prison. The new paper was extremely dull, and closed in October 1928, having lasted only four months. A projected lecture tour of the Empire lasted no longer; it seemed no one wanted to know him.

In February 1930 his wife Eliza died at The Dicker. His daughter Florence, whose first husband Jefferson Cohn had remarried in 1921, was herself remarried soon after to a planter named Moreland, and subsequently left for South Africa. Bottomley eventually lost The Dicker completely to Cohn, and was left alone, a tired and broken man. The real love of his life, Peggy Primrose, took pity on him and offered him a place in her flat. He could get no contracts of any kind, for newspaper articles or lecture tours, and in desperation Peggy Primrose arranged for him to be engaged at the Windmill Theatre, where he appeared in September 1932. His 'act' consisted of a string of anecdotes from his colourful past, but his delivery was tired and pathetic, and the audience, who had come to see the Windmill Girls, were not in the least entertained. A few days later he collapsed on stage with a heart attack, and was rushed to hospital, where he recovered. In 1933 he applied for the old-age pension, arguing that his war services had entitled him to it, but he was turned down. In May he collapsed again, and this time there was to be no recovery. He died in the Middlesex Hospital.

Ironically, he was remembered in death, and many people attended his funeral, which was held at the Golders Green Crematorium and paid for by Peggy Primrose. Like many financial crooks before and since, Horatio Bottomley was a larger-than-life character. If it had not been for his selfish way of living and his appalling vanity, his natural talents might have taken him far in any one of several legitimate fields – the law, politics, business. However, as he became involved in all of these fields, he sought to twist them for his own greedy profit and self-aggrandisement, a habit he was unable to break even after declaring in 1914 that he was determined to 'wipe out everything pre-1914'. It is easy to speculate about his motivation – those crushing early years at the orphanage which moulded his personality, forcing him into a fantasy world from which he never really escaped. Perhaps he felt that the only way to redress the balance of those traumatic years was to become a rich man. The truth of that will never be known, but in Bottomley the MP-turned-businessman-turned-crook we can see the shadow of Robert Maxwell – a man who outshone even Bottomley in charisma – when he appeared upon the scene more than forty years later.

9

John Poulson – 'Governed by warm-hearted and generous impulses' (according to his wife)

John Garlick Llewellyn Poulson was born in 1910. The son of a pottery maker, he left his Methodist public school without gaining any school certificates, joined a firm of architects, and was sacked in 1932. Yet he was destined to become a household name in Britain. The expansion and diversification of his business deals over a period of some twenty years from the 1950s made John Poulson head of what was at one time the largest architectural practice in Europe, earning him more than £1 million a year from a business that employed 750 people. He opened offices in London, Middlesbrough, Edinburgh, Lagos and Beirut. He was involved in the design of a £1 million international swimming pool in Leeds, the Cannon Street Station redevelopment in London, and – his biggest project – the £3 million Aviemore tourist centre in Scotland. Along the way he gained a reputation as a philanthropist who contributed generously to charities. He became Chairman of the National Liberty Party for Great Britain, and also of the Goole Conservative and Liberal Association. He was, moreover, a leading figure in the Methodist Church and held strong moral views, once sacking a man because he was having an extramarital affair.

But it was for his links with the unpleasant aspects of political and local government corruption that his name was to be remembered by those who lived through the 1960s and 1970s. Despite his subsequent conviction he always maintained that he had been misunderstood, and that what he did was simply the result of a too generous nature, particularly when it came to his friends and business colleagues. Poulson's rise and fall is one of the abiding stories of the great redevelopment explosion in Britain's towns and cities in the decades after the war. He began his career by landing a job as an articled clerk to an architectural firm as a young man of seventeen, though he was dismissed, allegedly for the poor quality of his work. He did not let this setback put him off, and studied part-time for four years at Leeds College of Art, although he never passed an examination. In 1932 he borrowed £50 and started up on his own in rented offices at Yorkshire Penny Bank Chambers, Ropergate, Pontefract. With two young assistants he built up a business by taking what work he could get, and by developing his contacts with local politicians and Freemasons; indeed with any useful or potentially influential person he met. He offered fast results at a low price, and his business grew. In 1942 he was elected as a licentiate (the category for non-qualified architects) of the Royal Institute of British Architects. By the late 1950s he had become very successful, attracting good staff, and even winning the Ideal Home 'House of the Year' award for one of his designs. He was also beginning to become involved in the contracts then being awarded for public projects, which had resulted from the increase in local and central government spending at this time. He applied some of the sales techniques that had worked for him in the past in order to turn these contracts towards his firm; but then he simply started to go too far. Did he deliberately set out to bribe people, and to set up consultancies staffed with his own appointees, or was it simply misguided 'generosity'?

Poulson's network of devious working practices was strongest in the North-East of England, in the Teesside local government area. He promised fast results, and he wined and dined local government officials and councillors, hiring them as 'contract scouts' to inform him in advance of potential business. At Eston he designed the Civic Hall, Town Hall, swimming baths, sports hall, Labour Club and several housing schemes in a contract worth some £3.5 million in all. Once he had received local government approval for the first part of the development – the swimming baths – the contracts for all the other projects went through unopposed, senior councillors blocking all opposition. He had a reputation for getting his work done ahead of time: for one swimming pool project his completion date was twenty-one months ahead of that of rival bidders. As his career developed so did the scale of his schemes. In 1963, as consultant architect for the £2.5 million Southport town centre development, he proposed additions to the initial plan – a conference centre, hotel, and car park. He was strongly supported by the Mayor, Dr Sydney Hepworth, who also happened to be Chairman of Southport's Development Committee. However, the plans came to nothing following a victory in the local elections which swept the Conservatives into power.

Back in Yorkshire, Poulson continued to cultivate local contacts. In five years he had collected £300,000 in fees from Pontefract Urban District Council, where he was a close friend of the Mayor, Joseph Egan, and his predecessor, Joseph Blackburn. In 1969 the Town Clerk of Pontefract, Fred Rook, was appointed to a Poulson company, Open System Building Ltd (OSB), when he retired. It was not surprising, therefore, that Poulson obtained work for his company from the local water board, given that Blackburn sat on the board, and Fred Rook was the Town Clerk. On a wider scale, Poulson collected fees amounting to £6.5 million on a total of 54 county-wide contracts between 1964 and 1970. Equally unsurprising, both Egan and Blackburn sat on the County Council; the Clerk of the Council, Sir Bernard Kenyon, cropped up at Open System Building in 1966, whilst he was still a serving local government officer.

But local authorities were not his limit. Poulson also made use even of chance acquaintances, especially if they were associated with nationalized industries. He had met Norman

Hudson during a chance encounter on a train back in 1952, and had discovered that Hudson was a commercial manager with the North-Eastern Gas Board. Later Poulson designed the Gas Board headquarters in Leeds and its showrooms in Pontefract, as well as a training centre and several offices. Trains seem to have been lucky for Poulson, for it was on another that, in 1963, he met Alfred Merritt, Principal Regional Officer at the Ministry of Health (as it then was). Merrit was given the job of liaising with the Leeds Regional Hospital Board over a new style of hospital to be built by Poulson at Airedale, and then took the latter's side in a controversy over the experimental design of the hospital. This design was also argued for by William Shee, Secretary of the Leeds Regional Hospital Board. Shee had Freemasonry in common with Poulson, together with a shareholding in a small property company, Ovalgate Investments; he later received a consultancy in the Poulson organization when he retired, having by then also recommended the architect to the South-West Metropolitan Hospital Board. As if this were not sufficient, Poulson managed to follow up another contact with South-West; a brief acquaintance with Wendy Braithwaite, wife of the Board's Secretary. From her he learned that she and her husband had purchased an old manor house in 1961, which now needed £7,200 spending on it for modernization and repairs. Poulson saw to this work, presumably out of a spirit of generosity. Meanwhile, the South-West Hospital Board had awarded contracts to Poulson worth £81,000 in fees; projects worth a further £3 million were also signed up with him, but in the end a lack of funding meant that they fell through.

John Poulson was a personable man who often developed contacts into contracts by 'looking after' people, ostensibly out of a spirit of generosity or friendship. The sums he paid to or spent on these contacts were not vast, and possibly seemed innocuous, coming as they did from the expense accounts or other resources of the giant Poulson organization. Bill Sales, of the National Coal Board, enjoyed going to the races, so Poulson paid for accommodation, meals and chauffeur-driven cars. He also arranged for Sales to receive a mortgage from the Wakefield Building Society when he wanted to buy his NCB-owned house: it helped that Poulson happened to be a director of the building society. Two 'friends', Andy Cunningham and George Pottinger, a senior civil servant, who were later tried with Poulson, were also recipients of his generosity. Cunningham once said that he was jealous of the foreign holidays Poulson took, so his friend paid for him to take a break. And Pottinger claimed that his son's poor performance in Greek was 'because he'd never been there' – an educational oversight which Poulson managed to rectify by giving the family a holiday in Greece. Pottinger also joined the growing list of those who enjoyed a Poulson mortgage through the Wakefield Building Society.

All these 'presents' were, on the face of it, at least, given to private individuals, and ostensibly, as Poulson was later to argue, without regard to any return. If any of these people were, in their official capacities, to put any business his way, it would be simply out of friendship or because he was the best person for the job. Letters to his colleagues tend to show a different picture, however. When Harry Vincent wrote in 1962 that a contact of Poulson's at British Rail, Graham Tunbridge, was 'rather a broken reed, and I do not think we will get anything from him', Poulson replied: 'there is far more left in the reed ... but don't you go around telling everybody.' All of these contacts had, in fact, been cultivated with an eye to future advantages.

Poulson's activities certainly received a boost through his friendship with Harry Vincent and T. Dan Smith. Poulson had met Vincent, then managing director of the construction company, Bovis, at a function at the former's old school. He told him about Ropergate Services, a company he had set up on the advice of Sir Herbert Butcher, MP, one of his long-standing friends, which combined surveying, engineering and architectural services in one firm, an arrangement which saved tax, allowed the build-up of funds, and permitted Ropergate to offer composite quotes in one package, as well as a single point of contact on site. Harry Vincent was immediately attracted by this neat deal. Bovis, like Poulson, was aware of the enormous growth of local government contracts, especially from Labour councils. Vincent brought in one of his old acquaintances, the planning consultant T. Dan Smith, to form a triumvirate of builder, architect and consultant, in order literally to cash in on the many town centre redevelopments then being mooted. Smith would receive 1 per cent of the cost of each scheme, plus an extra $\frac{1}{2}$ per cent if Bovis were accepted as the developer. Smith was therefore employed in selling Poulson's package deal, a convenient solution, and one that proved attractive to many smaller councils, which often did not have the necessary expertise amongst their own staff.

Smith set about the business of creating his 'national organization specially for the purpose of propagating J.G.L. Poulson organization ... under my direct control by selection of a number of individuals who ... must of course work for me and be unaware of any tie between J.G.L. Poulson and me ...' This organization was really a series of public relations companies fronted by Smith and run by Roy Hadwin and Peter Ward. Smith would try to persuade a local authority that Bovis was interested in any redevelopment schemes in the pipeline, with, of course, Poulson as consulting architect. There was soon a string of key councillors employed by Smith as 'consultants' in return for their promoting Poulson; they were found to be very keen in their pursuance of their employer's interests.

The activities of these 'consultants' are illustrative of their methods. In 1965, Smith made a note on a letter from Poulson about a contract for Durham Technical College that 'Roy H. [Hadwin] can no doubt see Sid D. about this and other appointments' ('Sid D.' was Sid Docking, then Chairman of Durham County Council). In Yorkshire, OSB continued to seek housing contracts by legitimate means, whilst Hadwin and Ward signed up councillors in several towns, including Tom Roebuck in Mexborough and Colin Dews in Castleford. Roebuck actually went on to Smith's payroll, sponsoring and touting for OSB. Dews received a retainer from a Smith company for promoting OSB, and was Chair of the sub-committee that awarded a £1 million contract to that company. Letters from Dews to Smith that were read out during the trials in 1975 show how open was the nature of the business relationship between them, Dews writing at one point that 'I must look out for myself', and that Smith can be assured of his 'best endeavours and loyalty'. In 1967 Ward told Smith that if a contract was not secured by Dews, 'there should be some straight talking with him as to what he reckons he can do for us in other authorities'.

Poulson's ambitions did not remain wholly in Britain. In the early 1960s, he set up Construction Promotions Ltd (CP), and in 1966 selected Reginald Maudling, MP, to succeed his friend Sir Herbert Butcher as Chairman. Poulson's wife, Cynthia, held the bulk of the shares. However, all did not go smoothly; there were boardroom rows with the company's co-founder, Leslie Pollard, over the amount of work going to Poulson companies. In consequence, Poulson first reorganized, and then closed, CP, and Maudling was removed from the organization. Maudling, who trained as a barrister, had been one of 'Rab' Butler's 'backroom boys' at Conservative Central Office in 1945, and in 1950 entered Parliament. Marked as a high-flyer, he was Economic Secretary to the Treasury in 1952, and in 1955 was made a Privy Councillor and Minister of Supply. Paymaster-General in 1957, he was promoted to the Cabinet, then becoming, successively, President of the Board of Trade in 1959, Colonial Secretary from 1961 to 1962, and Chancellor of the Exchequer from 1962 to 1964. He was only narrowly defeated by Edward Heath in the election for leadership of the Conservative Party in 1965, and thereafter became deputy leader. In time, he would come to rue his involvement with Poulson. Clearly, though, for the architect to attract such a senior politician to his company was a major coup. Poulson then set up International and Technical Construction Services Ltd (ITCS) in association with Dr Kenneth Williams, managing director of Vickers's medical division. ITCS would act as management consultants for Poulson's companies, Vickers being interested in any equipment deals for hospital building.

The rest of the world was, however, beginning to catch up with the activities of Poulson and his associates. The diversification of his organization and the front-end loading of expenses and costs from the trawl for contracts had attracted the attentions of the authorities. In February 1968 his bank told him to cut his overdraft and replace the shortfall with a loan. This loan came from the Industrial and Commercial Finance Corporation, secured on a Poulson office. In November 1968 the Inland Revenue sued him for back tax totalling £210,000 in surtax, income tax, and PAYE. He turned to his brother-in-law, John King, now Lord King of Wartnaby, and formerly Chairman of British Airways, to rescue the practice, but it was too late. By January 1969, Poulson's senior staff had to tell him that his organization was bankrupt, calling in the accountants and solicitors. The newspapers and media began to pay attention.

Ray Fitzwalter, a journalist on the *Bradford Telegraph and Argus*, began investigating the story of a Yorkshire architect called John Poulson just as police were beginning to inquire into the Bradford City Architect's Department. His article appeared in April 1970, and was illustrated with photos of Poulson, Maudling, Smith and Sir Bernard Kenyon. Fitzwalter met Laurie Flynn of *Construction News* and Paul Foot of *Private Eye* on 15 April, and on the 24th the first major article on Poulson appeared in *Private Eye*, under the headline 'The Slicker of Wakefield'. The article outlined the structure of the Poulson organization, and suggested that a number of people were hoping that 'if Mr Poulson goes down, he goes down alone.' Poulson declared himself bankrupt in January 1972. The first day of the bankruptcy hearings were not well attended, but *Private Eye* ran 'The Slicker of Wakefield, Chapter Two', with the result that many more reporters attended for the rest of the hearing, thanks to this reminder of both the public figures and the sums involved.

The bankruptcy laws allow gifts which have been made in the bankrupt company's name, or on its behalf, to be recouped if the money can be used to pay off company debts. At the hearing counsel for the creditors, Muir Hunter, QC, with the aid of Poulson's files (which comprised some 27,000 documents), insisted that the architect explain what had happened to the £274,000 shortfall. Poulson's defence seemed to be a string of expressions of amazement that the transactions he was confronted with had actually taken place, or had been as substantial as they had been. It is instructive to quote a few of his answers:

On the £155,000 to T. Dan Smith – 'Phew! It's fantastic, I had no idea it was that big ...'

On why payments were made to civil servant George Pottinger – 'Because he had been a very good friend of mine.'

On payment of £100 made to the civil servant Alfred Merritt, of the Ministry of Health – 'I cannot remember what that was for ...'

On holidays for Alderman Cunningham – 'There is no explanation.'

On £500 to a millionaire – 'I am as surprised as you.'

On £2,500 to George Braithwaite – 'They had to educate their children.'

That he ran ITCS – 'That is ridiculous.'

Of a letter to Reginald Maudling, in which Poulson had written that Deputy Sheikh Kabil el-Khury of Beirut 'wants paying', and that ITCS was to make the arrangements – 'I have no idea.'

On being asked by Muir Hunter whether he was a man 'with an immensely generous heart' – 'I think now, when I see these figures, "stupid" would describe it.'

The bankruptcy hearing was, however, only the beginning, for the political consequences of having associated with John Poulson had yet to be felt. In July 1972 the Prime Minister, Edward Heath, made a statement to the House of Commons on 'matters arising out of the public examination in bankruptcy of Mr John Poulson.' In his statement, Heath told the House that the Inspector-General in Bankruptcy had forwarded to the Attorney-General, the Lord Advocate and the Director of Public Prosecutions, the Official Receiver's preliminary report into the conduct and affairs of Mr J.G.L. Poulson. He added that after consultation with the Attorney-General and the Lord Advocate, the Director of Public Prosecutions had requested that the Metropolitan Police conduct an investigation and report back to him.

This put the Home Secretary in rather a difficult spot. Reginald Maudling was at the time one of Britain's best-known politicians. His first association with Poulson was in 1966, when, as has been said, he had been invited to become Chairman of Construction Promotion, the company which Poulson hoped would win him contracts abroad. The Conservatives had been thrown out of office in 1964, thus bringing to an end twelve continuous years of ministerial appointments for Maudling, and doubtless a position as chairman of a company in some way compensated for this. Once the investigation into Poulson's affairs had been authorized, however, Maudling's position as Home Secretary became untenable. He had no other choice than to resign. This is how the Prime Minister, Heath, informed the House:

> In this connection there is one other matter of which I should inform the House. I have received a letter from the Home Secretary, Mr Reginald Maudling, who has asked me to read the following extract from it to the House:
>
> 'We discussed the assertions made by Mr Poulson during his bankruptcy hearing. Among them was one referring to myself, to the effect that before I accepted this invitation to become chairman of an export company, for which post I took no remuneration, he had made a covenant in favour of a charitable appeal which had my support. I do not regard this as a matter either for criticism or investigation. However, there are matters not relating to me that do require investigation, and I entirely agree that this should be carried out in the normal way on behalf of the Director of Public Prosecutions.
>
> 'The difficulty arises that the task must fall upon the Metropolitan Police, and in my particular office as Home

Secretary I am police authority for the Metropolis. We both agreed that it would not be appropriate for me to continue to hold this office while the investigations are being pursued in view of the fact that my name had been mentioned at the hearings.

'You were good enough to suggest that I might for the time being hold some other office in your Government, but this I do not wish to accept. For more than 20 years now I have held office continuously, as a minister, or a member of the shadow cabinet. I think I can reasonably claim a respite from the burdens of responsibility and from the glare of publicity which, inevitably, surrounds a minister and inexcusably, engulfs the private lives even of his family.'

Heath went on to tell the House that though he understood and respected the reasons for Maudling's decision to leave the Government, it had been 'only with the greatest reluctance' that he had accepted the Home Secretary's resignation.

But the Poulson fall-out was only just beginning. First there was to be the criminal trial of Poulson and his cronies, then the House of Commons Select Committee hearing into his links with three named MPs, Maudling, Albert Roberts, Labour MP for Normanton in Yorkshire, and John Cordle, Conservative MP for Bournemouth East – at one time police were investigating links between Poulson and 300 politicians. In the end, seven people were gaoled after a series of corruption trials which started in 1973 and spanned two years. Poulson was sentenced to seven years, but served only three before being released in 1977 on grounds of ill health. His right-hand man, T. Dan Smith, the former leader of Newcastle-upon-Tyne City Council and a man once known as 'Mr Newcastle', was gaoled for six years. He too served half his sentence.

T. Dan Smith was the son of a miner. His father was frequently unemployed during his childhood and drank and gambled heavily. In later years, Smith would often recall how his mother had risen at 5 am each morning to clean the

Wallsend telephone exchange, before moving on to wash floors at the Shell-Mex office. 'She cracked up under the strain and died of a broken heart,' he would say when explaining his allegiance to socialist principles long after he had entered the world of commerce. Indeed, he refused to give ground to any attacks on his mixture of socialist principles and capitalist practices. At the height of his success, he had added a public-relations consultancy to the painting firm he had established, and which had grown to employ 250 people. The man who lorded it over Newcastle in his Jaguar with a DAN 68 registration, who sent his three children to private schools and had a pied-à-terre in London's St James's, said that he saw nothing incompatible between, on the one hand, making money and achieving power, and, on the other, being a socialist. He claimed that the mixture gave him the opportunities to do something practical for the people of the North-East; indeed, he unveiled a £200-million plan to transform the centre of Newcastle so as to make it the 'Brasilia of the North'. Wilfred Burns, the designer of Coventry city centre, was appointed to execute the task, and in 1960 Smith was voted 'Man of the Year' by the *Architect's Journal* for his contributions to town planning. It was, however, other, more substantial contributions that were to get him into trouble.

There were, for example, payments of £150,000 to Smith's companies from Poulson, out of the total of some £500,000 which the latter gave away in bribes and kickbacks. But early in 1970, even before this had become public, Smith had been summonsed in connection with alleged corruption involving one of his companies and Wandsworth Borough Council. This case hung over him for eighteen months – but he was defended robustly by none other than Richard Crossman, who devoted a front-page leading article in the *New Statesman* to championing him as the kind of man who got things done. Eventually, however, Smith fell, and was sent to prison for his part in the Poulson affair. Also gaoled was George Pottinger, the civil servant who had brought about Poulson's most lucrative contract, the Aviemore holiday village in the Scottish

Highlands – Poulson rewarded him with a £30,000 home overlooking Muirfield golf course. Andrew Cunningham, the Chairman of Durham County Council and a member of the Labour Party's National Executive, was also among those detained at Her Majesty's pleasure.

For those who served custodial sentences, the ordeal was finite. It started when the prison gates opened to admit them, and finished when they were released. For the politicians who were smeared by association with Poulson's corrupt ways, the nightmare somehow never really went away. Maudling and Roberts retained their seats in Parliament (though the former had to resign from the Cabinet), Cordle was eventually forced to resign his. Of the three MPs whose affairs were examined, he had been most heavily criticized by the House of Commons Select Committee. He had first been approached to lobby on Poulson's behalf by Leslie Pollard, a director of Construction Promotion and that company's driving force. Cordle had good links with West Africa and Poulson's company was interested in winning contracts there. The MP claimed he agreed to become a consultant to Construction Promotion only after his solicitors had made a rigorous check on the company. Late in 1963 he received a draft agreement, and the next year, while Poulson and Pollard were scouring Africa in search of projects, he made two speeches in one day in the House of Commons, urging more encouragement for British civil engineering firms in West Africa. But Cordle did not, however, receive money he had been promised under the terms of the draft agreement with Construction Promotions, and on 2 March 1965 he therefore wrote an eight-page letter to Poulson, explaining what he had been doing on his behalf. In it he included a reference to a speech he had made in the House of Commons about the Gambia, in which he had pressed Her Majesty's Government to help British firms: 'It was largely for the benefit of Construction Promotions that I took part in the debate in the House of Commons on the Gambia and pressed for HMG to award construction contracts to British firms.' Cordle also reminded Poulson in the letter that he had not received the promised retainer, and had only been paid £150 expenses. Shortly afterwards a five-year agreement, providing Cordle with £1,000 a year, was signed. In a statement to the Select Committee, Cordle said: 'The letter I wrote [to Poulson] was completely proper. My suggestion of an increase in my remuneration was totally separate from the speech I made earlier in the House of Commons. I have done nothing of which I am ashamed or of which any fair-minded criticism could be made.'

But the Committee took a different view. It accused Cordle of promoting 'a matter in Parliament for reward', and of having abused his membership of the Commons with conduct amounting to a contempt of the House. On 22 July 1977, the sixty-four-year-old John Cordle told the House of Commons that he was resigning his seat. The night before, a majority of his Conservative colleagues had said that he should 'do the honourable thing' and not fight on in the face of the damning criticism of him by the Commons Select Committee. Having made his resignation speech, after eighteen years as an MP, he was in tears and stumbled as he left the chamber. In the following week, Reginald Maudling and Albert Roberts faced their colleagues in a House of Commons debate. It is interesting to note that Poulson himself gave evidence before the Committee, having been released on parole in May of that year. Though he claimed that he could not remember a great many of the details about payments he had made to MPs, or for which services the politicians had provided, the Commons was clearly concerned about the depth of some of its members' ties with Poulson. For his part, Maudling resented the Select Committee's criticism that his conduct over his resignation letter was 'inconsistent with the standards which the House is entitled to expect of its members', the Committee having given as its considered opinion that the letter was insufficiently honest about his links with Poulson. Maudling and his family held shares in Poulson companies, and his son, Martin, was a director of one of them. As for Albert Roberts, he had received a salary of £208 a month as a consultant to John Poulson for four years until 1968. He was criticized by the Committee for having written a letter to the Ministry of Works in Malta on Commons notepaper, for having telephoned the Crown Agents, and for having written to George Brown, then Secretary of State for Economic Affairs, on matters affecting Poulson, without having disclosed his interest.

In a television programme in 1974 on the subject of Poulson, Reginald Maudling had denied that he had written a letter to the Maltese Government in 1966 urging it to award a hospital contract to Poulson. Subsequently he admitted having written the letter, and said he had denied it because he had forgotten all about it. Poulson designed the £1.5 million Victoria Hospital on the Maltese island of Gozo, and was presented to the Queen when she laid the foundation stone. Though both Maudling and Roberts survived in the Commons, the fall-out from Poulson both smeared, and effectively finished, their careers. This was much more damaging for Maudling, who had been thought of at one time as a future Prime Minister. In 1979, two years after he had had to face a vote on his expulsion from the Commons, which he won by 331 votes to 11, Maudling died.

In 1977, at the age of sixty-seven, Poulson was released from Lincoln Gaol, having served just under half of his sentence. Despite having been labelled 'an evil man' and the centre of 'a web of corruption' which enmeshed many public figures by the judge at his trial, Poulson always maintained that he was not a criminal. When, for a time, he was in Wakefield Gaol, he used to hold open house in his cell each evening, telling his fellow prisoners about the corruption which, he said, riddled British public life. But he left prison crippled with arthritis, and only a shadow of his former self. (When his wife, Cynthia, was told of his release she was about to take a class of five-year-olds at All Saints Infants School in Pontefract. She said: 'I'll be at the prison in good time to drive him home for a nice cup of coffee.') In 1980 he was discharged from bankruptcy. He received social security benefits, and was paid £20,000 to write his memoirs, but although a 200-page book, *John Poulson – The Price*, was printed, it was withdrawn for fear of libel writs. Poulson spent his retirement years gardening, and was being treated for Parkinson's disease when, in February 1993, at the age of eighty-two, he died in hospital, peacefully in his sleep. His wife was at his side.

Less than six months later, at the end of July, T. Dan Smith died aged seventy-eight. Though twenty years had passed since he and Poulson had last been in the public eye, both commanded lengthy obituaries in the newspapers. *The Times* described Smith as

> a city boss along the lines of Chicago's Mayor Daley ... He was not merely a show-figure for Labour but a favourite in Whitehall ... Over the past 16 years he had worked for the rehabilitation of offenders and campaigned for the rights of prisoners. As the years went by an odour, if not of sanctity, then at least a sort of rugged decency began to hang about him. There was an increasing tendency for people to remember what he had done for Newcastle rather than the methods by which he had achieved his aims. In 1987, after years in the political cold, he was readmitted to the Labour Party in Newcastle Central constituency.

Despite the passing of both Poulson and T. Dan Smith, there are many left who suffered at their hands. In December 1991, at the age of seventy-nine, John Cordle, former Conservative MP for Bournemouth East for eighteen years, requested a meeting with the Clerk of the Commons, Sir Clifford Boulton, to ask him to put on record the sequence of events which had surrounded his resignation. The former proprietor of the Church of England newspaper, and a lay reader, Cordle had been elected in the General Election of 1959, when Harold Macmillan's 'Never Had It So Good' government had come to power. Ever since he had resigned following the criticism over his links with Poulson, the ex-MP claimed 'a shadow has lain across my life' and that he had 'suffered irretrievable sadness through the slurs and innuendoes cast upon me'. Sir Clifford agreed to see Cordle, and afterwards wrote him a letter in which he concluded: 'Your personal decision to bring your Parliamentary career to an end was completely out of scale with the single incident to which the Committee drew attention.' Whether that made the former MP feel better or worse cannot be known.

10

Banco Ambrosiano, the Vatican Bank – And the archbishop who said 'At least I'm not in gaol'

The Banco Ambrosiano collapsed in 1982 with debts of more than $1.3 billion, and in June of that year its Chairman, Roberto Calvi, was found dead in rather macabre circumstances, hanging beneath London's Blackfriars Bridge. His demise has never been fully explained – was it suicide or murder? What would become clear, however, was that the Vatican Bank – the Istituto per le Opere di Religione (IOR) – which was a shareholder in Banco Ambrosiano, was to lose heavily when the latter collapsed. The Vatican made a 'voluntary' contribution to creditors of Banco Ambrosiano amounting to $244 million, and altogether the scandal probably cost it a further $160 million in losses. However, the extent of the Vatican's dealings have never fully come to light, because Archbishop Paul Marcinkus, the American who headed IOR from 1971 until his retirement in 1990, was deemed to be outside the jurisdiction of the Italian courts. In February 1987 a Milan court issued a warrant for his arrest and that of two of his associates, Luigi Mennini and Pellegrino de Strobel, on charges of fraudulent bankruptcy (which carried a penalty of up to fifteen years in prison). With this hanging over his head, the Archbishop was for a time confined to his state rooms in the Vatican, which was tough for the sports-loving cleric, who particularly enjoyed a round of golf. (Marcinkus, who was always contemptuous of the Roman siesta, often used to creep out of his carpeted office for a few quick holes at the Aquassanta Golf Club whilst the rest of the Vatican slept.) But at the Ambrosiano bankrupcty trial – Italy's largest – which ended in April 1992, neither he nor the IOR's senior officials were defendants. Long prison sentences were handed down to thirty-five accused – including Licio Gelli and Umberto Ortolani, heads of the P2 Masonic Lodge, and the men who had been able to obtain crucial permits for Calvi from the Italian Ministry of Foreign Trade because a high official there was a member of P2. It appeared that the IOR had been used by some Italian businessmen to recycle part of the $100 million paid in bribes by the Montedision chemical conglomerate in an unsavoury financial deal back in 1989. Calvi, it transpired, had allowed the bank to export lire illegally from Italy; over a five-year period some 50 billion lire was moved in this fashion.

The Vatican Bank became involved with the Banco Ambrosiano in the early 1970s, at which time it bought shares and made large deposits. In the latter part of that decade the Banco Ambrosiano, through its Luxembourg subsidiary, then set up ten shell companies in Panama. These companies were nominally controlled by the Vatican Bank, but whether the bank really owned them is still not clear. Calvi ran them. At the outset he lent $1.3 billion – $600 million of it borrowed from 120 foreign banks – to the shell companies, which then used the money to manipulate the share price of the Banco Ambrosiano. This rise in the latter's share prices was in turn used to borrow more money with which to fund various investments in other companies. Much of the $1.3 billion vanished when the stock collapsed.

The IOR – which is tucked away in a medieval tower in the Vatican that once housed a dungeon – has no branches, and in the late 1980s only had thirteen employees. It maintains, too, a certain ecclesiastical, if occasionally eccentric, manner of doing things; before the Second World War, for instance, it demanded that prospective depositors present their baptismal certificates as proof that they were Catholics. It is a holy Savings and Loan, a type of building society, which takes in money from religious orders and Vatican employees, paying them paltry interest. The bank in turn lent money to diocese and religious orders all over the world at bargain rates, enabling them to obtain funding for schools and church construction. At the time at which the bank had had links with Roberto Calvi it was headed by Archbishop Paul Marcinkus, a 6-foot-4-inch native of Cicero, Illinois, who had once served as a papal bodyguard. A man known for his flamboyant wielding of an oversized Prince tennis racquet on the Vatican courts, this former American football player was well thought of by Pope John Paul II, who was particularly vigorous in his defence of Marcinkus when the accusations started to fly about the Archbishop's involvement with Calvi and Banco Ambrosiano.

When, in 1988, the regulators began to close in on Calvi, he asked the Vatican Bank to help him out and supply proof that it had backed the ten Panamanian companies. Marcinkus has always maintained that it was only then that the bank knew of the loans to these shell companies. The Vatican decided to give Calvi a year in which to resolve the tangle. Officials in the Holy See wrote 'letters of patronage' stating that, directly or indirectly, the Vatican Bank controlled the ten shell companies. In return, Calvi furnished a letter acknowledging that Banco Ambrosiano, not the Vatican Bank, owed the $1.3 billion. But the episode ruined Calvi, who probably took his own life. In the subsequent collapse, creditor banks seized on the opportunity that the letters of patronage gave them to demand that the IOR reimburse them, and even threatened to drag the Vatican to court. Under pressure from the Italian Government, in 1984 the Vatican Bank coughed up that $244 million 'voluntary' contribution, but without admitting any wrongdoing. An arrest warrant for Archbishop Marcinkus was nullified by the Italian Supreme Court, on the grounds that Italy had no jurisdiction on Vatican soil. It prompted Archbishop Marcinkus, this son of a Chicago window cleaner who had climbed a religious ladder to the top, to quip, 'I may be a lousy banker, but at least I'm not in gaol.'

11

Savings and Loan – Spendthrift, or the biggest crisis since the Great Depression?

The American savings and loan (S&L) industry – the nearest equivalent in Britain are building societies, which were set up initially simply in order to lend money to people so that they could buy their own homes – was hit in the 1980s by a series of scandals which rocked the financial foundation stones of the United States. When President Bush took office, he said that it would cost $50 billion to rescue American's savings banks. By June of 1990, however, that figure had soared to an estimated $500 billion, or $2,000 for every man, woman and child in America. The money for such a rescue had to come from taxpayers, which prompted US Congressman, Peter Smith, to lament that it threatened 'our gravest economic crisis since the Great Depression'.

To understand how this crisis came about, it is necessary to look back in time. The S&Ls were traditionally rather staid and old-fashioned operations which took in the savings of America's working class, and lent the money out in long-term, fixed-rate mortgages. It was the S&Ls that financed the home-ownership boom of the 1970s, and all was going well until they were suddenly hit by spiralling inflation. While the home-owners were paying back their loans at 6 per cent or even less, interest rates elsewhere soared into double figures.

At the same time, the commercial banks were invading the home-loan market with variable-rate mortgages. Perhaps the S&Ls should have been allowed to wither and die upon the altar of the free market, but in the US, with its 13,000 independent banks and more than 3,000 independent S&Ls, finance can become an intensely parochial business. Their boards of management are, of course, also packed with the worthies of the region, whose influence counts heavily with local politicians, both Congressmen and senators. In order to keep the S&Ls alive, therefore, the rules were changed, and these companies were freed from old restrictions which had been designed to ensure that they steered clear of risky investments. Now they were to be allowed to play the money markets, and even to get into those darlings of financial wheeler-dealing in the 1980s, junk bonds (securities that offer a high yield, but often with a concomitantly high risk of default). In keeping with the prevailing ideology of the time, which believed in lessening the bureaucratic ties that hampered business, the Federal Regulators, the watchdogs of the S&L industry, had their budgets cut. To reassure nervous investors, however, the maximum $40,000 federal guarantee on deposits was raised to $100,000 – a move which in itself proved to be a recipe for fraud.

In the early 1980s, as property values began their glorious rise, the S&Ls prospered, and in the so-called 'Sunbelt states' of the southern United States their performance was dazzling. Then, suddenly, an external event triggered a crisis. The price of oil collapsed, and though this was good news for the majority of America, it was a nightmare come true for oil-reliant states like Texas and Oklahoma – and for their local S&Ls. The slump in the oil states left local developers bankrupt, unable to pay back their loans to the S&Ls, which were in turn left with half-built or otherwise unsaleable properties in lieu of the loans they had made. On paper, too, the S&Ls were also bankrupt, but under political pressure from local representatives, both senators and Congressmen, federal investigators were held back and did not make pronouncements about the financial health or otherwise of the 'thrifts' (another common name for the S&Ls). Meanwhile, unsurprisingly, property prices began to fall.

As the property slump spread and a collapse in junk bonds brought a new cash crisis to the strained system, the S&Ls sank deeper into trouble. The problem began to be as much a political as it was an economic one. There were many tales of S&Ls giving substantial donations to campaign funds in return for political assistance from incumbents. One such case came to be known as that of the 'Keating Five'. Five senators – four Democrat and one Republican – received re-election donations from the director of a failed S&L in California, Charles H. Keating, Jr. Senator Bob Kerry from Nebraska even referred to George Bush as the 'savings and loans president' – particularly after one of his sons, Neil Bush, was caught up in the evolving scandal. This, of course, then raised other issues. For example, did the rich and famous – or their offspring – receive more favourable treatment at the hands of law enforcement officers or regulators than did the ordinary citizen?

Neil Bush's alleged misdeeds as a director of Silverado Thrift in Denver, Colorado, were, however, small beer in comparison with the overall S&L picture, but they received undue attention from a scandal-hungry media. And, of course, the political opposition had a field day claiming that the President's son had received favourable treatment from the regulators.

The S&L débâcle also brought to the surface many of the perennial fears deeply ingrained in the American psyche. Various reports suggested – probably correctly – that the Mafia milked S&L institutions, and that S&L money was used to hire prostitutes and pay for businessmen's hunting trips and beach parties. Other reports claimed that the federal intelligence and espionage service, the Central Intelligence Agency (CIA), had used some thrifts as front organizations, diverting large sums of money which had then been used to fund covert operations during the Reagan years.

Since the savings and loan scandal two distinct theories have been expounded in attempts to explain how such a cataclysmic catastrophe could have happened. In a nutshell, the two divergent theories are these: first, that unscrupulous businessmen and criminals hijacked the system; or, second, that politicians and regulators had effectively set up a system which encouraged gambling and incompetence. In January 1994 two economists from the University of California at Berkeley, George Akerlof and Paul Romer, published 'Looting: The Economic Underworld of Bankruptcy for Profit', a paper for the prestigious Brookings Institute. In it, as the title suggests, the authors claim that deliberate looting by their owners accounted for much of the losses incurred by failing S&Ls, particularly those owned by relatively small groups of shareholders. Indeed, Akerlof and Romer allege that this looting stimulated criminal activity in junk bonds and property, which led, in turn, to the dramatic collapse of those markets. Thrift deposits were and still are insured by the federal government, something which made the regulators' burden that much heavier, since depositors, safe in the knowledge that they could not lose their money, took little notice of how the thrifts were run, or of whether or not their life savings were being prudently invested. In other words, according to some commentators, this lack of analysis on the part of depositors was in itself a contributory factor in encouraging a large number of unscrupulous traders. When the investment rules governing S&Ls were changed many of them were already in trouble. These associations had little to lose by putting their money into ever riskier ventures, and everything to gain if such gambles happened to pay off.

According to Akerlof and Romer, however, the rational course for many owners would not have been to gamble in order to save their companies, but to loot the remaining assets as fast as possible. The reason for this is because the amount an owner could steal by deliberately bankrupting the thrift exceeded its value as a going concern; moreover, there was only a slim chance of being caught. A key factor here was the easing of accounting rules in the 1980s, which enabled S&Ls to boost current profits artificially by making loans that added to long-term liabilities, but which provided significant short-term gains.

One trick was for S&Ls to lend to property developers sums which included reserves to pay the first few years' interest. In this way a thrift could lend on a shaky project at an exorbitant rate of interest, gleaning what appeared to be good profits but which were actually paid out of the thrift's own money. Or thrifts could buy junk bonds that paid high interest but were unlikely to be paid back in full. By making investments that boosted short-term profits but risked loss in the long run, S&Ls distorted the markets in which they dabbled. The commercial property market tends to follow a boom-and-bust cycle anyway, but in cities like Dallas, Texas, where lending to developers by S&Ls was particularly high, this was exacerbated by looting thrift-owners, according to the Brookings Institute study. Even though office vacancy rates there had reached 20 per cent of available space by 1983, significant development took place until 1988. The reason for this was because crooked thrift-funded projects raised land prices, misleading some honest developers into thinking that the underlying demand was strong.

In terms of the effect on local property prices, the 'strategy' whereby these values were artificially raised was probably accidental. This was not the case with junk bonds, however. It is no coincidence that the 'king of the junk bond', Michael Milken, used friendly thrifts to refinance (at high interest rates) the troubled junk-dependent firms he was helping. Without that finance such firms would probably have failed, but the backing of the thrifts helped convince other investors that the bonds Milken sold were actually better than they really were.

All these strategies had one crucial advantage – they had the appearance of being legal but risky, rather than downright crooked. It is for this reason that the prevailing view is that most thrifts were badly run, their investment decisions far too risky, but that they were not actively criminal. This philosophical view also helps to account for the fact that prosecutors have secured relatively few convictions of owners and others involved in dubious S&L deals. At the time when Akerlof and Romer were writing, the S&L industry had generated an estimated loss to the federal government of $170 billion, and it was the general opinion that only around $25 billion of that total loss was attributable to criminal activity in the S&Ls. Akerlof and Romer, however, believe that crime accounted for at least twice the latter amount, and that figure does not include losses incurred by investors in property and junk bonds. The two authors do not, however, provide sufficient evidence in their paper that criminality lay at the root of the S&L scandal. Their most convincing argument is that the majority of the owners of the thrifts behaved as if there was no tomorrow, rather than with actual criminal intent. It was behaviour shared by many entrepreneurs who had accumulated vast fortunes during the 1980s, but who lost them just as quickly as the decade turned the corner and recession destroyed the unwary.

At the heart of the S&L crisis, at least according to the other point of view, were not criminality or profligacy, but lax regulation and ridiculous deposit insurance, both to be laid at the door of the federal government. Writing in the November 1993 edition of the American Bankers' Association *Journal*, John West, President and CEO of First National Bank of Livingston, Texas, recalled that in February 1982 he had assumed the management of a $55 million independent bank in a community just north of Houston. He said:

> The oil boom in Texas had ended, but no one knew it yet. Deals were still being done with the expectation of $50–$60 per barrel oil prices. Houston was a boom town. Real estate prices and population growth were ballistic. The major international energy-related companies and local real estate developers were expanding exponentially. There was an atmosphere of success – everyone seemed to have a Midas touch.

He went on to say that, contrary to public perception, the real estate and energy explosions were not caused by 'a greedy and crooked bunch of businessmen and their bankers; they were the result of federal government policies and programs …'

The area in which West's bank was marketing itself was some thirty-five miles north of downtown Houston, and there were four S&L branches and one other bank in that 'marketplace'. As he explained:

> Its [i.e. the area's] rate of population growth from 1981 through 1984 was one of the highest in the United States. It sometimes seemed that everyone wanted to build something – anything – there, whether it made any sense or not. Money was plentiful, price appreciation was rampant, and the federal tax laws could not have been more accommodating. By the beginning of 1984 there was an additional bank and there were several S&L branches within walking distance of our bank. The S&Ls had few if any deposit account service charges and the rates they offered for their interest-bearing accounts were usually 30% to 50% higher than our highest. We were usually at least 75% loaned up, but still could not generate a yield that would allow us to increase our rates paid to compete with the thrifts.

West went on to recall the 'anything-goes' atmosphere of the time. Several of his friends were builders, and they described to him the lending arrangements they had with the thrifts 'in a manner similar to how a young man might describe being stranded on a lush island with a bevy of beautiful women. Real estate appraisals were contrived so that they were able to borrow 100% of their costs ...' And their costs included any kind of expenses they could imagine. If the builders went bust the thrifts could continue to develop the property or sell it whilst maintaining a very high price for their investment on their balance sheets. In the final analysis, too, thrift management knew that no matter how reckless their investments the federal government's insurance arm was standing behind them, duty bound to bail them out. As John West puts it: 'The entire process was underwritten in various ways by the federal government.' He continued:

None of it was illegal. None of it was visited upon our society by unscrupulous businessmen or bankers. The scoundrels who later gained such notoriety, and whose reputation still taints out industry's public image, were not the cause of the problem – they were part of the effect. The Reagan administration opened the door to the vault, the Congress laid out the 'Welcome' mat, the rest of the country looked the other way and the scoundrels walked right in. With the taxpayers taking all the risks, the greater a thrift's irresponsibility, the greater its potential rewards.

The S&L débâcle destroyed about a third of the industry, but whilst the drama was unfolding few politicians even mentioned it. During the 1988 presidential election campaign there was only one mention of it – by Democratic candidate Michael Dukakis, who said the S&L problem was a big one and blamed it on the Republicans' deregulation policies. But the subject was immediately dropped at the urging of the Democratic Speaker of the House of Representatives, Jim Wright of Texas, who was heavily involved with many savings and loan executives. Indeed, the biggest operators in the thrift industry – Charles H. Keating, Jr, of Arizona's Lincoln Savings and Loan, David Paul of CenTrust in Miami, Tom Spiegel of Columbia Savings and Loan in Los Angeles, and Donald Dixon of Texas Vernon Bank (known to regulators as 'Vermin Savings and Loan') – donated money to campaign funds on both sides of the political fence. Keating, when asked whether his large contributions to politicians bought him influence, replied with remarkable candour, 'I certainly hope so.'

There is no doubt that the politicians have to shoulder their share of blame for failing to prevent the S&L crisis. But in a country where local vested interests exercise immense power in Washington such a failure is not surprising – particularly as Dukakis's Republican opponent for the presidency, and the eventual winner, George Bush, had headed the task force on deregulation while he had been Vice-President under Ronald

Reagan. Quite apart from anything else, the S&L disaster had a cast of thousands, apart from the outright crooks – all were lured by the opportunity to make use of a no-lose situation offered by federally insured deposits. Amongst the prominent members of this all-star cast were lawyers, accountants, appraisers, business consultants and investment advisers. The S&L scandal was a warning, particularly to the lawyers and accountants, that professional advisers have a duty to make sure that their clients are acting legally.

It is worth studying the consequences of the disaster for a moment. The three bodies which now regulate the savings and loan industry in the US are the Federal Deposit Insurance Corporation (FDIC), the Resolution Trust Company (RTC), and the Office of Thrift Supervision (OTS). Apart from regulating the thrifts of today they are also charged with recouping as much money as possible for the federal government from those professional advisers to S&Ls who might have been negligent in their duties in allowing them to go bust through mismanagement. Another of the tasks of these three bodies is to restructure the thrifts in such a way as to make them stronger in the future, more resilient, and less likely to be the cause of another S&L collapse. In November 1992 the accountants Ernst & Young reached a $400 million (£263 million) settlement with these regulators over thrift audit failures. Arthur Young, one of Ernst & Young's predecessor firms, audited the accounts of 400 of America's 2,500 thrifts, among them some of the most notorious of the industry's failures – Silverado, based in Denver, Colorado, Lincoln Savings and Loan in California, and Western Savings and Loan in Phoenix, Arizona. The failed thrifts to which Ernst & Young had been accountants cost the taxpayers an estimated $6.6 billion. The charges against the accountancy firm ranged from claims that it failed to review adequately property appraisals and to make sufficient allowances for loan losses, to assertions that it had not required necessary disclosure of transactions between the thrifts and 'related parties'. Ernst & Young neither admitted nor denied guilt, but the decision to settle out of court helped both it as well as the regulators. For a start, three-quarters of the $400 million payment was covered by insurance. The remaining $100 million was to be paid out over a four-year period – solely by the US company, and not by any of its international arms – and funded from current earnings. While this might have reduced the firm's future payouts to partners, it would not have upset its business too badly; after all, Ernst & Young's fee income in the United States for 1991 alone was $2.2 billion. In addition, the settlement is only a fraction of the total damage claims, which would have run into several billion dollars, while alone the potential costs of fighting it out in the courts would have exceeded $100 million. It is worth remembering, too, that for the $100 million that Ernst & Young is in effect paying out of its own pocket the accountants receive immunity from prosecution for both the specific charges and for any potential charges. However, as part of the settlement some of the firm's partners have agreed to be retrained, and others have been banned from working on insured financial institutions.

In August 1994 another accountancy firm, KPMG Peat Marwick, agreed a $186.5 million payment with US thrift regulators in a global settlement of thirty-four malpractice cases stemming from its role in the savings and loan débâcle. Under the terms of the deal, $128 million in cash was paid to the Resolution Trust Corporation, $58.5 million in cash and promissory notes to the Federal Deposit Insurance Corporation, the accountants also consenting to accept quality-control mandates imposed by the Office of Thrift Supervision. KPMG Peat Marwick had said that it had served more than 40 per cent of the financial institutions during the 1980s when the S&L crisis began to emerge, and that it still leads the profession in bank and thrift work. The settlement represents about $129,334 for each of its current partners. The firm asserted the payments would cause no financial burden, not least because its professional indemnity insurance would cover 'a substantial portion' of the settlement. In addition, the FDIC received only $23.5 million in cash and the rest by way of a two-year promissory note.

With the KPMG Peat Marwick settlement S&L regulators have essentially closed the book on what had become known as the 'Big Six litigation'. Ernst & Young were the first to settle, then Arthur Andersen & Company paid $82 million. In March 1994 Deloitte & Touche paid $312 million, using moneys from a special fund established when Deloitte Haskins & Sell merged with Touche Ross & Company. There are less than a handful of federal cases pending against the two other Big Six firms, Coopers & Lybrand and Price Waterhouse. In total, the FDIC has only seven cases against accountancy firms pending and the RTC fewer than half a dozen. Some of these cases are against very small firms, or firms that have gone out of business.

It is not just accountants that have had to pay out, however. Early in 1992 the New York law firm of Kayel, Scholer, Fierman, Hays & Handler agreed to pay $41 million to settle a legal case being brought against them by the OTS, which charged the lawyers with withholding from regulators information about Lincoln Savings and Loan. Originally the federal authorities had claimed $275 million in damages for allegedly misleading regulators about the true state of Lincoln's finances, and had also sought to freeze the firm's assets and bar it from practising banking law. The firm had received $13 million in fees for representing Keating's Lincoln Savings and Loan Association. Other lawyers also paid a high price for their association with Lincoln Savings and Loan and Keating. In 1991 the Chicago-based firm of Sidley & Austin agreed to pay $7.5 million to settle malpractice charges against them. Sidley & Austin had gained a certain notoriety when a 1988 memo to Keating from one of the firm's Washington partners, Margery Waxman, was made public. In it she had boasted of putting the regulators on the defensive: 'You have them right where you want them,' she wrote. Later she told a Senate panel that her comments were hyperbole designed to impress her client. Charles H. Keating, Jr, was himself convicted of state tax-fraud.

As if the problems caused by the thrift débâcle were not enough in themselves, the clean-up operation mounted so speedily by the federal government is in danger of causing massive problems of its own unless those involved remain vigilant. There are many critics who believe that the legislation the S&L crisis spawned – the Financial Institutions Reform, Recovery and Enforcement Act of 1989 and the Federal Deposit Insurance Corp. Improvement Act of 1991 – were precipitate and flawed.

One of the difficulties for those tasked with clearing up has been caused by the sheer size of the crisis itself. Where the failed thrifts were concerned, the problem of disposing of their assets fell to the Resolution Trust Corporation, the agency charged under the 1989 thrifts bail-out act with cleaning up the mess. In economically and financially cautious times it has proved much more difficult to offload the assets, many of which are in property and commercial loans. The feeling in Texas, for example, was that the quick disposal of thrift property further lowered an already depressed local property market. At the end of 1991, though, the RTC had $129 billion-worth of such thrift assets on its books. The RTC also took over defunct thrifts, and tried to amalgamate some of the more viable ones. In 1989 the agency 'owned' 606 thrifts, but that figure had dropped to 110 by February 1992. There is no doubt, however, that giving the RTC the task of husbanding the assets of the failed S&Ls, and then selling them off, did create many problems. Following its formation, the federal agency became overnight America's largest owner of property and caretaker of a cumbersome array of loans, office blocks, family mortgages and white-elephant condominium complexes. Golf courses, luxury apartments in Houston, hotels, swimming pools and tennis courts have all passed through the RTC's hands.

The Resolution Trust Corporation was the cornerstone of President Bush's efforts to get to grips with the S&L crisis when it was formed in 1989, the year in which he assumed the presidency. The RTC's mission was to rehabilitate the industry by selling weak institutions to new management and by liquidating the assets of those beyond repair, in order to recoup some of the funds it had to pay out to depositors under the federal guarantee scheme. By January 1990 the RTC was warning that it was about to become insolvent itself and needed up to $100 million in cash to keep the thrift lifeboat from sinking. This new crisis forced an emergency bond auction, at which the government had to increase interest rates on the bonds being sold in order to attract investors. Critics of the strategy claimed that the cost of carrying all these sick S&Ls until buyers could be found for them actually pushed up the cost of borrowing across America as a whole, and led the country to the brink of the recession which, we now know, it careered into.

In 1992 there were once again reports of misuse of funds by the new generation of S&Ls. The Office of Thrift Supervision had been set up with unprecedented powers to ferret out corruption and safeguard depositors' money. Any one of the 3,000 OTS examiners could descend on a thrift anywhere in America at a moment's notice. Yet the same old stories of thrift executives squandering hundreds of thousands of dollars on penthouses, pleasure trips and hunting expeditions were still being heard. Unlike the frauds of the 1980s, however, it was not just depositors' money they were wasting, but billions of dollars from the government's generous S&L bail-out scheme. To take Texas as an example again, First Gibraltar, one of the twenty largest thrifts in the US was formed as part of the Southwest Plan, a government strategy put forward in 1988. At the core of this plan was the idea of creating safer, easier to regulate S&Ls by lumping together eighty-eight troubled Texas thrifts into a handful of 'megathrifts'. After pouring in billions of dollars in federal aid, the government sold the new institutions to a few lucky investors. First Gibraltar, the result of the amalgamation of five defunct thrifts, was sold to the Chairman of Revlon, Ronald Perelman, and run by the banking magnate Gerald J. Ford. It was one of the biggest megas, with a capitalization of around $11 billion. But the thrift also received $5 billion in federal money and a wealth of other perks, including guarantees of $600 million in tax benefits and a promise to cover losses from the thrift's bad loans until 1998. The setting up of First Gibraltar ended up costing taxpayers $2.4 billion more than if the five thrifts of which it was comprised had been closed and their depositors paid out. Furthermore, in 1990 examiners discovered that funds had been squandered on private jets, and when, a year later, First Gibraltar broke the rules again, the OTS mildly rebuked the Chief Executive Officer and levied a fine of $25,000 against him for violations 'regarding the leasing of aircraft and reimbursement expenses'.

What then is the upshot of the savings and loan scandal? Well, it undoubtedly helped to tarnish further the already tarnished image of American banking. In 1980 five of the ten top-performing banks in the nation had their headquarters in Texas; by the end of 1989, nine of the ten largest banks in the state had gone bust. The problem, of course, was not confined to one state – in November 1993, the President of the American Bankers' Association, Bill Brandon, said that the industry's nationwide share of the market had declined from 40 per cent to 20 per cent in the previous twenty years. In addition, there appears to be still a fundamental and as yet unresolved problem – the issue of financial companies being 'too big to fail'. If the legislation still enshrines within it the concept that the federal government will pick up the full tab for depositors if an S&L fails, then no matter how much more efficient the policing of the industry, or how much better run the majority of thrifts are, or even if there is an upgrading in the education of depositors so that they are able to tell a bad thrift from a good one, sooner or later disaster will strike again. And once again, a crook will get his hand into the cookie jar, knowing that if he eats the cookies someone else will have to replace them.

12

'Greed Is All Right ...' – The tale of Ivan the Terrible

Ivan Boesky made his first money at the age of thirteen, selling ice creams from a van which he was too young to drive legally. Like Robert Maxwell, he was a man who never really changed as he grew older – all that happened was that the deals got bigger. He started his New York investment business with £500,000 after his father had sold the family's bars in Detroit. By working twenty hours a day, with just two hours' sleep each night, he turned it into a multi-million-dollar empire. Within four years he had $45 million. That, however, was nothing compared with the riches that awaited him. Boesky used confidential information from his contacts to buy shares in companies that were targets of takeover bids – and by the end of 1986 his financial empire had recorded a profit of £1.6 billion.

Addressing a group of business students a year earlier, he had said: 'Greed is all right by the way: I want you to know that. I think greed is healthy. You can be greedy and still feel good about yourself.' And feel good he certainly did, as he entertained America's most powerful figures, including Ronald and Nancy Reagan and former Secretary of State Henry Kissinger and his wife. He lived amid splendid surroundings, he and his wife, Seema, owning a 200-acre estate in Westchester County, in the midst of the exclusive stockbroker belt, and only some twenty miles from Manhattan. That property alone was worth more than £6 million. Their home in Mount Kisco had twenty bedrooms, most of them equipped with their own marble bathrooms; it also had a squash court, two swimming pools – indoor and outdoor – and a cobbled courtyard for the vintage Rolls-Royce.

The profits from Boesky's twenty-two different companies enabled him to buy properties such as the famous Beverly Hills Hotel in Los Angeles and to set up companies in tax havens like the Bahamas and Bermuda to protect his money. He built up his fortune using simple and age-old methods – he greased the palms of key contacts to tip him off when firms were about to be taken over. Then he illegally used this privileged information to make quick investments in the companies before anyone realized that a takeover was in the wind. In short, he was 'insider dealing' (or 'trading'), a crime in which a person connected with a company uses for his own ends confidential information that would, if generally known, affect the share price of the company in whose securities he or she is dealing. Often Boesky would disguise his purpose by suggesting that he was interested in taking over the company himself, but in fact all he really wanted was to make as much money as possible in the shortest time. When the target company's shares rocketed on news of a takeover bid, Boesky sold – and walked away with massive profits. The key to his crime was a large bank of 300 telephone lines that sat on the mahogany desk in his white-carpeted office in Manhattan. Only Boesky knew who was at the end of each line. He never dialled the numbers, but used a code known only to himself – the machine did the rest. On the direct-line number were a variety of people in the know – senior industrialists and businessmen, waiters from top restaurants, hotel doormen, chauffeurs, anyone with inside information about company takeovers, but mainly either executives in the companies involved, one way or another, in a takeover who had privileged information, or people in strategic positions who could overhear the conversations of the rich industrialists and financiers making takeover bids. Boesky was even in contact with an official at one of New York's airports who fed him vital information about the movements, to and fro, of private jets. He also rewarded his informants with money, other business information, and sex; he had a direct line to a top brothel in Manhattan, and used its services as a means of rewarding some of his informants.

When he was on the top of the heap (to quote the most famous song about New York), Ivan F. Boesky, the self-made billionaire son of a Russian emigré, was known by a number of nicknames: 'Ivan the Terrible', 'The Rambo of Wall Street', 'King Midas', 'the Shark of the New York Stock Exchange'. He admitted that he was addicted to risk, saying that this was what had drawn him to arbitrage – the highly risky business of speculating on companies locked in takeover deals.

So how did Boesky's love affair with risk arbitrage start? – to which the answer is that it began in his native Detroit. In June 1960 he met Seema Silberstein, whose father was a wealthy Detroit real-estate developer. A relative of hers, a federal district court judge, hired Boesky for a one-year clerkship, and soon afterwards the young Ivan and Seema were married. Whilst in Detroit Boesky had spent two years at Cranbrook, a prestigious prep school (in the US, a private secondary school, and not to be confused with the British prep school) where he had excelled as a wrestler. In later life he was to compare wrestling with his work on Wall Street: 'Wrestling and arbitrage are both solitary sports in which you live or die by your deeds, and you do it very visibly.' So when one of his wrestling colleagues from Cranbrook, by then working for Bear, Stearns in New York, told him about arbitrage, Ivan Boesky decided that he was going to make his fortune on Wall Street. He had, in any case, begun to feel that Detroit was too small for him.

Seema's father installed the couple in an elegant Park Avenue apartment, and Boesky landed a job as a trainee with L.F. Rothschild, which lasted a year. He moved on to First Manhattan, where he obtained his first taste of arbitrage, before moving again, this time to Kalb Voorhis, where he promptly lost $20,000 in a single deal and was sacked. Boesky was contemptuous of a firm that should take such action over such a small amount. After a brief spell of unemployment he joined a small member firm of the New York Stock Exchange, Edwards & Hanly. Remarkably, given his employment history and limited experience, they gave him permission to set up his own arbitrage department. He made a splash in his chosen field almost immediately. Using his wits, he managed to convert Edwards & Hanly's modest capital into $1 million and even $2 million positions (a position is a dealer's market commitment), large enough to move individual stock prices from time to time. He was considered bold. Once, for selling stock short (i.e. selling stock he hadn't actually got in the hope of buying it back cheaper as the stock price fell, thus making a profit in between) he was fined $10,000 by the federal regulatory authority, the Securities and Exchange Commission (SEC). But some of Boesky's tactics contributed to his firm's demise – by 1975 Edwards & Hanly was bankrupt. Boesky, by now sick of trying to convince others of his talent, decided to go it alone. He stunned his colleagues by taking out advertisements in the *Wall Street Journal* asking for investors and extolling the profit potential of arbitrage. He allocated just 55 per cent of the operation's profits to the investors, keeping 45 per cent for himself – however, he assigned to investors 95 per cent of any losses! He was unable to attract enough capital to meet his requirements, and so it was his wife's family money, therefore, which provided him with the capital that allowed him to move forward.

From the first day of the Ivan F. Boesky Co. in 1975, its founder arrived at work by limousine. If he wanted something quickly he paid private couriers to deliver it, but he did not waste – as he saw it – any money on the firm itself. It was housed in an ageing office building in Whitehall Street, in a single room so small that the Stock Exchange Auditor ordered him to move to larger premises. Boesky also hated his employees to leave their desks at lunchtime, so he bought their lunch and had it delivered, but only up to a $5 limit per person.

He would arrive every day at work at 7 am. If, however, he was not going to be in on a particular day, he would call at 7.01, and if the phone wasn't answered immediately he would fly into a rage. (Once, years later, Boesky called when a fire drill was in progress. No one answered the phone immediately. The next day a memo appeared on everyone's desk. 'Yesterday, at 3.15 pm, I called in,' it began. 'My phone rang 23 times. I understand there was a fire alarm. Certainly, I don't want you to risk your lives. But I extend my appreciation to those of you who stayed behind.' Nor did Boesky's generosity of spirit extend to days off; indeed, he disliked his staff taking any time off. He himself would never come into the office on the Friday after Thanksgiving, when most Manhattan businesses are reduced to skeleton staffs. But none of his employees were allowed to take the time off. Boesky would check up on them by calling throughout the day, to such an extent that his staff thought that it would have been easier for him if he had come in anyway.

Boesky, like Maxwell, was a workaholic, spending more time working than doing anything else; indeed, the two men were rarely happy unless they were working. During a romantic evening in Paris, Boesky's wife, Seema, made a remark about the beautiful moon, to which he replied: 'What good is it if you can't buy or sell it?' Money was obviously what turned Ivan Boesky on. In an interview he once fantasized about climbing to the top of a huge pile of silver dollars: 'Imagine – wouldn't that be an aphrodisiac experience?'

Maxwell and Boesky also shared a curious attitude to food and eating. Neither believed that stopping to eat was time well spent. Both were browsers – they ate whilst going about their working day. The difference between them was that Maxwell was constantly eating, while Boesky hardly ate at all. One London solicitor who acted for Maxwell told me that he put on a stone in weight during the three years he worked for 'Captain Bob'.

> Going up to Bob's office was like going to a wedding feast. I wanted to ask where the bride and groom were.

There was always a long table full of food: toasted cheese, smoked salmon, buckets of caviare and brown bread. The executives always dined well: good food and fine wines. I remember at coffee time Robert Maxwell had his own cup, on which was printed 'I am a very important person'. It resembled a soup bowl and Maxwell had to use two hands to drink out of it. Often small snacks would arrive in the middle of meetings and were handed out by his butler, Joseph, from a large silver tray. We would all take one and the tray would then be passed to Maxwell who would finish off the rest. He was always eating, particularly in the afternoons around five or six o'clock.

Boesky's eating habits could not have been in greater contrast. For breakfast he would order a single croissant and would pick at it, eating no more than a flake or two. Once he invited to lunch Meshulam Riklis, the Chairman of Rapid-American Corporation, and husband of film star Pia Zadora. Boesky had found out beforehand the sort of food Riklis liked and persuaded him to eat heartily, despite Riklis's initial protestations that he was going to work out with his personal trainer after lunch and therefore did not want to eat too much. Boesky ate a single grape.

His eating habits did not prevent Boesky from making money, however. In 1981 he liquidated his interest in Ivan F. Boesky Co. and set up another company. He had failed to persuade any of his employees to take over the firm he had founded, and so had recruited an arbitrageur from Morgan Stanley to take over and rename the company Bedford Partners, though his wife still had $8 million in the business, which made her the largest investor. Boesky's new firm was named the Ivan F. Boesky Corporation. As a corporation rather than a limited partnership, the company's shares were divided between common stockholders and preferred stockholders. Investors mostly received preferred stock, and the profits were allocated heavily to the common stockholders, which meant principally to Ivan Boesky himself. The past pattern of the greater proportion of losses being picked up by the investors once again held, and the preferred holders had to shoulder most of those. The corporation was launched with less than $40 million, Boesky setting up shop in an unused partner's office at the Manhattan law firm of Fried, Frank, Harris, Shriver and Jacobson, where Boesky's principal lawyer, Stephen Fraidin, was a partner. With the arbitrageur was Lance Lessman, who had come from Boesky's now renamed company, and Michael Davidoff, a trader he had lured away from Bedford Partners.

At this point it is necessary to introduce another character who was to play a vital role in the Ivan Boesky story. His name was Michael Milken. His particular part of this story starts ten years earlier with the merger between Burnham & Company and the old Wall Street firm Drexel. Working for Drexel at the time was Michael Milken – though not happily, having for long complained that the starched-shirted Drexel WASPs (white Anglo-Saxon Protestants) tended to treat him as a second-class citizen. After the merger Tubby Burnham, grandson of the founder of the I.W. Harper distillery, allowed Milken to set up a semi-autonomous bond-trading unit within the firm, and in 1975 gave him a compensation package crafted to provide strong performance incentives. Like nearly all of Wall Street, Drexel paid relatively low salaries, most employees making up for that with performance-related bonuses. Milken's deal, however, was unusually generous: he and those working for him were awarded 35 per cent of all the firm's profits derived from their activities. Milken was given the discretion to allocate the money among his staff, keeping the remainder for himself. Burnham also gave Milken additional 'finder's fees' of between 15 and 30 per cent of the profits attributable to any business brought into the firm by Milken or his people. Burnham paid out 35 per cent of its profits to the people actually doing the work and up to 30 per cent of the profits to those who landed the client, the company keeping as little as 35 per cent to cover overheads and the partners' share of profits. Milken's deal was, though, a closely guarded secret. It was clear, however, that he wasn't just another employee – he was, in fact, one of the highest-paid people on the staff. Having started with $2 million in capital in 1973, he was generating astounding 100 per cent rates of return, earning bonuses approaching $1 million a year. And he was doing it in a relatively obscure area of trading: high-yield, unrated bonds.

The American bond market is dominated by two giant bond-rating agencies, Moody's and Standard & Poor's, which for generations have guided investors trying to gauge the risk in fixed-income investments. The value of these investments depends on an issuer's ability to make the interest payments it has promised until the bond matures, and to repay the principal loan. Top blue-chip corporations, like the telecommunications giant AT&T or computer company IBM, are rated triple A by Standard and Poor's, which means that there is little or no risk of them not making their payments. Companies with weaker balance sheets or other problems are correspondingly lower rated, while some companies are deemed so risky that they receive no rating at all. Interest rates on corporate debt fluctuate with market rates. The lower the debt rating, therefore, the higher the rate a company has to pay in order to attract investors.

In the mid-1970s there was not a great deal of low-rating or no-rating debt around, and in any case most investors would not touch either. The big investment banks were not interested; they were too hard to sell, too risky for the firms' reputations, and tended to alienate the mainstream, top-rated issuers. Much of the high-yielding debt around was the paper of companies which had once had high ratings but which had fallen on hard times – known on Wall Street as 'fallen angels'. Milken was drawn to this quiet investment backwater.

Milken came from an upper-class background, and grew up in the town of Encino, in the San Fernando Valley north of Los Angeles. His father was an accountant, and at the age of ten Milken began to help him sort cheques and reconcile chequebooks, and later to help with tax returns. From his early years he dazzled schoolmates with his mental arithmetic, for he was able to do quite complex sums in his head. He went to Birmingham High School, where the movie star Sally Field was a classmate, then on to the University of Southern California at Berkeley, graduating in 1968. He married his girlfriend from his schooldays, Lori Anne Hackel, shortly after graduation and they moved to Philadelphia, where Milken enrolled at the University of Pennsylvania, attending the prestigious Wharton Business School. He studied hard, graduating with As in all his subjects after working part-time at the local office of Drexel Firestone. Once he had qualified he stayed with Drexel, commuting from a Philadelphia suburb to the firm's Manhattan headquarters. He appeared to be oblivious to the tradition that promising business graduates went into investment banking – into corporate finance, not sales and trading. Indeed, Milken actively sought out sales and trading, coming to focus almost exclusively on the low-rated and unrated securities that would become his hallmark.

In the years to come his success would help feed the myth that he was a 'genius', the man who discovered the profit potential of what became universally known by the pejorative title 'junk bonds'. But Milken never made any secret of the fact that while still at Berkeley he had come across and assimilated research which formed the basis of his analysis. Indeed, W. Braddock Hickman, analysing corporate bond performance between 1900 and 1943, demonstrated that a diversified long-term portfolio of low-grade bonds yielded a higher rate of return for no further risk, than a comparable portfolio of blue-chip companies. A later study from 1945–65 reached the same conclusion. Like a zealot, Milken proceeded to preach this particular gospel. It was hard work, largely because virtually no research was being done on Wall Street, with the result that he had to handle his own fact-finding. With a bulging briefcase he travelled around trying to persuade investors to gamble on high-yielding securities which, he believed, would make their payments and which were, as a result, undervalued. He began to succeed. Among his early successes was a group of wealthy, mostly Jewish, financiers who had acquired insurance companies. None was a member of the Wall Street establishment. They did not worry about the stigma associated with the type of business Milken was putting to them – and they liked his ideas. Saul Steinberg, Meshulam Riklis (who would one day have the uncomfortable lunch with Boesky) and Carl Lindner became early converts. As their annual returns met or exceeded Milken's predictions they became heavy backers, and they also became clients of Drexel. For his part, Milken was unconcerned that Lidner was the subject of an SEC investigation, and that he was shunned by Cincinnati society; or that Steinberg had annoyed the banking establishment by daring to stage an unsuccessful hostile bid for the giant Chemical Bank; or that Riklis had started as a poor Israeli immigrant who had made his money in movie theatres and booze. By early 1977, Milken's operation controlled a remarkable 25 per cent of the market in high-yield securities, and was really the only business maintaining an active market-making operation whilst trying to enhance the amount of money in the market – its 'liquidity', as it is known in financial circles. (A market-maker assures a holder of a security that it will buy it whenever the holder wants to convert it into cash. The market-maker in turn sells it on, keeping as its profit the difference between the 'buy' and 'sell' prices obtained.) There were banks, such as Lehman Brothers, the market-maker in high-yield bonds, which would underwrite some new issues and husband those they had previously underwritten, but this was mostly a service to existing clients; other firms were not interested in being market-makers. So Milken became, in effect, the market for high-yield bonds. He had an incredible memory, and knew who owned what issues, what they had paid, the issues' yields to maturity, and who else wanted them. As his reputation grew, so his clients developed such confidence in his abilities that when he urged them to invest in a particular issue, they did. They did not care that there were no published prices, or that Milken never told them how much he was earning (in other words, what the spread was between 'buy' and 'sell') – all they were interested in was the size of their own profits.

In 1977, Milken's team had a corporate finance bonus pool of $1 million. That year, a company called Texas International wanted to raise capital but had too much debt to draw in investment by the usual means. Milken decided to do a public high-yield issue – that is, an original new yield issue direct to the public, rather than the secondary offerings that were the mainstay of Drexel. He sold the $30 million issue easily, earning himself an underwriting fee of 3 per cent in the process. He went on to do another six issues that year for companies which were unable to obtain capital in any other way. At around the same time he sold the idea of allowing small investors to invest in a diversified portfolio of junk bonds via high-yield mutual funds. The mechanism for a revolution in finance was in place, right under the noses of the Wall Street establishment.

Michael Milken first met Ivan Boesky in 1981, through Stephen J. Conway a former investment banker at Drexel in New York. Like Boesky and Maxwell, Milken was another financier who seemed to need no sleep, so he and Boesky found plenty of time to talk on the telephone. (After 1977, when Milken's operations had been moved to Beverly Hills, he would arrive at his office at 4 am, and Boesky at his office in New York at 7 am – given the time difference between the two cities, they effectively arrived at work at the same moment.) Boesky wanted to raise $100 million and Milken and Drexel were willing to help. When his father-in-law had died in 1979 he had left large portions of his estate divided equally between his daughter – and Boesky's wife – Seema, and her sister, Muriel Slatkin. The Beverly Hills Hotel was one of the properties the two women inherited. Built in the 1930s, it was legendary: Katharine Hepburn had swum there, fully clothed, after a tennis game, and Eddie Murphy had been known to hurl himself off the diving board.

After Silberstein's death, ownership was divided between Seema and Muriel, with a vital 5 per cent stake in the hands of other relatives. Boesky set about getting his hands on that stake, knowing that, with his wife's share, it would give him a controlling interest. He managed to do so, and then changed the name of the company from Vagabond to Northview Corporation. Ivan the Terrible now saw himself becoming what in Britain is described as a 'merchant banker' – that is, an investment banker who acquires shareholding stakes in companies. After he had obtained the $100 million Vagabond/Northview financing in mid-1983, the Boesky-Milken financial connections became heavily intertwined. Most of Boesky's capital was now Milken generated. This presented Drexel, his own investment bankers, with a potential problem in that Boesky, as an arbitrageur, should not be given access to confidential information about takeovers which he might then be able to use to his advantage. This is supposed to be prevented by the use of so-called 'Chinese walls' within an investment firm (a Chinese wall is an investment barrier between investment bankers and traders intended to prevent the latter from acting on confidential information entrusted to investment bankers by their clients). But though some Drexel employees were impervious to Boesky's advances, others were not. Dennis Levine, who had joined Drexel in early 1986, was a thirty-two-year-old whiz kid in its mergers and acquisition business. He began to cultivate a friendship with Drexel's biggest individual client, Ivan Boesky. Levine was hired on a $1 million-a-year salary, but he soon found that Boesky could top that up. After all, Boesky's touch on Wall Street, where he seemed able to predict takeovers and mergers moments before they happened, had brought with it a loyal following which had enabled his investment bankers, Drexel Burnham Lambert, to raise close to $1 billion to commit to his arbitrage fund. Dennis Levine began to supply Boesky with information, and notably with advance notice of the R.J. Reynolds merger with Nabisco, valued at $4.9 billion. Boesky made a profit of $4 million on the information supplied by Levine, which had come from inside Shearson Lehman Brothers, Nabisco's advisers. Also that year Boesky netted another $4 million profit during the InterNorth takeover of Houston Natural Gas, Levine's information coming this time from inside Lazard Frères, HNG's advisers. In addition, Boesky profited from intelligence about takeovers or restructuring at Boise Cascade, General Foods, Union Carbide, American Natural Resources and other companies, for a total profit of around $50 million. In one month, Levine earned $4 million in commission for the valuable information he passed to Boesky.

How then did this elaborate scam fall apart? The simple fact is that, as in most financial scandals, it was the snagging of a small thread that led to the unravelling of it all. The process began towards the end of May 1985 when an anonymous letter arrived on the desk of the vice-president of compliance at the Wall Street investment house Merrill Lynch. The letter implicated two of Merrill Lynch's employees in South America in small irregular share transactions, which had all been made through the Bahamas branch of Switzerland's oldest bank, Bank Leu. After an internal investigation Merrill Lynch took immediate action and sacked the two men involved; however, it also passed the information on to the regulatory body, the Securities and Exchange Commission. In turn, the SEC looked into the matter further, and noticed that on twenty-eight occasions transactions had occurred in the shares of companies which had then been the subjects of takeover bids. The SEC contacted the bank. The transactions were all connected with one account – Diamond Holdings, operated by Dennis Levine. When Levine first became aware of the SEC's interest he was inclined to take the view initially that a combination of the Swiss secrecy rules with Bahamian law would protect him. He then proposed that the bank should engage US lawyers, and himself put forward the name of Harvey Pitt, a former SEC general counsel now in private practice with Fried, Frank, Harris, Shriver & Jacobson at its Washington office. Levine further suggested that Bernhard Meier, the man at Bank Leu who handled the Diamond account, should tell the SEC that he had made the investments for a general portfolio of bank clients. The problem with that as a means of covering up the crime was that Pitt wanted to see evidence of it, which of course Meier was unable to supply. Pitt and his team of lawyers knew that if the transactions had been carried out by one person, then they could be sitting on the world's biggest insider trading scandal.

Eventually, Bank Leu sent over its own lawyer from Zurich. The bank, which wanted to expand in the US, had no wish to fall foul of the American regulatory authorities. The Swiss lawyer therefore told Meier to let Pitt know what was involved, but not the identity of the man behind the Diamond account; however, Pitt was told that the operator of the account was an investment banker with Drexel Burnham Lambert. In the light of all this, Pitt then informed Bank Leu officials that he hoped to keep them from prosecution by brokering a deal with the SEC whereby the identity of the dealer might be divulged in return for immunity from prosecution for bank employees. This required sensitive handling not only of the SEC but also of the Bahamian authorities, but eventually a deal was drawn up. The net was tightening around Dennis Levine.

Question: 'What's the definition of an arb?'

Answer: 'Someone who's never seen, heard of, or talked to Dennis Levine!'

This was the joke doing the rounds on Wall Street shortly after May 1986, when Levine was arrested as a result of the SEC investigation. When the SEC managed to obtain a continuation of a temporary freeze it had placed on Levine's $10 million account in the Bahamas, it quickly became apparent that the investment banker wanted to deal. He offered to identify four other young bankers who had taken part directly in the insider-trading ring, as well as one other person 'who's bigger'. A deal was worked out under which Levine was allowed to keep his Park Avenue apartment, his BMW but not his Ferrari, and an account at Citibank which he described as 'walking-around money' but which the men from the SEC thought would largely be spent on legal fees. He identified for the authorities three of the four investment bankers he had promised to name, saying that he had never known the name of the fourth one but that he had been recruited by one of the others and worked in the mortgages department of Goldman, Sachs. Finally, Levine confirmed the investigators' suspicions by telling them that Ivan Boesky was involved, and that he himself had first begun dealing with Boesky by sending him confidential documents on Boise Cascade and Elf-Aquitaine. He went on to describe how he had phoned Boesky and offered to supply him with tips, and that they had met for a drink in order to discuss the arrangement and payment for the service.

A short time after agreeing this deal, Levine contacted his co-conspirators on a tapped telephone line. The only one to speak to him, though he knew the line was probably bugged, was his friend Robert Wilkis of the firm E. F. Hutton. The others, Boesky included, put the phone down on him. On the next day, however, lawyers acting for Ira Sokolow called the SEC to negotiate a plea; so too did those representing David Brown, the Goldman, Sachs investment banker. Sokolow confirmed that Brown was a close friend of his from Wharton Business School, and that Brown was the man he had recruited to the scam and whose name was not known to Levine. Each agreed to plead guilty to two charges and pay substantial financial penalties to the SEC. Sokolow was later sentenced to a year and a day in prison; Brown received thirty days.

Wilkis too eventually co-operated, pleaded guilty to four charges, and paid more then $3.3 million dollars as well as the proceeds of the sale of his Park Avenue apartment. He was allowed to keep an apartment in Manhattan's West 78th Street, his Buick car and $60,000 – which, by then, was about all he had left. He wept as he was sentenced to a year and a day in prison and five years' probation. Ilan Reich, a partner in the law firm Wachtell, Lipton, also co-operated in the end. Although he had never received any payment for the tips he had passed on and had left the scheme in 1984, Reich was still sentenced to a year and a day in prison after pleading guilty to two charges. He agreed to pay $485,000 and was left with his house on New York's West Side, his Oldsmobile car and $10,000.

On 20 February 1987, hundreds of reporters, television crew members, and idle passers-by stood outside the federal courthouse in White Plains, a suburb of New York, to hear the sentence handed down to Dennis Levine. It had been suggested in court that Levine had managed to hide some money from government scrutiny, but Judge Goettel seemed more impressed with the fact that the banker had co-operated with the investigation. Levine was sentenced to two years in prison and fined $362,000, on top of the $11.6 million he was paying to the SEC. That just left Boesky.

In late July 1986, two months after Levine's arrest, Boesky had flown to Los Angeles for a meeting with Milken, at which the latter suggested that, given the media attention and the government's watchful eye on the markets, they should limit their deals for a while. Boesky agreed. The two of them then tried to find a formula with which they could substantiate their phoney explanation for a $5.3 million 'consultancy fee' which Boesky had paid Milken. Drexel, they agreed, would have to produce more documentation showing research work that had been done but which had not culminated in a deal – the accounting records, however, had to be destroyed.

In the middle of August Harvey Pitt, Bank Leu's lawyer, telephoned Gary Lynch of the SEC at the cabin in Maine which he and his family traditionally booked for their summer holidays. Pitt wanted to meet Lynch, who replied that 'it had better be good'. It was – Pitt told Lynch that he was not representing the Bank Leu in this instance, but Boesky. Over the coming weeks a deal was again worked out. Boesky had confirmed to his lawyers the details of his dealings with Dennis Levine, and also of various transactions between him and Milken, as well as between him and a West Coast broker, Boyd Jefferies, and a number of other prominent businessmen besides. Before co-operating, he had wanted to know from his lawyers the answers to three questions: what would happen to his wife and children?; what would happen to his employees and investors?; and would he be sent to prison? He was told in reply that his family's assets and trust funds, including those generated on their behalf by his illegal activities, would probably be unaffected since they had played no part in his deals. He was also informed that in all likelihood he would be barred from the investment industry, which would mean that his employees would lose their jobs, but investors probably would not be hurt. As to time in gaol, he would almost certainly have to serve some, he was told, but the period of the sentence would be far shorter if he co-operated than if he went to trial, pleaded not guilty, and was then convicted. This then was the advice of Boesky's lawyers to their client, and it was on the strength of these opinions that he decided to settle with the SEC. At first his legal team tried to obtain an assurance that Boesky would not be prosecuted, but the SEC would not buy that, nor could those who worked for it say whether a plea agreement could be worked out – that was up to the US Attorney's Office or the Justice Department.

Back in New York the District Attorney, Rudolph Guiliani (later the city's Mayor), said immunity was impossible – but a plea could be negotiated. This would mean that Boesky would have to plead guilty to at least one charge. He would also have to give the authorities the names of those he had been dealing with, and in addition a heavy fine would be levied. The SEC's annual budget at the time was $105 million, so a $100 million fine was suggested. The idea was that such a large, round figure would dazzle the public, while the comparison with the SEC's budget was also seen as something that would look good in the media.

The negotiations between Boesky's lawyers on one side, and the SEC and the US Attorney's Office on the other, were shrouded in secrecy. They were held at the offices of Fried, Frank, Harris, Shriver & Jacobson – Boesky's legal representatives – in order not to attract attention, while in telephone conversations he was never referred to by name – the SEC codename for him was 'Irving' and that of the US Attorney's Office 'Igor'. In discussions it emerged that Boesky would be charged with conspiracy to commit securities fraud, an indictment which, if he was convicted, carried with it a maximum five-year prison sentence.

After the two sides had agreed a framework for a deal, Boesky himself began to be questioned. The first thing he did was name those he had been dealing with – and what names they were, a galaxy of the stars of the securities world. The most important was Michael Milken, the junk bond king, but there were also Martin Siegel, Drexel's star investment banker, Boyd Jefferies, head of Jefferies & Co., the West Coast brokers, and Carl Icahn, the corporate raider (that is, a person or business that makes a practice of acquiring substantial shareholdings in companies in order to take them over, or force their managements to act in certain ways). Boesky's lawyer, Harvey Pitt, had promised that his client's evidence would provide 'a window on Wall Street', and so it was to prove. Like many outsiders who had heard of Boesky and knew of his reputation, both the SEC officials and their colleagues in the US Attorney's Office believed that he himself was the big fish on Wall Street. It soon emerged, however, that Boesky depended upon Milken and Drexel – they could make him richer, or they could destroy him. In mid-October 1986 Boesky again went to Los Angeles for a meeting with Milken. This time, however, he was there for only one purpose – to try to trap Milken into discussing their previous illegal dealing, for which purpose Boesky had a microphone taped inside his clothes. The conversation between the two men was then recorded in Harvey Pitt's room at the Beverly Hills Hotel, where Boesky, not unnaturally, also had a suite. At the meeting, they chatted briefly in general terms about the financial markets, and Boesky then told Milken that the SEC had subpoenaed his records, adding that the Commission was breathing down his neck. He then tried to get Milken to be more explicit about their dealings together. Though he never volunteered information, Milken did not refute assertions Boesky made about the $5.3 million payment, thus indicating that he had taken part in illegal transactions.

On Friday, 14 November, at about 3.20 pm, Boesky gathered all his staff together. They knew something unusual was happening when their employer was followed into the room by a team of lawyers headed by Harvey Pitt. Boesky began by reading from a prepared statement. He said the past few weeks had been 'very difficult' for him because he had been unable to discuss anything with his staff, and had also avoided contact with them. He went on to say that what he was about to tell them must not leave the room until after 4 pm and that they would not be allowed to make any calls until a quarter past that hour. He paused, then, after taking a deep breath, he told them that at 4 pm it would be announced that he had reached a settlement with the SEC in which he would pay $100 million, and that he had agreed to plead guilty to one count of conspiracy to commit securities fraud. The Government, he said, 'justifiably holds me and not my business associates or business entities responsible for my actions'. He then continued, in a sombre and perhaps rather sententious vein:

> I deeply regret my past mistakes, and know that I alone must bear the consequences of those actions. My life will be forever changed, but I hope that something positive will ultimately come out of this situation. I know that in the wake of today's events, many will call for reform. If my mistakes launch a process of re-examination of the rules and practices of our financial marketplace, then perhaps some good will result.

His statement over, Boesky turned his gaze towards his employees and offered to take questions. There was total silence.

At 4.28 pm in dealing rooms, financial offices and newsrooms across the country the stunning news came rattling on to the teleprinters – 'SEC Charges Ivan Boesky With Insider Trading'. Beneath that headline, the report went on to say that: 'The Securities and Exchange Commission charged Wall Street arbitrageur Ivan Boesky with trading on inside information provided by Dennis Levine.' The news became even more startling, however, for the item continued:

> Boesky has agreed to co-operate with the SEC in its widening investigation of insider trading on Wall Street, SEC officials said. In addition, the United States Attorney in New York said Boesky entered into a criminal plea

agreement in which he will plead guilty to one federal felony charge. The US Attorney's Office, which declined to identify the specific charge, said Boesky is co-operating in its continuing criminal investigation arising from the Dennis B. Levine insider trading case.

Boesky and Milken had fuelled the bull times of the 1980s; indeed, they had in large part been responsible for the takeover fever which had gripped the country. Boesky's admission of guilt marked the end of an era. But for many it was the beginning of a brief but perhaps rather fearful period, since almost all the top people on Wall Street had spoken to Boesky at one time or another. For a while paranoia swept the skyscrapers.

At Milken's offices in Beverly Hills, he and his colleagues had had a busy week. When the news came through Milken stayed at his desk and acted as though nothing had happened. He then went to the office of his brother, Lowell, and spent more than an hour with him. At the time he had no idea that subpoenas from the Justice Department had already been issued concerning Milken and Drexel – a criminal investigation was under way. When the New York Stock Exchange heard the news of Boesky's plea, shares fell, but the exchange shrugged off the news and closed only 13 points down. Drexel and Milken was a different and potentially far more damaging case, however. On the day on which the *Wall Street Journal* revealed Drexel to be a target of an SEC investigation, the Dow-Jones Industrial Average dropped 43 points. Stocks in companies which rumour held were the targets of takeover bids – the sort of stocks Boesky would in the immediate past have been interested in – fell heavily. Junk bond prices plunged. Some Drexel clients pulled out of pending deals; Ronald Perelman abandoned his Drexel-backed hostile bid for Gillette, causing further turmoil on the markets. Rumours swept the floor of the stock exchange, and almost hourly news came through that Milken had resigned.

Far from resigning, Milken intended to fight – after all, he had been investigated by the SEC before, and had won. It was clear from the subpoenas Drexel received in November and December of 1986 that Milken's relationship with Boesky was at the heart of the investigation. Almost all the deals they had done together were identified, Fishbach, Pacific Lumber and Wickes amongst them. The $5.3 million 'consultancy fee' from Boesky figured prominently. The subpoenas called for the production of a vast quantity of documents and gave Drexel thirty days in which to respond. The Drexel executives accepted Milken's explanation that the $5.3 million payment was for research – even though Drexel did not usually bill its clients for research work.

Milken's defence lawyers described him as an innocent victim of the true criminal, Ivan Boesky, and even suggested that their client was a genius, a hero of the American economy. Such a positive characterization, together with the support he had inside Drexel, made it hard for Milken to back down and accept a guilty plea. But on 20 February 1990, more than three years since Boesky had agreed himself to plead guilty, it finally happened. The deal this time was that Milken agreed to pay a $600 million fine and to plead guilty to six charges. On Tuesday, 24 April, Michael Milken arrived in a dark limousine at the Manhattan Federal Courthouse. The largest courtroom was packed and there was a ripple of laughter when Judge Kimba Wood, parroting the standard judicial advance to defendants, told Milken that the court would appoint a lawyer for him if he was unable to afford one!

The mood quickly changed, though, as Milken read out a detailed confession to the six charges: conspiracy with Boesky; aiding and abetting the filing of false statements in connection with the Fischbach scheme; aiding and abetting the evasion of net capital rules; securities fraud for concealing the ownership of MCA stock; mail fraud for defrauding investors in Finsbury; and assisting the filing of a false tax return.

Milken argued that his admission of guilt was 'not a reflection on the underlying soundness and integrity of the segment of the capital markets in which we specialized and which provided capital that enabled hundreds of companies to survive, expand and flourish.' But he concluded more sombrely: 'I realize that by my acts I have hurt those who are closest to me;' then, clearly having difficulty speaking, he added an emotional, 'I am truly sorry ...' As he said that he started to fall forward and his lawyers rushed forward to prop him up. While they supported him, he put his face in his hands and began to cry.

Milken was not sentenced for another seven months, finally reappearing in the same courtroom on the morning of Wednesday, 21 November 1990. Once more brushing away his tears, he heard his own lawyers ask for leniency. The prosecution, however, wanted a custodial sentence. Judge Wood then spoke. In measured tones, she emphasized the 'extraordinary interest' in the proceedings, and said that she wanted to dispel several misconceptions, among them that Milken should be punished for the ills of the economy and the collapse in the savings and loan industry (by this time boom had turned into recession and the S&L scandal was out in the open). Judge Wood then noted the 'legitimate' principle 'that everyone, no matter how rich or powerful, obey the law', and 'that our financial markets in which so many people who are not rich invest their savings be free of secret manipulation. This is a concern fairly to be considered by the court.' Then the judge went to the heart of the matter:

> When a man of your power in the financial world, at the head of the most important department of one of the most important investment banking houses in this country, repeatedly conspires to violate, and violates, securities and tax laws in order to achieve more power and wealth for himself and his wealthy clients, and commits financial crimes that are particularly hard to detect, a significant prison term is required in order to deter others.

In a final flurry, she added: 'This kind of misuse of your leadership position and enlisting employees who you supervised to assist you in violating the laws are serious crimes warranting serious punishment and the discomfort and opprobrium of being removed from society.'

Judge Wood asked Milken to rise, and proceeded to sentence him to a total of ten years in prison, two years each for counts two to six, to be served consecutively. She then said that Milken might sit if he wanted. As the judge left the courtroom it seemed to many observers there that Milken had not understood what had happened – he appeared to think that he had been sentenced to only two years (which would have been the case if the sentences were to have been served concurrently). He was taken to a small witnesses' waiting room, and there collapsed when he was made to realize just how much time he would have to serve behind bars. Michael Milken began his sentence at the federal minimum-security prison in Pleasanton, near San Francisco, California, in March 1991. Judge Wood had recommended that he serve a minimum of thirty-six to forty months in gaol.

Of the other players in this drama of insider trading, Martin Siegel, who had left the Mergers and Acquisitions Department at Kidder Peabody to join Drexel, from where he supplied inside information to Boesky, had to sell his house in Connecticut and his apartment in Manhattan, and bought a home in Florida. As part of his deal with the government he was forced to hand over to the SEC his bonus cheque for 1986 – it was for $3 million. When Siegel was eventually sentenced the view of officialdom was that he alone of all those caught up in the scandal had shown true remorse. The judge praised him as a 'credible and reliable' witness who had co-operated with the investigation despite 'an intense campaign of vilification'. Siegel was sentenced to two months in prison and five years' probation.

Robert Freeman, who was head of arbitrage at Goldman, Sachs, was arrested in spectacular fashion at his company's offices, where he was frisked and handcuffed before being marched through the main dealing room. Two other Wall Street insiders were similarly badly treated – Richard Wigton was arrested in some style at his desk at Kidder Peabody, and Timothy Tabor, who had just lost his job at Merrill Lynch, was arrested in the foyer of his apartment block on the Upper East Side. Both men had the cases against them dismissed, however.

John Mulheren ran his own firm, Jamie Securities, having previously worked for Spear Leeds. He became involved with Boesky's schemes when the arbitrageur approached him for a favour. On a number of occasions Boesky's business associates asked Mulheren to take shares off their hands – the idea being that they would buy them back at a future date and would indemnify Mulheren against any losses he might incur. Such an arrangement was known on Wall Street as 'parking', and occurred when the real owner of the shares had built up too high a holding and was as a result in breach of securities regulations. Boesky entered into this arrangement with Mulheren on different occasions and with a number of stocks, notably those of Unocal, KKR, Boise Cascade and Warner Communications. However, Mulheren refused to accept that he should be indemnified against losses, knowing that this was against the law, and preferred instead to take over the shares as a favour for which he received no financial reward. When he came to trial, he rejected any idea of plea bargaining, even though he faced charges of multiple parking, tax fraud, evading net capital requirements, and stock manipulation. Boesky was the main prosecution witness, but performed badly and was unable to remember many of the deals he said had been done. Conspicuous by his absence was Carl Icahn, the corporate raider who was prominent in the Gulf & Western stock manipulation charges and whose name had been one of those given up by Boesky in his initial deal with the Government. Despite this, Icahn had not been charged with any crime, and the investigation into his affairs had been halted. Mulheren testified on his own behalf, emphasizing that he believed that he had borne all the risks in the stockholdings he took at Boesky's request. In some damaging admissions, however, he did admit to the court that he had inflated invoices in order to repay a debt to Boesky. After six and a half days the jury found him guilty of conspiracy and securities fraud, but said that it was hopelessly hung on the twenty-six counts of parking. The judge declared a mistrial on those counts, but on the other charges Mulheren was sentenced to a year and a day in prison and fined $1.5 million. The Appeal Court, however, took a very different view of the Mulheren case; his conviction was entirely reversed, and his prison sentence and fine were set aside.

As for Ivan Boesky himself, on 18 December 1987 he was sentenced to three years in prison, and was released to a half-way house in Brooklyn after serving eighteen months. Four months later he was a free man again. There have always been suggestions that, particularly in financial terms, Boesky got off lightly – despite his $100 million fine. Indeed, of the initial $50 million payment, he eventually only paid half of that, for he managed to set the rest against his tax bill for 1986. In June 1993 he even managed to claw back $20 million in a divorce settlement with his wife Seema, from whom he also received $180,000 a year, as well as the Malibu beach house she had bought after his release from prison.

Boesky will always be associated with the greed of the 1980s, which seemed to come to an end with his fall and that of his co-conspirator, Michael Milken. One of 'Ivan the Terrible's' most important legacies, however, was in a sense simply a sideshow to the main events in America. This was the revelation that a share-support scheme had been employed effectively in the £2.7 billion hostile takeover bid by Guinness for Distillers. That piece of information, of little interest to those prosecuting Boesky, was passed on by the SEC to the British regulatory organizations, and went on to cause a sensation in the City of London.

13

Barlow Clowes – Are taps a gilt-edged investment?

The investment management company Barlow Clowes was not one of the blue-blooded darlings of the City of London. The company was based in the unfashionable North-West of England – but like many such financial services groups during the 1980s, this did not stop the company making money. The problem was that as fast as the group could make it, its founder, Peter Clowes, was spending it. Investors' money was used to provide him with an extravagant and lavish lifestyle. New investments were taken in and used to pay the unrealistically high returns that had been promised to investors already with the company. This constant recycling of money worked as long as there was an equally constant source of new cash available to feed the increasingly hungry investment machine. Here was a classic 'Ponzi' scheme – one of the oldest forms of investment fraud.

The Barlow Clowes case, however, was also a watershed for Britain's financial regulatory system, for the public's confidence in investment firms, and for the non-interventionist stance of the Government. In a way, what was most extraordinary about the Barlow Clowes affair was not that Peter Clowes pulled an old trick to such good effect and managed to lead the good life at his investors' expense, for many financial demigods have done just that ever since capitalism was invented; but that, in an unprecedented campaign, the 18,500 mainly elderly victims managed to put enough pressure on the Government to force it to cough up £150 million in compensation.

At his trial in 1991–2, Peter Clowes was described as 'the instigator and driving force behind the fraud'. He was found guilty of eight charges of fraud and ten charges of theft totalling at least £13.2 million. He was cleared of one charge of conspiracy, and sentenced to ten years in prison. His right-hand man, Peter Naylor, was jailed for eighteen months on one theft charge arising from the collapse – he was found guilty of stealing £19,000 from clients. Naylor was cleared of three other theft charges, totalling £3.38 million, and of criminal involvement in obtaining the money spent on a country house in Surrey, which he bought for £365,000 in 1985, and an adjoining farm, which he bought for £515,000. Peter Naylor was a computer consultant who developed sophisticated trading models of gilts markets, and rose to become deputy chairman of Barlow Clowes, as well as a director of three other Clowes firms. He had joined the company in 1983 after leaving Exeter University with a double first-class honours degree in Maths and Physics; he also obtained a doctorate from the Aeronautics Department of Imperial College, London. During his trial, Anthony Glass, QC, defending Naylor, described Clowes's 'total control' of the company and how Naylor had been taken in by him: 'They are the men surrounded with the trappings of wealth, a number of homes, cars and jets. They are very generous with money which later turns out was not theirs to dispense ... such a man was Peter Clowes.'

Also awaiting the verdicts on 11 February 1992 at the Central Criminal Court – the Old Bailey – alongside Clowes and Naylor, were Guy von Cramer and Christopher Newman. Cramer, then aged thirty, had six years earlier become the youngest ever head of a British public company – James Ferguson Holdings, the firm that acquired Barlow Clowes in 1987. His rise had been even more spectacular than Peter Clowes's. Brought up in Bradford, West Yorkshire, he began his working life, like Clowes, at the age of fifteen, selling crockery in Leeds market, though he made his first serious money by trading property. After the trial, in which he was acquitted of six charges of theft and one of conspiracy, Cramer said that there had not been a scrap of evidence against him to show that he had known that Clowes had been diverting cash from investors' funds; the Serious Fraud Office he continued, should never have brought the case against him. Though the SFO had been successful with its prosecutions in the first Guinness trial two years earlier, Barlow Clowes had certainly been a major investigation for them. The trial lasted 112 days – the same length of time as the initial Guinness trial – and at the height of its investigation the SFO had had a squad of sixteen people working on it, who travelled to Gibraltar, Switzerland, Jersey and the Isle of Man to collect evidence. The investigation cost a total of £2 million – though that was just a foretaste of what was to come in other fraud cases. None of this impressed Guy von Cramer, however. He said the prosecution had run the case on a guilt-by-association basis, and that throughout the time he had known him, Peter Clowes had always given him the impression of 'extreme wealth and a man of integrity. Clearly that has been proved wrong.' The two had teamed up in 1986 at James Ferguson, before launching share purchases in other firms, culminating in the takeover of a Welsh brewery, Buckley's, a year later. Until the collapse, business with Clowes had been kind to Cramer. Cramer was best known in the Yorkshire hamlet of Micklethwaite, where he lived, for his high-performance cars – a Ferrari Testarossa, an Aston-Martin, and a chauffeur-driven Bentley Turbo. He also used a red helicopter.

The fourth man investigated, tried and, like Cramer, acquitted of all charges, was the latter's finance director, Christopher Newman. He was charged with seven counts of theft totalling nearly £11 million. Neither he nor Cramer gave evidence in court, but the hearing was told that Peter Clowes had lent Newman money after the finance director had suffered losses in the stock market crash of 1987. Newman's defence argued that this was no more than generosity to a valued employee, and that their client had always believed that the lavish lifestyle enjoyed by Clowes had been paid for out of his own money.

Sentencing Clowes, the judge, Mr Justice Phillips, told him:

> I do not believe any judge in this country has ever been called upon to pass sentence on a worse case of fraud than yours. The scale of the fraud was breathtaking. You deliberately picked on small investors, many of them pensioners who were interested in security. It was your intention to help yourself to those moneys and to use them for schemes, some of them highly speculative, which you hoped would make you rich. What you were doing, in effect, was gambling the money dishonestly.

During the trial the prosecution, led by Alan Suckling, QC, on behalf of the Serious Fraud Office, said that the Barlow Clowes fraud was massive, flagrant and 'as old as the hills' in style. Investors were persuaded that their money would be safe, securely invested in gilts – gilt-edged securities, i.e. British government stocks – when in reality it was spent on 'living the life of Riley'. In the course of the hearing the jury were shown a photograph of Clowes's yacht moored in Gibraltar – the vessel had been owned by Christina Onassis – and were told that if they looked closely that could see 'the only gilt-edged object bought with investors' money'. Suckling then asked them: 'Can you guess what it is? The taps.'

After the case was over, a list was compiled showing just where Clowes clients' money had gone:

The yacht, *Boukephalos*, cost £1.3 million, and Clowes had also placed a £1 million deposit on a sister ship, the *Yara*.

Investors' money was also spent on a château, with its own vineyard, in the Gironde region of France; the cost was £600,000.

One Learjet had been bought and others were on order.

The Clowes family home at Paddock Brow, Prestbury in Cheshire cost £250,000.

More than £1 million of clients' capital had been illegally ploughed into the loss-making jewellery company F. R. Stanhope.

Buckley's Brewery in Llanelli, Dyfed, was bought using £16 million of investors' cash.

Money was also spent on fast cars and on funding corporate raids. The company brochures sold the Barlow Clowes concept of investment by emphasizing that clients' money would be invested in gilt-edged securities – a crucial selling point for those anxious to find a safe haven for their lifes' savings. But contracts contained clauses authorizing non-gilt investment, which Clowes maintained enabled his company to adopt an alternative investment strategy. This strategy, far from being gilt-based, saw Barlow Clowes operating as a small merchant bank, funding takeover bids for public and privately owned companies which it wanted to control. In a four-year period up to 1987 more than £113 million of the funds invested in the offshore companies and partnerships in the Barlow Clowes fund-management empire was milked from investors. At the end of 1987, when the Department of Trade and Industry inspectors began investigating the company, strenuous efforts were made to throw them off the scent. Documents were shredded, bogus letters were filed to indicate accounts had been closed, and £16 million of clients' money was used to plug holes in the accounts. The true position only emerged later when, in May 1988, the firm collapsed. More than £225 million had been invested by clients, and a £115 million liability to them remained. At the same time, less than £2 million was found to have been invested in gilts. The value of other assets recovered by the receivers and liquidators totalled £60 million. These sums apart, there were no other assets to speak of.

What, then, was the background of Peter Clowes? He was a working-class boy who left school at the age of fifteen and began work in his parents' hardware shop in Manchester. After ten years of selling ironmongery over the counter he decided it was time to move on and joined International Life, a

British life insurance company linked to the notorious Investors' Overseas Services run by entrepreneur Bernie Cornfeld. International Life eventually went bust, but Cornfeld's philosophy took root early in Clowes, especially the former's famous catchphrase (which was actually a question): 'Do you sincerely want to be rich?'.

It was whilst working at Investors' Overseas that Clowes met Elizabeth Barlow, a sales representative like him and also a branch manager. In 1973 the two of them left to form an investment company specializing in gilts, and Barlow Clowes was born. Seven years later, by which time Mrs Barlow had left to pursue other interests, the company had £10 million under management; by 1987, as a result of widespread advertising, it had £190 million of investors' money to deploy.

Barlow Clowes made great play of the practice, now banned, of 'bond-washing', which involved buying gilts after a dividend had been paid and selling them before the next dividend payment. The device was used to turn income into capital gains, and appealed to investors seeking to minimize their tax liabilities, with the result that the money came pouring in. Clowes had by now expanded far beyond his original brief. He had investments in property, jewellery and aviation, hidden behind a web of offshore companies and nominee names. In 1985, as Britain soared into one of the strongest surges in stock market prices this century, Barlow Clowes Gilt Managers, as it was then called, won the Department of Trade and Industry's stamp of approval. Barlow Clowes International was founded the next year, based in Gibraltar. Two years after that, the entire empire fell apart. In May 1988 Barlow Clowes Gilt Managers was placed in provisional liquidation at the request of the newly formed regulatory body, the Securities and Investments Board, now known everywhere in the City as SIB. Three weeks later Clowes was arrested by Fraud Squad officers outside his home in Cheshire as he drove to buy his morning papers. The headlines next day could not have pleased him – '£10 million spree of spend, spend Clowes' screamed one, while another declared that '£100 million may be lost for ever in jet set tycoon's big crash'. For the first time, investors learned about the 101-foot floating palace which had once belonged to Christina Onassis, but which now belonged to Clowes. They read of the sixteenth-century Château d'Auros, near Bordeaux, with its 50-acre estate and its own wine label, and of Far Coombes, a 292-acre sheep farm in the Derbyshire Peak District. Investors also learned from the newspapers of Clowes's £80,000 silver Porsche coupé with its can-can red leather upholstery, and his £68,000 Bentley Turbo.

Anger against Clowes was compounded by two factors – by the fact that most of the investors were elderly people, and by the lavishness of his lifestyle. Over the course of the 109-day trial, 113 witnesses gave evidence, among them a succession of investors who described why they had been attracted by Clowes and his schemes. One woman who had lost £440,000 said that she had put the money into the hands of Barlow Clowes because she had been given to understand that her savings would be 'as safe as the Bank of England'. During the trial, Clowes admitted that although the group had billed itself as a gilts specialist, it did indeed act as a merchant bank. He went on to deny that his dealings had been dishonest, claiming that the contractual clauses allowing other investments had meant that his conduct had been 'absolutely honest'. He also asked the jury to believe that the complex arrangements for handling investors' funds were not a laundering operation, as the prosecution had claimed, but a means of maintaining clients' confidentiality. This was cold comfort to some of the many backers who had placed total trust in Barlow Clowes. Jim Hinton, a former oil company executive from Dorset, invested £22,000 with Barlow Clowes. He said: 'This affair must have been responsible for quite a lot of people passing on to the next world rather earlier than they would have done. A good 75 per cent of investors were elderly. They thought they were making a safe investment.' John Bohn from London, who invested the proceeds from the sale of his company, said: 'The sad and scandalous thing is that this case involved so many people who were trying to get richer. They were mainly elderly people who had never invested outside a building society in their lives. They thought this was going to be the safest investment they could make.' He then went on to describe how the twenty-month ordeal – the time between the exposure of Barlow Clowes and the payment of compensation – had affected the swindled investors. 'This resulted in quite a few attempted suicides, quite a few nervous breakdowns – some people are still on tranquillizers even now. Even though people got their money back, that is no compensation for the loss of their health.'

Barlow Clowes investors also point out that 500 elderly investors had already died by the time the then Trade and Industry Secretary, Nicholas Ridley, bowed to their pressure and announced the Government's compensation scheme. That announcement coincided with the publication of a report by the ombudsman, which criticized the DTI on five counts of maladministration regarding the licensing and regulation of Barlow Clowes. After paying out to Barlow Clowes investors, therefore, the Government began to look to recovering money from others to help offset its costs, and the DTI issued more than 800 writs against those thought to be liable. Touche Ross, the accountancy firm, as well as solicitors and stockbrokers connected with Barlow Clowes's parent company, James Ferguson Holdings, were being sued by the DTI. So too were investment advisers who had recommended Barlow Clowes to investors, as well as all four major high street banks and Allied Dunbar and Legal & General, the life assurance groups. Many of these actions are still not resolved today. The Government claim is that they were negligent or in breach of their contracts. Investors in Barlow Clowes assigned their rights to take legal action against anyone involved in the Barlow Clowes scandal when they accepted the Government's compensation deal. In June 1994 newspapers reported that six financial institutions involved in the Barlow Clowes affair were close to agreeing a secret deal with the Government which would require them to pay back some £35–£45 million; among those involved in the negotiations were the Midland Bank and

Touche Ross. The other parties in these talks are the professional indemnity insurers of Spicer & Pegler, who were the auditors to Barlow Clowes and who were subsequently taken over by Touche Ross; the merchant bank Singer & Friedlander, which acted for Clowes's parent company, James Ferguson Holdings, and was originally being sued for £53 million; Ferguson's brokers at the time, Rensburg & Company; and the law firm Simpson Curtis.

The liquidators are likely to recover about £76 million from the ruins of the Clowes empire, so that securing a deal with advisers, accountants and bankers involved in Barlow Clowes would bring the Government's compensation pay-out down from £150 million to £74 million. Peter Clowes and his wife, Pamela, were also forced to pay damages to the Department of Trade and Industry. In April 1992 at the High Court, the Vice-Chancellor of the Supreme Court, Sir Donald Nicholls, ordered Mr and Mrs Clowes to make an interim payment of £6 million. He said the exact amount of damages had yet to be fully assessed, but that it was 'inevitable' that the figure would exceed £10 million, and probably £15 million, with interest to be added.

The fallout from the Barlow Clowes affair – as is true of all major fraud cases – continues long after the guilty have been punished. Of course, the more complex the crime the longer it takes to sort out. In the meantime, investors continue to suffer, either directly in financial terms, or from the anguish of the past events. The legal process can always be relied upon to take many years to run its course – and so it has proved, even with a case as relatively simple as that of Barlow Clowes. In October 1993 there was another manifestation of the shock waves of the fraud when the accountancy firm Touche Ross was told by the Treasury that thirteen of its staff would, in effect, be barred from Government contracts because of their role in the Barlow Clowes affair. Touche Ross had become embroiled in the investment company following the latter's takeover by James Ferguson Holdings in April 1987. Touche Ross then became auditors to Barlow Clowes, taking over from Spicer & Pegler, the outgoing company expressing the view that there was no reason for concern over their resignation as accountants to Barlow Clowes. By now, the DTI had become concerned about Barlow Clowes, but the quality of the latter's advisers, and notably the accountants overseeing the books, helped to persuade the Department to allow the investment firm to continue trading. A little over a year later, however, following a DTI investigation, Barlow Clowes was shut down. The knock-on effect for Touche Ross has been damage to its reputation and the blacklisting for government work of some of its employees. Such banning, though, is standard practice if a client has, as the Government had at the time, a lawsuit outstanding against the firm in question. Touche Ross had been one of the Government's most important advisers on privatization work. A senior partner, John Roques, issued a statement on behalf of the company in which he said that the firm was '... proud to be a major supplier of consulting and other advisory services to government. We have every expectation that we will continue to be selected on our merits to serve a wide variety of government departments.'

There is a final, almost poignant, note to the Barlow Clowes affair. The financial repercussions for Peter Clowes also continue. The judiciary has already ordered him to pay out millions of pounds, and has said that this order should be enforced even if it means that he and his wife are declared bankrupt. In October 1994 Clowes once more found himself the centre of controversy, though he was still in prison. He had served the first part of his ten-year sentence behind bars at Wandsworth Prison, but was then moved to Sudbury Open Prison, near Ashbourne in Derbyshire. The controversy came about when a Greek businessmen, George Anagnos, head of the South London computer programming company Zebra UK, offered Clowes a job writing specialist computer programs for the legal profession. The prison Governor, Peter Salter, agreed to allow Clowes to work and set him up with phone, computer and fax facilities in the prison chapel; in return, Clowes was paid £150 a month. But some of the investors who had lost money when the Barlow Clowes empire came crashing down objected to the man they viewed as the villain of the piece making money in this way. One seventy-four-year-old, Arnold Acroyd of Hoddesdon in Hertfordshire, said: 'I am shocked and surprised. If he is allowed to work like this he should be using the money to pay back those he defrauded. I believe in prisoners being allowed to work to earn their keep. But there are many people still out of pocket because of this man. Even a pound a week would help some people.' After a brief furore the Director-General of HM Prison Service, Derek Lewis, was forced to put an end to Peter Clowes's employment. He said: 'Given the nature of Mr Clowes's offences, this practice is quite unacceptable.'

14

The Hong Kong Stock Exchange – A cosy club?

Ronald Li cut a flamboyant figure in Hong Kong's financial circles. A member of one of the Colony's oldest and best-known families, he was the man who had almost single-handedly welded Hong Kong's four independent stock exchanges into a unified body. He was a major player on the local market himself, and had a network of friends and allies which stretched into every corner of business. He came to international prominence during the worldwide stock market crash of October 1987, when he appeared on television wagging his finger at an inquisitive reporter, and demanding that this representative of the fourth estate should be gaoled for questioning why Li had deemed it necessary to close the Hong Kong Stock Exchange for four days in the aftermath of the crash.

Before the dreadful events of 'Black October', Li had prospered. In Hong Kong share prices had, if anything, risen even more rapidly than had those on the exchanges of any of the world's other major financial centres. It was not surprising, therefore, that international investors poured into Hong Kong, or that companies queued up for a stock exchange listing there. As Chairman of the Hong Kong Stock Exchange, Li's position was pivotal. Eventually, however, rumours began to circulate about what criteria had to be fufilled in order to persuade Li and his friends to grant a place in the listings queue to companies keen to cash in on the rising market. Some of the rumours later formed the evidence in Mr Li's trial. When he was arrested he faced twenty-five charges – though these were eventually whittled down to just two. In October 1990, Ronald Li was found guilty of corruption involving preferential share allocations.

During his trial – which lasted seven weeks – Li was accused of running the Hong Kong Stock Exchange with his relatives and friends like a 'very cosy club', of which he was the 'captain'. This view echoed an official report produced after the 1987 stock market crash, which had said that 'an inside group treated the exchange as a private club rather than a public utility.' Li's elder son was the exchange's legal adviser until 1981, his other son was the medical adviser, and a company run by his son-in-law even manufactured the exchange's souvenir tie-pins!

The corruption charges against Ronald Li related to his purchase of 500,000 Cathay Pacific new-issue shares in 1986 and 200,000 Novel Enterprise shares in 1987, when he was also Chairman of the exchange's Listing Committee (Novel was a knitwear manufacturer). The prosecution alleged that he had received the shares as a reward either for assisting, or for using his influence to prevent the obstruction of those two companies' listings on the Hong Kong Stock Exchange. In answer to the charges, Li had argued that he had simply been pursuing his normal business by acting as sub-underwriter for the two issues through SPS Investment Services, a company in which he held a majority interest.

At his trial, however, the judge, Justice Bokhary, said Li had benefited from profits of £58,000 from the sale of the shares shortly after flotation: 'Not a single share went to SPS or a single cent of the profit went to SPS.' There was no evidence that the shares had been passed on to Li as a gift or reward, or that he had employed any of the traditional (and legal) means of buying them. He had neither made a formal application for them, nor had to pay for them in advance. In the case of Novel, Li's shares came out of the Chairman of the Hong Kong Stock Exchange's personal share allocation; in the other case, the Cathay Pacific shares had been drawn from shares allocated to Wardley, a firm of merchant bankers. In all, it was estimated that Li had made around HK$ 870,000 in profits on the share allocations.

15

The Recruit Scandal – The Japanese Prime Minister takes his share of the blame

When, in November 1987, Noboru Takeshita took over from Yashurio Nakasone as Prime Minister of Japan, political commentators urged him to forge a brand of leadership that would bring him – a hard-working, naturally shy man – out of the shadows and make him and Japan front-page news. In April 1989 he did just that, although perhaps not quite in the way that the leader writers would have wished – he resigned, the latest sacrifice to what became known as 'the Recruit shares scandal'.

The scandal had broken in the summer of 1988, when newspaper reports first began to appear suggesting that senior members of the ruling Liberal Democratic Party had been given shares in a subsidiary of the employment agency, Recruit, before those shares had been listed on the stock exchange. In this way they were able to make substantial profits when the companies in question actually went public. A month later, newspapers claimed that in fact the net spread wider; it now appeared that Recruit had sold shares to Cabinet ministers and their aides, including, among the former, Prime Minister Takeshita and the Finance Minister, Kiichi Miyazawa. Later that month the Chairman of Recruit, Hiromasa Ezoe, and Ko Morita, a president of Japan's top financial daily, *Nihon Keizai Shimbun*, resigned over share purchases. Less than three months later a former Recruit executive, Hiroshi Matsubara, was arrested on suspicion of trying to bribe an opposition MP, and in November a Japan Socialist Party MP, Takumi Ueda, resigned after admitting that he had received Recruit shares. He was the first political victim of the scandal. The former Chairman of Recruit, Hiromasa Ezoe, was summoned before parliament to testify about the affair.

The aftershocks from the scandal continued to be felt. In December the resignations of politicians were still being handed in – three of them in that month alone. Finance Minister Miyazawa was forced to resign after it became clear that shares had been bought in his name. Next on the executioner's block was the Chairman of the telecommunications giant, NTT, Hisashi Shinto – he resigned over Recruit share purchases made by his secretary. The Justice Minister, Takashi Hasegawa, also resigned, suggesting that this was because of his involvement with Recruit. Nor did the political resignations stop there. It was almost as though someone had ignited a slow-burning fuse which, once lit, could not be put out until it had burned to the end. Thus it was that this particular fire began, as most scandals do, in an innocuous way with rumours and reports, led inexorably through minor casualties to some of the bigger names who, having thought they could weather any storm, finally fell victim themselves. So in January 1989 the Economic Planning Minister, Ken Harada, became the latest victim when he too resigned. The next month the Chairman of the Democratic Socialist Party, Saburo Tsukamoto, stepped down over the Recruit affair, and four prominent businessmen and a former Labour Ministry official were arrested on suspicion of corruption. In March 1989 Hisashi Shinto, the former Chairman of NTT, was arrested and charged with accepting shares as a bribe. Finally, in April 1989, the fuse that had been lit ten months before reached its bitter end. The Prime Minister, Noboru Takeshita, informed parliament that he had received large donations from Recruit. Increasing numbers of his colleagues in the ruling LDP, as well as business leaders, called for him to step down. He obtained the approval of his party leadership to do so, and resigned.

16

The Guinness Affair – Not necessarily good for you

Britain's Serious Fraud Office – or, as it has more recently become known, the 'Seriously Flawed Office' – was set up in the late 1980s by a government increasingly worried about the image of the City and its ability to police itself, a code of conduct known, sometimes laughingly, as 'self-regulation'. The SFO, as it is more usually known, was born out of the idea of bringing together a number of specialist disciplines in order to fight financial crime. Within the organization, therefore, accountants, lawyers and policemen all work closely together. The SFO's first case was also its most successful to date. During a 112-day trial in 1990 four of Britain's most prominent businessmen appeared in court charged with a variety of offences arising out of the Guinness takeover of the drinks group, Distillers. All were found guilty, though with hindsight and in the light of subsequent events, it might well be thought that they were simply scapegoats selected by a public which demanded action in the austere 1990s to punish the excesses of the late 1980s.

The story actually starts in 1981, when Ernest Saunders joined the brewing group, Guinness, from the Swiss giant Nestlé. In early 1982 he was made managing director. Up until that time the company had been run largely by aristocrats associated with the Iveagh family, one of their ancestors, Arthur Guinness, having founded the brewing company in

Dublin back in 1759. Edward Guinness, who became the first Lord Iveagh, took hold of the company in 1876 and it was he who floated it on the London Stock Exchange. The sale of stout has continued to grow across the world ever since the firm's foundation, but in the 1960s there were some not too successful attempts at diversification. When Saunders took over, the company was in the doldrums run by absentee aristocrats who, although they only held 25 per cent of the shares in the company, acted as though they owned 75 per cent. Nor were they used to having a managing director who actually wanted to *run* the company – Saunders himself tells the story of how, at one Guinness family wedding, he was seated on the tradesman's table!

All that was to change, however. Saunders was a man of vision who had ambitious plans for Guinness. He spent two years assessing the situation, and then began to put his plans into effect. In June 1984 Guinness made its first major acquisition under Saunders when it bought Martins, the newsagency business with 500 stores, for £45 million. Saunders wasted no time – he had his corporate chequebook out again buying Nature's Best Health Products, a vitamin producer, and in February 1985 acquired Neighbourhood Stores, and with it the UK franchise for '7-Eleven' outlets, for £12 million. Then, in June of that year, Saunders stepped up a gear, launching a £330 million hostile bid for the whisky producer Arthur Bell. In August Guinness had to increase its offer to £370 million, but by the end of the month the battle was won. Then came the big one, Guinness's bid for Distillers. Originally, according to Saunders, the company had not intended to bid for Distillers, but then, in December 1985, a bid had been made by the supermarket group, Argyll. It was only when that happened that Saunders began to realize that perhaps the acquisition of Distillers by Guinness would help to fulfil his global ambitions.

Argyll's original bid for Distillers, a hostile one, had been worth £1.87 billion. About a month afterwards *The Times* carried an article speculating about a possible Guinness bid for

Distillers. In the third week of January 1986 the Distillers board, which was opposed to the Argyll bid, decided after a long meeting to recommend to its shareholders that they accept a bid from Guinness, an offer worth £2.2 billion. On 27 January Argyll complained to the City regulatory body, the Takeover Panel, that Distillers had agreed to pay Guinness's bid costs. The panel rejected the complaint. From then on the fight became even dirtier.

It is time now to introduce some of the key players in what was to become a long-running drama. Ernest Saunders, Guinness's MD, has already appeared. But what of the three other men who were implicated alongside him in running an illegal share-support scheme? One was Gerald Ronson, the founder and boss of the Heron Corporation and the man who was credited with having introduced to Britain modern petrol stations as we now know them. Ronson was an associate of one of the other defendants, Tony Parnes, known as 'the animal' for his long hair and not for displaying, as some of the popular press continue to claim, somewhat 'basic' habits as a trader on the London Stock Exchange. The fourth defendant, Sir Jack Lyons, then seventy years old when Guinness began to make its bid for Distillers, was a consultant with Bain & Company, an American firm of management consultants, and was known to have political contacts at the highest level. These were the four who stood trial, but there is one other player to be mentioned. Olivier Roux had joined Guinness in 1982, aged thirty-two, as a management consultant with Bain & Co. He became director of financial strategy and development in 1984, and had a key role as financial adviser to Saunders. He stopped working at Guinness in December 1986, and resigned in January 1987. He was to prove to be the prosecution's star witness in what was, for the City, the most important trial it had ever seen.

It is quite possible that had it not been for Ivan Boesky, the disgraced Wall Street arbitrageur, Ernest Saunders might have continued at the helm of Guinness. But Boesky had volunteered to the US authorities information about his part in a share-support scheme which had helped Guinness win control of Distillers, a scheme which was the main, although by no means the only, strategy employed in the vicious campaign against Argyll. Boesky's connection to Guinness was through Gerald Ronson, and he had been a guest on the latter's £10 million yacht, *Gail III* – named after Ronson's wife, a former model. Despite the suggestion that Mrs Ronson could not stand Boesky – she is reported to have said that she never wanted him on board again – he and her husband did quite a lot of business together. According to Boesky, Ronson had first contacted him about the Distillers bid in early April 1986, having apparently agreed to get the American involved after a lunch with senior Guinness executives at the company's head office in London's Portman Square. Saunders had undertaken to indemnify Heron against any losses the group might make on £25 million of Guinness shares it bought, and to pay a £5 million success fee should Guinness win control of Distillers. Boesky's deal was that he too would be indemnified against losses on Guinness shares, and would be paid interest at 5 per cent per month on any sums invested. He also kept another of America's big traders informed of Guinness/Distillers developments – Meshulam Riklis, of the Rapid American cosmetics, casinos, retailing and drinks distribution empire. Riklis committed an estimated £60 million to purchases of Guinness shares, using a London firm and the ill-fated Drexel Burnham Lambert. His purchases were so substantial that for a brief period he owned more than 5 per cent of the company – a fact which he failed to disclose, as he was required to do by British law under the Companies Act. After the Guinness bid had gone through the Dewars whisky trademark was transferred to Riklis in a deal said to be worth £50 million, which some people inside Distillers thought odd. According to Riklis, the trademark transfer was intended to protect the brand, which his company distributed, against parallel imports in the US. He told inspectors from the British Government's Department of Trade and

Industry that his share purchases were not indemnified in any way, and that he had made the investment purely to protect his own commercial interest as a Dewars distributor in the US.

As for Boesky, a number of different ways of paying him off were considered, including giving him a Californian vineyard or selling him property at an under value, and these schemes were examined by Guinness following the Distillers success. He said that he had lost some $30 million dollars on Guinness shares after investing $1.1 billion, and eventually suggested that the company should invest in his limited partnership, which was seriously underfunded at the time. On 21 May 1986 Guinness instructed a bank in Amsterdam to transfer $100 million to Barclays in New York for Boesky's limited partnership. This transfer of funds took place five days before it was approved by Guinness's executive committee, and nearly two months before it was reported to the full board.

This background to Guinness's bid for Distillers is almost complete – except for some mention of their opponents, Argyll. It is important to sketch in a little detail about that company and its Chairman, James Gulliver, not only in order to complete the scene-setting, but also because of the fact that the Guinness bid was welcomed by the board of Distillers, whereas the Argyll bid was vehemently opposed. A large part of the reason for that opposition has to do with James Gulliver's perceived background, while another part of it has to do with the tactics that Saunders and his team employed. Gulliver was a Scotsman, and had been born in Campbeltown in 1930 (he was thus five years older than Saunders), a distilling town on the Kintyre peninsula in the West Highlands. He went to Campbeltown Grammar School and then on to Glasgow University, where he gained a first-class honours degree in engineering, and went on to win a prestigious Fulbright Scholarship to the Georgia Institute of Technology in Atlanta, where he took a Master of Science Degree. A four-week course in marketing for managers at Harvard was later misrepresented in his *Who's Who* entry as signifying that he had attended that university, something which was to bring him trouble during the bid for Distillers.

Gulliver was as well educated as many other managers – Ernest Saunders, for example, had a second-class honours degree from Cambridge. But it was typical of the way the battle was fought that he was quite often described as the 'grocer's son from Campbeltown' who had gone on to run his own grocery chain. The Distillers board took the view that he was not worthy enough to take them over, and this snobbery was exploited by Saunders (who, ironically, had suffered the same sort of thing from the Guinness family) in his bid for the company. Gulliver's business track record, though, was impressive. By the age of thirty-three he was running Headway Construction, a subsidiary of Fine Fare, and a year later he was in charge of the entire business. When Gulliver moved in the supermarket chain was losing £300,000 a year; by 1972, some eight years later, it was making profits of around £5 million. He next borrowed £1 million to buy a 30 per cent stake in Oriel Foods, persuading his friends Alistair Grant and David Webster to join him. In 1974 Oriel was sold to the American corporation RCA for £11 million. Gulliver and his partners did the same thing with Alpine, the double-glazing company – having bought in for £1.9 million, they sold out to the Hawley Group for £16 million. In early 1981 he bought Oriel Foods back from RCA for £20 million in cash, and early the next year took over Allied Suppliers from Sir James Goldsmith for £104 million. It was a good price for a variety of stores ranging from Liptons to the fast-growing chain, Presto, and it was the latter company which became the centrepiece of the Argyll Group when it was formed in November 1983. It was not, therefore, Gulliver's business acumen to which Distillers objected. The company saw itself as being a cut above other busines and traced its ancestry back to the 1870s when the Buchanan brothers had set up a distillery and whisky retailing business. In some ways Distillers saw itself as being in the aristocratic mould, and its board believed that this fitted better with the image of Guinness, which still had Lord Iveagh as Chairman and which could trace its lineage back to the late eighteenth century.

On 9 January 1986 Argyll's initial bid for Distillers received the green light from the Department of Trade and Industry, the then Secretary of State, Leon Brittan, having decided that the bid need not be referred to the Monopolies and Mergers Commission. The directors of Distillers were horrified – they had thought that at the very least the Government would block the deal. It was then that they decided they must find a 'White Knight' – Stock Exchange terminology for a company that rides to the rescue of another company threatened by a takeover bid. Against advice, Saunders had decided that to win Distillers he had to win its board's support. He therefore invited the other company's Chairman, John Connell, on a family skiing holiday in Switzerland, the clear purpose being for the two men to discuss terms. Once there, the Guinness MD proposed that there should be a holding board, with the existing Guinness and Distillers boards operating as a second tier; Connell, Saunders said, would be Chairman, and he would work to him as Chief Executive. To the embattled Distillers man – faced with the problem of fending off Argyll's unwanted attentions – this plan seemed to be heaven-sent: he could accept the chairmanship of a new group without loss of face. Connell therefore said that he was interested, but added that he would have to consult the Distillers board. In the event, the other directors were given little choice in the matter – their advisers, Kleinwort Benson, told them there was almost no chance of the company remaining independent, and if it was to escape Gulliver's clutches then a merger with Guinness was all that was left open.

At this point, what might be called 'the Risk factor' enters the picture. Sir Thomas Risk was the Governor of the Bank of Scotland and one of Scotland's most respected businessmen. On Friday, 17 January 1986 he was due to fly down to London for a business meeting when his car phone rang. The message asked him to call Ernest Saunders at Guinness; when he did so, Saunders asked him if he could come to Guinness's offices in Portman Square on his arrival to discuss an urgent matter. Risk was shown into Saunders's office; already there was Roger Seelig, corporate finance director with merchant bankers Morgan Grenfell, one of Guinness's advisers during the bid.

Saunders spent three-quarters of an hour outlining to Sir Thomas how close Distillers and Guinness were to agreeing a merger, a move which would create an international company and at the same time save the giant of the Scotch whisky industry. One of the areas still to be agreed upon, however, was the question of a chairman acceptable to both boards of directors, whereupon Seelig turned to Risk and said: 'The man we have in mind is you.' The banker's initial answer was 'no'; after all, he already had a demanding full-time job. But Saunders was persuasive, appealing to Risk's sense of community, and stressing that the deal needed to go through in order to safeguard the future of the whisky industry in Scotland. Risk's involvement was a vital ingredient in the merger, he believed. When Sir Thomas left for his other engagements he had agreed to consider the proposal further and to give an answer within twenty-four hours. He then spoke to all of his colleagues on the bank's board, and all urged him to take the job on. He therefore telephoned Saunders on the Saturday evening and said he agreed in principle to accept the post of Chairman. Almost immediately Saunders ordered up his chauffeur-driven car and set off for the Walton-on-Thames home of John Connell. Connell showed him into the living room and asked him if he wanted a drink, to which Saunders suggested that they toast the success of the merged company – he with a Johnnie Walker, Connell with a Guinness. The conversation then came round to the structure of the new board, with Saunders saying that the new company needed an independent chairman from outside the business, preferably a Scot, and that he had found the very man, Sir Thomas Risk. Connell began to protest, but Saunders spoke about the need for a chairman with standing in the financial community. Connell knew and admired Risk – he also knew that Saunders had outflanked him, for by now the merger strategy could not be reversed.

Disturbed by all the Guinness/Distillers rumours flying about, and by press reports based on leaked information, James Gulliver made continual efforts to corner Saunders to find out what his intentions were. The latter denied his interest, but the frantic activity at Guinness's headquarters – even on the Sunday morning – was obvious for all to see, including Gulliver and his advisers.

On 19 January 1986 the Distillers board unanimously agreed to the merger with Guinness, after heated discussions about whether or not their company would underwrite Guinness's costs. As has been said, the Takeover Panel, despite protestations from Argyll about unfairness, suggested that the deal could go ahead as Distillers' plan to reimburse Guinness's bid costs were not material. After all, at the time these were estimated to be no more than £20 million, in the context of a £2 billion bid. In the end, however, those costs were to soar to around £100 million. Had the regulators known that this would happen, then perhaps its decision would have been different.

On 6 February Argyll increased its offer for Distillers to £2.3 billion. Now both sides anxiously awaited a ruling from the Office of Fair Trading. The renewed bid for Distillers from the Gulliver camp was designed to aid the OFT in making a decision which favoured referring the terms of the Guinness bid for Distillers to the Monopolies and Mergers Commission; it would help the image of the OFT with Distillers shareholders if there were to be a bid of around the same value as Guinness's. Lobbying was intense – but all to no avail. On 11 February Sir Gordon Borrie, the Director-General of the Office of Fair Trading, sent his verdict around to the DTI. He said that while he was concerned that his office was referring only one of the two bids to the Monopolies and Mergers Commission, in the end he had had no choice. The reasons he gave were on the grounds of competition: he had added up the market shares in the UK of the Guinness-owned Bells and of Distillers and found that they came to 38 per cent of the home market, well past the 25 per cent benchmark for referral. Saunders and his team either had to give up, or go to the MMC with a new deal that was materially different, in terms of competition, from the first. And that is exactly what they did – Guinness agreed that in the event of its winning Distillers then it would sell off five whisky brands, bringing its UK market share, when combined with Distillers, down to below 25 per cent. The MMC agreed that under these terms the first Guinness bid could be set aside, to be replaced with the new one. The next day Guinness increased its bid for Distillers to £2.35 billion. The regulatory hurdles were finally put behind them when the whisky firm Whyte & Mackay, a Lonrho subsidiary, paid a knockdown price of £3.5 million for the five brands. But then, Saunders was desperate to offload the brands in order to keep the rest of the takeover on track.

There is no doubt that at the time of the Distillers bid most of the top management at Guinness could think of nothing else. The bid was unusual, too, in that there was a legion of advisers sitting alongside Saunders and his own team of executives. Guinness's merchant bankers, Morgan Grenfell, were represented by the forty-year-old Roger Seelig. Saunders's most trusty companion was the American lawyer Thomas Ward – the former had been linked with Ward's firm, Ward, Lazarus, Grow & Cihlar of Washington, DC, since his days at Nestlé. The share buying and selling during the bid was done by the City's leading institutional broker, Cazenove & Co., which was represented by David Mayhew and Anthony Forbes. The legal aspects were covered by the leading City law firm, Freshfields, in the person of Anthony Salz. The inner circle or 'war cabinet' for the bid was completed by Olivier Roux, the management consultant from Bain & Co., who was now also a director of Guinness. This was the era of management consultants, and Saunders and Guinness were at the forefront of their use. In the subsequent trial it emerged that at the time Guinness was spending £1 million a month on fees to Bain & Co.

There were two other figures who worked behind the scenes for the Guinness bid. One was the stockbroker Tony Parnes, whose role was to encourage buyers of Guinness shares and to keep a watchful eye on the movements of shares not only in Guinness, but also in both Distillers and Argyll. The other man was Sir Jack Lyons, who had been brought in for his political contacts. As a friend of the Prime Minister of the day, Margaret Thatcher, he knew just who to go to in the Government to argue the case for Guinness, and thus to ensure that the bid did not founder on the rock of regulation.

In order to understand why a scam was necessary and how it worked there is one fundamental fact that has yet to be established. The value of the Guinness bid was dependent on the Guinness share price because the company intended to buy Distillers using cash and shares. So, if Guinness shares dropped in value than it would have to pledge more shares in order to maintain the value of its bid. More importantly, however, a fall in the Guinness share value made the deal less attractive to Distillers shareholders, since they wanted to feel that the shares they were being offered would increase in value. There was, too, one other effect. When, at crucial moments in the bid, Argyll instructed its stockbrokers to buy Distillers shares, they were prevented from doing so by a rapid rise in the price of Guinness shares, since that rise also pulled up Distillers shares. It went higher than the cash alternative price offered in the company's bid documents. Under Takeover Panel rules, a bidder is not allowed to offer a higher price than the cash alternative listed in the official bid documents. So it meant that Distillers couldn't buy any more Guinness shares.

Eventually, after what Argyll always considered was a well-orchestrated share-purchasing scheme operating on a massive scale, Guinness declared victory. Just before 1 pm on Friday, 18 April 1986, Ernest Saunders announced to the City that he had won control of 50.7 per cent of the shares in Distillers. For Gulliver there was bitter disappointment – the battle had cost his company £55 million, though there was a £20 million profit from selling their Distillers shares to take into account. For Guinness, costs were around £120 million; in addition, ways had to be found to legitimize many of the illegal payments.

The first problem for the new company was that, following victory, the Guinness share price – which had been kept

The Guinness Affair 195

artificially high – started to fall steadily. Waiting to offload their shares were the supporters of Guinness who had been told that whatever losses they made would be underwritten by the company. If everyone offloaded their shares at once prices would spiral downwards and the costs to the company would be enormous. A plan for orderly disposal was therefore devised. The Swiss bank, Bank Leu, was to buy all the small parcels of shares in return for a £50 million deposit. The shares were then to be sold at a trickle and Bank Leu paid an indemnity on any losses it might incur. By the end of May that year the bank had taken in another 15 million shares, to add to the 26 million it had purchased during the bid (the Chairman of the bank's supervisory board was Dr Arthur Furer, former boss of Nestlé). And it was not just foreign money that was being used to underpin the Guinness share price. Soon after the takeover the Distillers pension fund – which had £500 million in its coffers – bought 5 million Guinness shares, and other Guinness company pension schemes also bought shares.

Ironically, whilst strenuous efforts were again being made to keep the Guinness share price steady, Saunders became involved in a row which in a week knocked 40 pence off the share value. It became known in the newspapers as 'the Risk Affair'. As has been said, Sir Thomas Risk, the Governor of the Bank of Scotland, had been promised that he would become Chairman of the new joint company following a successful Guinness bid; others, too, had been promised positions on the new board. These promises, as well as an undertaking to site the headquarters of the new company in Scotland, had been made in formal bid documents circulated to Distillers shareholders. Now it appeared that these promises were to be reneged upon, and that Saunders would take on a dual role as head of both the Guinness and the Distillers sides of the new company. There would in effect be no new board, and the headquarters of the company would stay in London. Risk and his friend Charles Fraser, Guinness's lawyer in Scotland, together with that company's Scottish-based stockbrokers,

Wood Mackenzie, all tried to persuade Saunders to honour his commitments, but failed, with the result that Fraser and Wood Mackenzie resigned their positions. Saunders and Guinness accordingly moved to try to limit damage to the company, announcing that the two-tier board which had been proposed was unwieldy. Finally, after lengthy discussions with Sir Thomas Risk, Guinness took the view that his participation in the new company was not in stockholders' interests, and that seemed to be the end of the matter. It is difficult to judge just how damaging the Risk affair was, but there is no doubt that from this time onward the Scottish business community – a powerful voice in Britain as a whole – was to make it clear that it had little time for Saunders.

Saunders's euphoria over the successful Distillers bid lasted just three months. On 1 December 1986 inspectors from the Department of Trade and Industry called at Guinness headquarters, and on the same day also visited the offices of Guinness's merchant bankers, Morgan Grenfell. There was, of course, much speculation about the inspectors' motives. Three weeks later it emerged that one of Riklis's companies, Schenley Industries, had acquired a 5 per cent stake in Guinness in April and had not declared it. This was a clear breach of the Takeover Code, although such breaches were considered to be relatively minor. But on 18 December evidence started to emerge linking Guinness executives with the disgraced Wall Street arbitrageur, Ivan Boesky. The newspapers suggested that Guinness had invested $100 million with Boesky shortly after winning Distillers.

Events now began to move swiftly. Shortly after Christmas, Morgan Grenfell stood down as merchant banker to Guinness, and Roger Seelig was forced to resign from the bank. On 4 January Ernest Saunders returned to England from a skiing holiday in Switzerland – and was grilled by DTI officials about the share operation by the two biggest investors in Guinness and Distillers, Warburg Investment Management and Prudential, which the banking firm, Henry Ansbacher, had operated for Guinness. Any hope of Saunders weathering the gathering storm clouds vanished the next day when the company's solicitor, Sir David Napley of Kingsley Napley, received a letter from Olivier Roux outlining his own role and that of Saunders during the Distillers battle. The so-called 'Roux letter' was said to be a damning indictment of Saunders, and it began to be suggested that Roux was co-operating with the investigating authorities. The management consultant's flat in Holland Park was besieged by television reporters, who stood in the cold for hours while Roux remained barricaded inside. I was one of those reporters, and remember him sending out word that he could not comment.

Still Saunders survived at Guinness, but it was not to be for much longer. On 9 January the London *Evening Standard* carried an interview with Jonathan Guinness, a non-executive member of the board, in which he said that he thought it was time for Saunders to step down. It appeared that the Chairman and Chief Executive of Britain's fifteenth largest public company had finally lost the support of the founding family. Later in the day Jonathan Guinness had sight of the Roux letter, and from it realized that nothing could be done to avoid Saunders's demise. The board duly asked him to go, and he replied by saying that he would 'stand aside' for the duration of the DTI inquiry; he did not resign. He never again set foot inside the executive suite at Guinness.

The final act came on the Wednesday following, when the company announced that its accountants, Price Waterhouse, had uncovered a £200 million share-support scheme. This, the company claimed, led via Saunders and Roux to Zurich and Bank Leu. The board immediately sacked Saunders, and demanded the resignations of Dr Arthur Furer of Bank Leu and of the American lawyer, Thomas Ward. The company's own lawyers, Kingsley Napley, were replaced by Herbert Smith. Nor did the resignations and sackings stop there. Lord Spens, of merchant bankers Henry Ansbacher, resigned, as did the Chief Executive of Morgan Grenfell, Christopher Reeves, and its corporate finance boss, Graham Walsh. Gerald Ronson's name was dragged into the public arena – and he returned a £5 million cheque to Guinness which he had received as a success fee, saying that he had not realized that what he had done was wrong. Into the frame too came Tony Parnes, the stockbroker who operated on half commission from Alexanders Laing and Cruickshank (he received $\frac{1}{2}$ per cent commission for all work he introduced to the brokers) – the broking firm severed all ties with him. Sir Jack Lyons lost his job at Bain & Company after it emerged that he had been paid £2 million for unspecified services to Guinness.

On Wednesday, 6 May 1987 Saunders was again interviewed by DTI inspectors. Later that same day two police officers from the Fraud Squad arrived at his solicitors' offices off the Strand, just behind the Law Courts. Saunders was arrested and driven to Holborn police station. He appeared at Bow Street Magistrates Court on the next day, where he was charged with intent to pervert the course of justice and with the destruction and falsification of documents – on the charge sheet he was described as aged fifty-one and unemployed. In the coming weeks and months charges against Ronson, Lyons and Parnes were also brought. The scene was set for the first Guinness trial, which ended on August Bank Holiday 1990 after 107 days.

My abiding impressions of that trial can be recalled in a number of starkly contrasting images. I remember Olivier Roux, the chief prosecution witness – he never spoke except in the witness box, and turned up day after day in his off-white raincoat. Ernest Saunders and Anthony Parnes were approachable, even friendly. The former was continually button-holing members of the press, telling them of the latest scheme to establish his innocence. Parnes, on the other hand, always looked more relaxed, even joked with some of us and often sat down in the rather barbaric surroundings of the court canteen to share a table and a chat over coffee. In contrast, Gerald Ronson and Sir Jack Lyons were completely unapproachable. Ronson's chauffeur-driven Jaguar would sweep up to the steps of Southwark Crown Court, on the south bank of the Thames, often with his wife Gail and a number of his daughters on board. It always seemed remarkable to me how, in a small, overcrowded courtroom where seating even for the press was at a premium, Ronson's family managed to turn up day after day and take the front row of the public gallery for themselves only moments before the judge appeared in court. Their timing was remarkable.

Remarkable, too, was the day of the verdicts, as it turned out. The judge, Mr Justice Henry, had from the start made one point abidingly clear to the jury: he wanted to dispel the notion, often prevalent in fraud and other 'white-collar' cases, that there was or could be any such thing as a victimless crime. He said that in this case it was important to realize that the Distillers shareholders, or, indeed, any potential investors in either company, had the right to believe that the stock market was operated fairly. In the Guinness case, such investors might have believed that the rise in the company's share price reflected the market's belief that the Distillers bid was the right thing to do, that Guinness would be a stronger, more effective company as a result of a win, and so on. But if a false market was created in Guinness shares, how then could investors have faith in the stock market? In the words of Judge Henry, investors must be assured that the stock market 'isn't a casino where the odds are rigged in favour of the rich few'. Furthermore, if potential shareholders were denied access to proper information, how could they make well-judged investment decisions? They might lose out financially as a result, so in that sense they were victims of a crime against them.

During the trial itself, Ernest Saunders claimed that he had not known what was happening. On his behalf, his counsel, Richard Ferguson, QC, had claimed that his client's primary role within Guinness had been as a marketeer and PR man, and one without much understanding of financial matters. Olivier Roux responded in court by saying:

> Mr Saunders was running the company, running the business, otherwise how do you think Guinness would have achieved what it did? You are painting a ridiculous picture.

> This was a big business run by a chief executive and a number of people – not two people one doing PR and the other doing finance. We were not running a Sock Shop.

Saunders, reflecting on his first sight of the Roux letter, told the court that it was a classic pre-emptive strike:

> Here was the most cynical implication that I had knowledge of, or worse, authorized matters which the letter claimed Mr Roux had been involved in. Clearly here was an attempt to do a buck-passing operation of the most cynical kind and I was absolutely livid. I remember what I wrote down on a piece of paper that I no longer have: pure poison.

It also emerged during the trial that for his eight weeks' work on the Guinness/Distillers bid the American lawyer Thomas Ward received £5.2 million, though the money was not paid to him direct – that would have been highly irregular, given his position as a director of the company – but to a nominee company, MAC, via the Channel Islands. Three million pounds of this found its way into a Union Bank of Switzerland account belonging to Ernest Saunders, the prosecution claiming this was his 'bonus' from all the share scams going on. In answer to this charge, Saunders said that he had lent the account to Ward because the American did not know how to open a Swiss bank account. The prosecution's response was that it was not to be believed that an international lawyer like Ward would not know how to open his own account. Though Saunders was never charged with theft, the prosecution successfully implied that the money had been destined for him. What was particularly damning was the fact that of the £5.2 million, £3 million plus the exact interest on the latter sum, had been transferred to Saunders's Swiss bank account. The prosecution's argument was, would the calculation have been so exact if the money had really belonged to Thomas Ward?

It emerged that in his dealings with the DTI inspectors and other fraud investigators, Olivier Roux had not always told the truth. In court he said this had been because he had wanted to help his friend Tony Parnes. Parnes had brought Ephraim Margulies, then the head of the commodities firm S.W. Berrisford, into the share-support scheme. When it went wrong, Margulies said it was up to Parnes to get him out. The stockbroker therefore appealed to his friend Roux, who agreed not to divulge the link between Margulies and the payment of nearly £2 million to a Panamanian company called Cifco. Roux agreed to help with a cover-up, which was to include back-dated letters, fictitious contracts and shadowy Swiss middlemen; he later changed his mind, however, when he realized that the truth could not be kept from the investigating authorities.

Gerald Ronson also blamed Parnes for his troubles. The Heron boss said that he had committed £25 million to the share-support scheme on Parnes's say-so, and had expected the stockbroker to have been aware of the law. For his part, Parnes claimed that he had known nothing about Ronson's £5 million success fee until after the bid – though Ronson counter-claimed that Parnes had helped negotiate it with Saunders. Parnes himself, however, had received a success fee of £3.34 million. As if there was not enough confusing and conflicting evidence, there was more of it to come over the involvement of Sir Jack Lyons. He had given three different explanations of a series of £25,000 monthly payments he had received from Guinness. He had first said that these fees were to pay off indemnities on Guinness shares bought by him and his clients. Then he had said that the money was a retainer for advice on the disposal of Distillers property. Finally, he returned to his original explanation. In Sir Jack's defence, it was said that he had been tired and confused at the time.

The four defendants were found guilty of twenty-eight of the twenty-nine charges of theft, conspiracy, false accounting and breaches of the Companies Act. When the judge sentenced Anthony Parnes to two and a half years in prison, he collapsed to the floor of the court and had to be helped up, whilst Gerald Ronson's wife Gail screamed, 'Murderers, murderers!' Ronson himself was given a one-year sentence, and proceeded to run his Heron Corporation from inside gaol. It was rumoured that he was paying up to £250 each for telephone cards worth only a few pounds in order to keep in touch with his business whilst incarcerated! Sir Jack Lyons received a thirty-month jail sentence but it was suspended because of his age and frailty – though he was later stripped of his knighthood. Ernest Saunders was jailed for five years. The marriages of both Saunders and Parnes broke down as a result of the stress of the investigation and trial. There were other consequences: among them the fact that the spectre of the Guinness case haunts the City even now.

All four of the men convicted in the first Guinness trial in 1990 were given leave to appeal by the Home Secretary, Michael Howard, after arguing that vital evidence had been withheld. The basis of their claim was that the Serious Fraud Office had known about widespread use of share-support schemes but had not made this evidence available to them. It was, however, given to Lord Spens, and used in his defence, during the second Guinness trial. That trial fell apart and Spens, of Henry Ansbacher; Roger Seelig, formerly of Morgan Grenfell, and David Mayhew of Cazenove were all acquitted. Lord Spens is now suing the Bank of England for damages arising from the Guinness affair. Thomas Ward, the US attorney who advised Guinness during the Distillers takeover, was acquitted in 1994 of stealing £5.2 million from Guinness. Outside the Old Bailey he told me that he would go and celebrate with champagne. In a final twist at the High Court in December 1994, Thomas Ward was sentenced in his absence to six months in prison for failing to co-operate with the continuing DTI inquiry into the bid; he had not complied with DTI requests to give evidence to inspectors.

In my initial investigations into the Guinness affair it became apparent that the four defendants in the first trial had not taken the best legal path towards protecting themselves. Some criminal lawyers I spoke to gave the opinion that it had quite plainly not been in their interests to speak to the DTI inspectors. The view in the City at the time, however, was that, if called to account by the DTI, a person simply had to answer – a potential gaol sentence for contempt lay in wait for anyone who did not. In short, there is no right to silence. But weighing it up, I believe that in that first Guinness case, many of those interviewed did not believe that what they said would form the nucleus of criminal charges against them. Nor had they foreseen that the sentences, when they came to lose the criminal case, would be far harsher than they had expected – and that they would have saved an awful lot of time and money if they had simply refused to talk to the DTI inspectors. It is surprising that no one under investigation has tried this tactic yet.

There is no doubt that all four men convicted in the first Guinness trial regret it bitterly. Of the four, the consequences have been harshest for Ernest Saunders and Anthony Parnes. Gerald Ronson was able to resume the helm of the Heron Corporation when he left prison, but the glory days for Saunders and Parnes were over. Both men have since become obsessed with trying to clear their names. So it came about that, at the end of November 1995, Ernest Saunders, Jack Lyons, Gerald Ronson and Anthony Parnes were once more named in a court action, though this time it took place at the Court of Appeal in London's Strand. Unfortunately for them, while the venue may have been different, the result was the same. Three judges, headed by Lord Taylor, the Lord Chief Justice, dismissed their appeal against their convictions, saying that the jury in the Guinness trial had been 'well justified'. Giving judgment, the judges said:

> Despite the mass of paper and the factual complexity of some of the transactions, the issues in this case were essentially stark and simple. They turned on the jury's view as to whether these appellants were proved to have acted dishonestly.

The combination of indemnities paid by Guinness to purchasers of its own shares [i.e. the share-support scheme], the false invoices, the huge success fees and the failure to disclose either indemnities or success fees to the Guinness board provided ample evidence of a dishonest scheme in which all the appellants played their parts.

The four men had all used two main arguments in their appeals. The first – cited by Michael Howard, the Home Secretary, when he referred the case to the Appeal Court in December 1994 – concerned the Serious Fraud Office's decision not to disclose to the defendants evidence of indemnities being used in other City deals. The second was the claim that ministers, along with civil servants from the office of the Director of Public Prosecutions and from the Crown Prosecution Service, had unfairly 'colluded' with inspectors from the Department of Trade and Industry. Counsel for the 'Guinness Four' argued that the DPP and CPS had delayed establishing a police investigation into the affair in order to enable DTI inspectors, using their powers to compel witnesses to answer questions, to obtain the maximum amount of information first.

Among the documents which had not been disclosed to Saunders, Ronson, Parnes and Lyons were some concerning seven transactions between TWH, a firm of share-dealers, and Lord Spens of Henry Ansbacher, the merchant bank. In due course Spens was charged over the Guinness affair and came to trial; he was subsequently acquitted, however, when the proceedings were abandoned because of the ill health of his co-defendant, Roger Seelig of Morgan Grenfell.

All seven transactions had involved Ansbachers giving an oral indemnity to TWH to persuade it to buy shares. Where TWH had suffered losses it had been reimbursed, false invoices being used to cover the payments. Other documents giving evidence of share-support schemes which the authorities had known about concerned the use of indemnities by Hill Samuel, the merchant bank, to persuade others to buy shares in Turner

& Newall during the latter's failed 1986 bid for AE Automotive Components, as well as a share-buying 'concert party' organized during the 1985 Burtons and Habitat bid for Debenhams. The four appellants claimed that these documents showed that practices similar to those at the heart of the Guinness affair had been common in the City and that therefore they had been acting honestly.

The Appeal Court ruled that the SFO should have disclosed the documents as a matter of procedure, but that these documents on their own would not have been enough to persuade a jury that the use of indemnities and success fees in the Guinness affair had been legal and honest. The court dismissed the argument over supposed collusion between the DPP, CPS and DTI, the judges opining that there would only have been wrongdoing by the state agencies if the prosecutors had interfered with the independence of the DTI inquiry, something which had not happened. The court quashed one of the convictions of Jack Lyons – a charge that he had conspired with Saunders over arranging one of the indemnities. Lyons will be repaid £500,000 of the £3 million he was fined after his conviction; he remains stripped of his knighthood, however. All four appellants had to pay around £50,000 each towards costs – and all four are now considering an appeal to the highest legal authority in Britain, the House of Lords. The main legal challenge to the Guinness convictions, however, remains the case being brought in the European Court of Human Rights by Ernest Saunders. It may just be that there is an end to the Guinness affair in sight.

As we have seen, these cases just seem to drag on and on. Astonishingly, even now the report on the DTI investigation into the 1986 bid battle between Guinness and Argyll for Distillers is not yet complete. It is at the consultation stage, and leading players in the £2.7 billion battle have recently been sent the provisional findings of the two DTI inspectors responsible for the report, David Donaldson, QC, and accountant Ian Watt. The report has taken almost ten years to compile at a cost of well over £2 million; however, it is unlikely to be published before the European Court of Human Rights rules on Saunders's challenge to the use of his evidence to the DTI inspectors in his 1990 trial. This will be heard by the full court of thirty-one judges in Strasbourg. Saunders is claiming that his trial was unfair because it infringed his right not to incriminate himself: people questioned by DTI inspectors have no right to silence. If the court agrees with him, the decision will throw the bringing of prosecutions for serious fraud in Britain into further turmoil.

17

The Robert Maxwell Affair – 'He could charm the birds from the trees, then shoot them'

On 4 November 1991 I was sitting at a fundraising dinner in one of London's plushest hotels, waiting to hear the guest speaker, Robert Maxwell. Unfortunately he was not present, and his speech had to be delivered by one of his sons, Ian, who told the hundreds of guests that his father had suddenly been struck down with a heavy cold. I remember wondering how it was that at the eleventh hour his son could deliver Robert Maxwell's speech without making any mistakes, almost as if he had been practising it for days. It was not until later – as the scandal surrounding Robert Maxwell began to unfold – that I realized that this ploy of agreeing to deliver a speech, then pulling out at the last minute and substituting one of his sons, was something Maxwell senior did all the time. Nor could I have known then, as I listened to Ian Maxwell delivering his father's speech to the dinner-jacketed guests sitting at tables laden with china and cut glass, that somewhere off the West African coast Robert Maxwell was living the last six hours of his life.

For Maxwell had indeed told everyone that he had a cold, and had decided to shake it off by cruising aboard his 190-foot yacht *Lady Ghislaine*. For the past few days he had been enjoying the sun and sailing in the waters around the Canary

Islands. But this was no ordinary 'get-away-from-it-all' holiday, however – for as Maxwell's luxurious yacht cut through the Atlantic waves, a wave of much greater proportions was about to wash away his financial empire. No one can ever be certain that Robert Maxwell did not kill himself, but in the early hours of 5 November 1991 the crew reported him missing at sea. His body was recovered within days.

If ever a man epitomized in his character the qualities needed to perpetrate fraud on a massive scale, then that man was Robert Maxwell. And the signs that sooner or later he would overstep that line between what is unethical and what is illegal, were writ large in him from an early age. Robert Maxwell began life as Ludvik, or 'Laiby', as he was known in the family, Hoch. He was born on 10 June 1923 in the village of Solotvino, in Eastern Czechoslovakia, and for the first seven years of his life did not own a pair of shoes: when he died he was said to be one of Britain's ten wealthiest individuals. Ludvik's father, Methel Hoch, was an itinerant labourer and was known locally as 'Methel der Lange' – Methel the tall – he stood 6 foot 5 inches. When Ludvik's father was unable to find work he bought cattle for the local butchers and received the hides by way of payment; these he sold on to the leather merchants. Unsurprisingly, given that he came from a poor family, the concept of making deals took root in young Ludvik from an early age.

He had an orthodox Jewish upbringing and studied at a Jewish academy or yeshiva. When he was fourteen he was sent to a larger yeshiva in Bratislava – his mother entertained hopes that he would become a rabbi – nearly four hundred miles from his home. It was while he was there that the young scholar first began selling – he dealt in cheap jewellery, and would often return home as a travelling salesman, his pockets stuffed with his stock in trade. In a family where presents were unknown the young Ludvik would give his elder sisters some of his necklaces, a generous gesture the memory of which was to stay with them through the dark days of the Second World War and beyond. The family soon had to accept that their son's destiny was not going to be fulfilled by his continued studying, nor was he to be the famous rabbi of which his mother had dreamt. Discarding his traditional dress in favour of a modern suit, and cutting off his sidelocks, young Ludvik began to plan a life in commerce.

For a while his plans had to be postponed, for Europe was plunging into war. Fortunately Ludvik had one particular talent which stood him in good stead during the war, and was to prove a useful tool in his renewed commercial activities after it – his linguistic ability. He had been brought up in a part of Eastern Europe which, although it had come under the Czechoslovakian flag at the time of his birth, straddled the borders, as they were then drawn, of Hungary, Poland and Romania. From an early age, therefore, he had spoken several of the local languages, as well as German. With the coming of war in 1939 he fled to Romania, and from there made his way to France, where he picked up that language too. In the spring of 1940 the Nazis invaded and conquered France, and Hoch was evacuated to Britain. At first he joined the Auxiliary Pioneer Corps – the only unit in the British Army open to 'aliens' at the time – and he began his military career as number 12079140, Hoch, Private L. Soon, though, he was befriended by people with influence, and with their help managed to join the Regular Army. He now changed his name to Leslie du Maurier (taking the surname from his favourite brand of cigarettes), and his rise through the ranks was swift. He was promoted staff sergeant during the battle of the Orne in the summer of 1944, after the Normandy landings, and in March the following year he married Elizabeth Meynard in Paris. In December of that year, however, Leslie du Maurier left his French wife to go back to England to accept a commission as Second Lieutenant Ian Robert Maxwell. He had taken the surname after his patron, Brigadier Carthew-Yorstoun, a proud Scot, had suggested that Maxwell was soundly Scottish.

Maxwell won the Military Cross for his bravery in leading a counter-attack which rescued a platoon that had been pinned down by the Germans. He was promoted Captain and, after the European war had ended in May 1945, took up a position with the Allied Control Commission, the body whose task was the administration of the British zone in Berlin (the city then being divided into Soviet, American, British and French sectors), as 'a Temporary Officer Grade 3, Information Services Control Branch'. This effectively made him censor of the newly emergent non-Nazi press in Berlin; he also became one of twelve British officers authorized to purchase goods, through the American-British Joint Export-Import Agency. It was through this agency that he was introduced to the elderly German publisher, Ferdinand Springer, whom he helped to restart his business in Heidelberg, and to import into Britain back copies of Springer's scientific publications. Maxwell set up a company specifically to handle these and similar transactions, and so it came about that, in 1947, he left the army to concentrate on his business interests. A year later Springer formed a joint venture with the British publishers, Butterworths, which was christened Butterworth-Springer. Although Maxwell had no financial interest in this company, it was to become the springboard from which all his other business interests were to be launched. His own company only distributed the publications for Butterworth-Springer, but when the British publishers decided that they no longer wanted to be in that business it was to Maxwell they turned. He bought the company in 1951, changing its name to Pergamon in the process.

Maxwell believed that the post-war world would see a thirst for scientific knowledge, and that the plethora of new universities, colleges of further education, polytechnics and the like would be only too willing to pay premium prices for the ever-increasing catalogue of scientific publications his company produced. What is more, the academics Maxwell involved in writing or editing his publications were usually so flattered that anyone should take an interest in their chosen field, that the last thing on their minds was any thought of payment for what they were doing. Here was a perfect business opportunity – publications written or compiled for next to nothing, and which could be sold to quasi-public bodies for high prices. Not surprisingly, business was brisk for several years. In 1969, however, came the Leasco affair, and with it the first public acknowledgement that Maxwell was not the honourable businessman he purported to be. Leasco was an American firm, founded and headed by Saul Steinberg, which leased computers; at the time, it was said to be the fastest-growing company in the world. Maxwell courted Steinberg, and it has to be said that the American, a man not easily impressed, was won over by Captain Bob's charisma (a trade union negotiator once said of Maxwell that he could 'charm the birds from the trees, then shoot them'). And Steinberg was impressed, remarking that when Maxwell came to New York and accompanied him to parties, the naturalized-British businessman knew more of the top people there than he himself did. This closeness between the two men prompted Steinberg to bid for Maxwell's company, Pergamon, the idea being that the latter's scientific database would then be loaded into Leasco's computers. But while Leasco's accountants were having difficulty obtaining information from Maxwell, it emerged that two of his family trusts had been selling Pergamon shares bought by Leasco at inflated prices. Then Leasco discovered that a large proportion of Pergamon's recent profits had been derived from dealings with private Maxwell companies, thus casting doubt on their true value. (He was to use this trick to devastating effect more than twenty years later.) Leasco withdrew its £25 million bid, but by then the American firm held 38.5 per cent of Pergamon's shares, and therefore banded together with institutional investors to vote Maxwell off the board. This did not please the academics who wrote for Pergamon's journals, however, and profits slumped accordingly.

After a struggle, Maxwell lost control of the company he had built up. Then, in July 1971, just as he was about to win it back, a Government report into the Leasco takeover dubbed Maxwell 'a person who cannot be relied upon to exercise proper stewardship of a publicly quoted company'. This damning phrase, from the report of the inspectors appointed by the regulatory department of the Government, was a devastating blow to a businessman who, in any case, always believed that the British Establishment was against him. But Captain Robert Maxwell – who came to be known in the satirical magazines as 'the bouncing Czech' – was not going to be put off either by the opinions of bureaucrats or by a few taunts. He still had the support of the academics at Pergamon, and by November 1973 had regained a seat on the board. At the end of 1974, with the company going through troubled times, Steinberg agreed to sell his shares to Maxwell, and thus to give him overall control. These shares, valued at 185p each only four years earlier, were now sold for only 10p. Steinberg had paid £9 million for his holding in Pergamon; Maxwell repaid him just £600,000 to regain control. To this day, Saul Steinberg refuses to speak about Maxwell.

Six years after regaining the helm at Pergamon, Robert Maxwell bought Europe's largest printing company, the ailing British Printing Corporation. BPC was losing £1 million a month and was racked by union troubles. Maxwell was seen by many as the only man able to handle the unions (an image he was keen to foster on many future occasions). At the end of 1982, BPC was renamed the British Printing and Communications Corporation, emphasizing Maxwell's intention to expand into cable and satellite television, computers and databanks, electronic printing and every other branch of communications technology. His dream was, as he put it, to 'build a company to rank among the world's ten largest communications corporations'. In September 1987 the name was again changed to the (ill-fated, as it turned out) Maxwell Communication Corporation (MCC).

Three years before that, however, Maxwell had finalized one of his sharpest business deals, when he bought the Mirror Group of newspapers (MGN) from the publishing giant Reed International (now the Anglo-Dutch group, Reed-Elsevier). The price was something over £100 million, and for that he gained control of some of Britain's best-known newspaper titles. This not only gave him a potentially profitable business, but also both a power base and a propaganda machine. It was probably the high point of his business career – and it almost certainly contributed to his downfall.

At this point it should be noted that back in 1964 Robert Maxwell had been elected to represent Buckingham in Parliament, becoming the youngest Labour MP in Harold Wilson's Government. He was ambitious – probably too ambitious – and wanted ministerial office immediately. His ultimate goal was to become Prime Minister, but his political career quickly ran into trouble because he did not know when to keep his mouth shut, with the result that he constantly rubbed his colleagues in the House and in the Labour Party up the wrong way. Before long, Maxwell soon realized that he was effectively condemned to a life in the political wilderness as a backbench MP, and so began to channel his energies into making money. Throughout his life, however, he continued to see himself as a world statesman, the equal of Gorbachev or Yeltsin, and on friendly terms with the American President, Ronald Reagan. He once told a journalist on one of his newspapers, the *Daily Mirror*, that Russian tanks could not possibly be on the streets in one of the Baltic republics 'because Gorbachev wouldn't do anything without consulting me first'. This attitude was in part self-delusion, and in part a ploy by which he hoped to be seen by others as a friend to the powerful. He once paid $100,000 to sit next to Ronald Reagan at a charity dinner in California. As foolish as that may sound, one has only to consider how cost-effective that particular piece of self-promotion was as a global image – pictures of the two seated together were flashed around the world. How much easier would it have been for him now – a friend, apparently, to the most powerful leader in the West – to go to the bank and negotiate a loan? And that is just what Maxwell often did. Furthermore, his acquisition of Mirror Group Newspapers catapulted him once more into the limelight which he enjoyed so much. At the same time, however, he started to believe some of his own publicity. He had in the past prided himself on his deal-making skills and on his ability to forecast the financial markets, but in the hurly-burly world of the 1980s things began to go wrong. Maxwell did what so many others did in those days – he simply borrowed too much. In his case, though, rather than give up his global aspirations, he devised an elaborate rescue plan which, he hoped, would keep the companies afloat until the good times came rolling back again and thus allowed him to sell off some of those expensive buys without incurring huge losses.

The deal that did for Robert Maxwell was made in 1988 when he bought, at the top of the market and against fierce rival bidding, the US-based Macmillan Publishing Group (he already owned, in Britain, both Pergamon and Macdonald & Co. Publishers Ltd), the *Official Airlines Guide*, and the Berlitz language guides. He borrowed nearly £3 billion to make the deal, repaying the loan being dependent on the sale of his printing group, BPCC. But he was not able to sell BPCC quickly enough, and thereby found himself unable to cover the loan. The stock market quickly figured this out. After having risen in the wake of its acquisition of Macmillan, shares in MCC began to drop. The burden of Macmillan was piled on top of other burdens: old debts, the flop of the launch of his new daily paper for London, the London *Daily News* in 1987, the prospective launch of the *European* newspaper in 1989. By the autumn of 1990, as the 1980s boom collapsed into recession, Maxwell faced a mountainous task in trying to fend off the mounting financial pressures on his media empire. In response to demands from his fifty creditor banks he agreed to sell businesses, but he also borrowed fresh money at the same time, and in order to do that he was asked to pledge additional collateral, by way of shares – many of them in the family – that is, his private – businesses. Once again there were problems. Maxwell had agreed that should the value of the pledges fall – in other words, if the shares fell in value beyond a certain price – then more shares would be placed in the bank's hands as collateral. When, almost inevitably, this started to happen, he used the complex web of his business empire and the methods of twenty years before, to obscure illegal transactions in a last desperate attempt to keep his global media companies from crashing down around his ears. It will never be known whether, if had he lived, he would have succeeded. But despite his undoubted charisma and formidable business skills, I believe that even he could not have got out of this one.

What Maxwell did was to bring into play some of the methods which he had employed during the Leasco affair. He used transactions between his public companies – Mirror Group Newspapers and the Maxwell Communication Corporation – and his private companies to obscure the fact that in effect he was robbing Peter to pay Paul. He also used this web, together with trusts set up in the secretive European principality of Liechtenstein, to obscure the true ownership of money and shares which actually belonged to various company pension funds.

How did all this come to unravel? To look objectively at that question, it is necessary to go back to 16 July 1991, the date of the beginning of the end of the Maxwell empire. On that date the former Conservative Cabinet minister, Peter Walker (now Lord Walker of Worcester), decided not to take up the chairmanship of MCC, after an internal review had shown that the company was in a difficult financial position with debts of around £1.3 billion. The shares fell, and as we now know that compounded the problem. In August there came the disclosure from the American investment bank, Goldman Sachs, that it held a 7.5 per cent shareholding in MCC and a 10.48 per cent holding in MGN; the shares, the bank added, were held as a 'security interest' against loans.

Maxwell had never been a figure much liked in the financial circles of the City of London. Nor had there been much love lost between him and other branches of the media. I particularly remember the animosity displayed and the tough questions asked by journalists from rival tabloid papers back in May of the year he announced a flotation of shares in the Mirror Group of newspapers. Now, only some three months later, it was the turn of the quality press and broadcast media to put him, his business empire and his ethics under the microscope once more. It began in September when the *Wall Street Journal*, bible of American bankers and investors, weighed in with a highly critical overview of the financial stability of the

Maxwell media empire. This was quickly followed by BBC Television's flagship current affairs programme, *Panorama*, which investigated Maxwell's sale of 49 per cent of his shares in Mirror Group Newspapers. In the course of this programme a former MGN employee alleged that the *Daily Mirror*'s Lotto and Spot the Ball competitions were unfairly run, so that the chances of the newspaper having to pay out large sums were cut down. The Mirror Group responded to the effect that these readers' contests were run in accordance with accepted newspaper practice. On the eve of the *Panorama* broadcast, Robert Maxwell wrote an editorial in the *Sunday Mirror* in which he complained that the BBC had not listened to his reservations about the programme. He accused the BBC Chairman, Marmaduke Hussey, the Director-General, Michael (now Sir Michael) Checkland, and the latter's deputy, John Birt, of being 'the three monkeys of broadcasting. They want to hear nothing, see nothing and say nothing.'

This attack on the media, the latest in a very long line, seemed curiously limp in comparison to the many times Maxwell had slapped writs on those individuals or organizations that had crossed him in the past. His most notable success had been against the satirical magazine *Private Eye*, from which he had won substantial damages, moving the jury when he broke down in court as he recalled how his family had been all but wiped out by the Nazis. Now, however, he seemed exhausted, unable to persuade observers of the situation that he really had a case against this latest flurry of harmful allegations about the way he ran his businesses. Disquiet began to be apparent amongst his financial backers.

Then along came Seymour Hersh, an American investigative reporter with a reputation that rivalled those of Carl Bernstein and Bob Woodward of Watergate fame. In his book, *The Sampson Option*, a study of Israel's highly secret nuclear weapons programme, Hersh alleged that in 1985 Maxwell and Nick Davies, the foreign editor of the *Daily Mirror*, had helped Mossad, Israel's intelligence service, to kidnap a renegade Israeli scientist bent on exposing his country's nuclear secrets. Both Maxwell and Davies vehemently denied any involvement in the kidnapping of Mordecai Vanunu – the scientist had been lured to Rome, snatched by Mossad, taken to Israel, and there tried and sentenced to eighteen years in prison for supplying Israeli secrets to journalists from the *Sunday Times*. Though questions about the reliability of Hersh's principal source, Ari Ben Menashe, who had served in the Israeli Defence Force for ten years, quickly arose, the damage was done. In the ensuing furore, the cashflow problems which the Maxwell companies were experiencing threatened to blow up into a full-scale crisis of confidence.

So, in the last days of his life, there developed 'the Max Factor' – the feeling that shares in his publicly quoted companies might trade higher if his name were not associated with them. But also behind this phrase lay a growing conviction in the City that Maxwell's time as an entrepreneur was up. In the past he had notched up some notable successes. He had been one of the first to realize the potential of academic publishing in the years after the Second World War, and despite the Leasco affair Pergamon Press – which had been among the first publishers to use computerization – was a flourishing business. From 1981, too, his printing interests prospered in the form of what he retitled the British Printing Corporation, and latterly, from 1984, his purchase of Mirror Group Newspapers for £113 million had proved to be a triumph. But as the high-risk strategies of the 1980s were replaced by the steadying hand of the managerial 1990s, it became clear that Maxwell had made one deal too many, buying Macmillan Inc., the *Official Airlines Guide*, and the Berlitz language guides. In a bitter contest Maxwell had paid $2.6 billion for Macmillan alone – most experts believed at the time that this was at least $600 million more than the company was worth. He then went on to spend $750 million on the *Official Airlines Guide*. Berlitz was small beer in comparison, and Maxwell moved to sell 44 per cent of its shares within a year of buying it.

But with the adverse publicity and the mounting debt, Robert Maxwell's bankers began to exact tougher and tougher conditions in return for easing his cashflow problems. Though he tried to sell off assets which he described as peripheral to the business – in October he sold Macmillan's directories publishing business to Reed for £83.5 million in cash – the disposals were proving too little, too late. The recession was biting, and no one was keen to spend money knowing that a few months down the line they could probably buy the same assets much cheaper. On the last day of October, five days before his death, Goldman Sachs sold 2.2 million of Maxwell's shares after having repeatedly asked him to repay his loans. The price of Maxwell Communication Corporation stock fell, and as Goldman Sachs again asked for repayment rumours swept London's financial community that other banks were also keen to call in their loans.

Then, before the storm could break, Maxwell was dead. Events moved rapidly from then on. On 6 November his sons, Kevin and Ian, were confirmed as Chairman of Maxwell Communication Corporation and Chairman of Mirror Group Newspapers, respectively. It emerged that there was £800 million of debt in the private holding companies and £1.5 billion in publicly listed MGN and MCC; the high street bank NatWest was approached to help the private companies suffering cashflow problems. Then, four days later, evidence emerged that, before his death, Maxwell's empire had been about to be investigated for illegal share dealings by the Department of Trade and Industry. On 18 November the Serious Fraud Office was called in by the Swiss Bank Corporation to investigate a £55 million loan the latter had made to an offshoot of Headington Investments, one of Maxwell's private companies. It later emerged that Maxwell had taken out the loan in order to buy a Japanese investment trust called First Tokyo, and had pledged as security certain shares held by the trust company; these, however, were never placed in the hands of the Swiss Bank Corporation. What in fact happened was that Maxwell took the money to buy First Tokyo, and had then sold that company's only asset, its shares.

But worse was to come. On 4 December the SFO launched investigations into how the Mirror Group and Maxwell Communication Corporation pension schemes had incurred potential losses of £526 million on loans to the Maxwell family's private companies. Administrators were called in to the main holding companies for these businesses, Robert Maxwell Group and Headington Investments. It quickly became apparent that the only assets many of them now had were residual pockets of shares, mainly in Maxwell's public companies, the value of which had tumbled on a daily basis as the extent of the financial crisis had become apparent. Finally, on 2 December, shares in both MCC and MGN were suspended, 'pending clarification of the financial position'.

The *Daily Mirror* was to claim that its owner had skimmed £930 million from pension funds and companies under his control in the weeks before he died. The administrators said that the Maxwell family businesses were $2.5 billion in debt. Then sources close to the probe into Maxwell's private companies stated that he had skimmed $720 million from MGN and MCC pension funds. Soon a pattern began to emerge. Hemmed in by his mounting debts to the banks, which rose as the share price in his publicly quoted companies fell, so that further securities had to be placed in the hands of his bankers, Maxwell had robbed his company pension funds, achieving this by encouraging those funds to buy shares in his own companies. Often these and other shares owned by the pension funds were then lent to other Maxwell companies, which would in turn pledge them to the banks as security for loans. In many cases, the fact that the shares were rightfully the property of the pension funds was disguised by moving the shares through a number of Maxwell companies, thus blurring their initial starting point and making it more difficult for the banks to question Maxwell's assertion that these were shares that belonged to him.

The linchpin of the whole operation was a little-known company called Bishopsgate Investment Management (BIM), which was found to be simply an investment vehicle for pension fund money. It was through BIM that most of the missing pension fund assets from the other Maxwell companies had been channelled. On 10 December, Neil Cooper of the accountancy firm Robson Rhodes, which had been appointed liquidator of BIM, announced that a total of £727 million was missing from the Maxwell pension funds, and that £450 million of that had been traced. So where did all the money go? Well, the £450 million that had been traced was largely in the hands of banks and financial institutions, having been pledged against loans made to Robert Maxwell. There followed the pension fund battle to establish legal ownership of these shares and securities, which came about because many of the banks and other institutions claimed that they had had no reason to believe that Maxwell was not the owner when he had pledged the shares, and that, of course, the cash he had been lent had vanished. The pension funds, not surprisingly, claimed the shares belonged to them. Of the rest of the money – some £277 million – a certain amount of it had no doubt been squandered on Maxwell's lavish lifestyle. He had been gambling heavily in the months before his death. He had his yacht, the *Lady Ghislaine* – named after his favourite daughter – to keep up, and its crew of eight to pay for. His budget for eating was as large as his reputation – $4,000 an afternoon when he was in New York! But by far the greater part of the missing money simply went in interest repayments on the loans, or in supporting the share prices of his two listed companies, MCC and MGN, in a futile attempt to keep those prices up, and thus obviate the need for further security to be pledged to the banks.

As to Maxwell's legacy, he always said that he would never leave any of his fortune to his children, and this now seems to have been the case. For the tens of thousands of Maxwell pensioners throughout Britain the first few months following his death were to prove a terrible strain, as each day seemed to bring fresh revelations or accusations, and as they worried about just how much the robber Maxwell had left them to live on in their old age. It now appears, however, that none of these people will go without a pension, though some have had to forgo lump sums, and others will perhaps receive less in the future than they would have done had the surplus in their funds been allowed to build up, as normally happens in most company pension funds.

This view was reinforced by a global settlement announced in mid-February 1995, and which had been brokered by a leading businessman, Sir John Cuckney. In essence, he arranged to bring £276 million back into the pension fund coffers from some of Maxwell's professional advisers who were by then facing legal action from lawyers acting for BIM. These lawyers contended that the institutions like Lehman Brothers and Goldman Sachs either knew, or should have known, that the shares which Maxwell pledged in return for loans actually belonged to his companies' pensioners. In the event, some of these lawyers would have liked to have tested their case in court, since they were convinced that the evidence would have upheld their arguments. The financial institutions, they believed, would therefore have been forced to cough up a great deal more cash than was actually paid as a result of the Cuckney deal, under which the legal actions were dropped, and which also offered the institutions immunity from criminal prosecution. Having had the shadow of the affair hanging over them for a number of years, however, the Maxwell pensioners were delighted when it finally looked as though only a handful of those hit by the worst cases would lose out, and only then in a relatively minor way – no one would actually go without a pension. For the institutions, there was the bonus that none of them would face a prolonged legal action, nor would they attract any lasting stigma as a result of their involvement in the Maxwell saga.

For the Government, the timing of the Cuckney deal could not have been sweeter, with the new Pensions Bill passing through Parliament – that legislation being, of course, the one truly positive measure to have emerged from the Maxwell pension débâcle. Clearly the law governing the administration of occupational or company pension schemes had to be tightened, and therefore the act provided for the balance of trustees

– that is, those from among the ownership or management, as compared to those from among the employees or union members – running pension funds to be made more even. In this way it has been made almost impossible for an overbearing entrepreneur like Maxwell to wield undue influence over where and how funds are invested. The rules governing self-investment (the company pension fund investing in the company's own shares) were also altered under the act to discourage massive reliance on one share which, if it crashes, can leave the pension fund bankrupt. So it has come about that what Maxwell did may protect pensioners in the future from the exploitation of men like him. As to his motivation, it is known that, in a desperate gamble, he stole pensioners' money, double dealt with the banks, and supported his own shares. It is possible, however, that he viewed the frauds only as temporary measures for keeping his companies afloat; a loan which he intended to repay as soon as the economy picked up, and his main businesses became more profitable. He would then have been able to realize better prices for his unwanted companies. In the event, he would not actually have had to have waited very long, but, as with all things in life, timing is everything. If that had indeed been his plan, Robert Maxwell's death was certainly badly timed.

Of course, theories about the cause of his death still abound. Initially, everything was mentioned, from suicide to death at the hands of some foreign government or terrorist organization. Of the tycoon's last hours this much is known. Maxwell flew from London to board the *Lady Ghislaine* at Gibraltar on Thursday, 31 October 1991, sailing to Madeira before going on to the Canaries. He was last seen alive at 4.25 am on Tuesday, 5 November, when a crew member saw him strolling on the deck. At 4.45 am he called to ask for the air conditioning in his cabin to be turned down. At 11 am a call from New York was put through, but when no reply was received the ship's captain, Gus Rankin, went to Maxwell's cabin to check he was there. Discovering he was missing, Rankin ordered a thorough search of the boat; then, following another fruitless search, he raised the alarm. Maxwell's naked body was found floating off Gran Canaria by a rescue helicopter at 5.55 pm that day. Lying face up, with arms and legs splayed, the body had apparently suffered no damage from the boat's propellers. It had resurfaced after only thirteen hours, at most, in the water, compared with the average time for victims of drowning of two to three days. A local judge, Luis Gutierrez, at first told reporters that the publisher had been dead when he fell into the water, the view being that he had died of a heart attack. However, a subsequent report for the companies insuring Maxwell's life, prepared by Dr Ian West, head of forensic medicine at Guy's Hospital in London, suggested that he had killed himself. From what I knew of Maxwell, such an act fitted in with the psychology of the man. He was a fearless war hero who had faced death many times before. He had lost his business empire, and had fought back to an even stronger position. But he was sixty-eight years old, and could not do that again. He could see no way out as the prospect of the collapse of all that he had built stared him in the face that dark night out on the ocean. Why not end it all there, rather than return to London and the humiliation that awaited him? In the end, this may very well have been what happened, though it is a view vehemently opposed by Maxwell's family.

After Robert Maxwell's business empire fell to pieces, Kevin and Ian Maxwell found themselves the focus of all the public hatred of their father that had built up over the years. As the country looked around for scapegoats in the aftermath of the scandal of the robbed pensioners, here were the two sons, flesh of his flesh, successful businessmen who had worked for their father – surely they were to blame? However understandable, there was something not altogether just about such a view. After all, as the brothers were to point out at their trial, none of the advisers to the companies, nor any of the bankers who had lent money on securities offered them by Robert Maxwell, ever appeared in the dock. For a brief while, Kevin and Ian Maxwell tried to hold their father's business empire together in the aftermath of his death, the former taking charge of the Maxwell Communication Corporation, and his brother becoming boss of Mirror Group Newspapers. Both had to relinquish their posts when it was realized how great were the missing sums of money.

Kevin and Ian Maxwell were arrested on 18 June 1992. Their trial opened a few days short of three years later, and they had to wait a further eight months to hear a verdict. With them in the dock were a former London School of Economics lecturer, Larry Trachtenberg, and an accountant, Robert Bunn. It was to become the most expensive trial in British legal history, costing more than £20 million and drawing in 76 witnesses. The jury also went into the record books, clocking up eleven nights in a hotel, breaking the previous Old Bailey record of eight nights in a hotel in 1982. Half the jurors had to be examined by a doctor during the 131 days of the trial, and two were declared unfit at different times. In the course of the trial both a leading lawyer and a defendant collapsed, the latter being the forty-seven-year-old Robert Bunn, who was later freed on the grounds of ill health. All the defendants pleaded not guilty to fraudulently using £122 million of pensioners' money.

From the outset, the prosecution suggested that Maxwell's younger son, Kevin, had been the financial brains behind the scheme to save his father's business empire from collapse. It was alleged that he had used pension fund assets as collateral to raise a loan with National Westminster Bank, money which was then used to prop up the ailing private companies owned by the Maxwell family – the Robert Maxwell Group. Kevin Maxwell was also charged, with his father, of having misused £100 million worth of shares in Scitex, an Israeli drugs company. He, his brother Ian and Larry Trachtenberg were accused of misusing £22 million worth of shares in Teva, another Israeli company, and it was further claimed that this second fraud had taken place in the days after Robert Maxwell's death at sea.

Kevin Maxwell, who until the trial had often appeared to the public as arrogant and privileged, began to look more human. He said from the beginning that he intended to appear in the witness box and outlined his defence. It would have two strands to it. In the first of these, he placed crucial responsibility on his father. Ironically, he was helped in his defence by many of those 'portraits' of his father to which the family objected. On 28 June 1992, Radio 4 had broadcast *Maxwell: The Final Day*, starring Alfred Marks as a foul-mouthed and paranoid Robert Maxwell. One run of the television series *Inspector Morse* had ended with the eponymous detective arresting an Oxford-based educational publisher clearly modelled on Maxwell; in the drama not only was the 'Maxwell' character implicated in a murder, but his supposed incarceration in a Nazi death camp was shown to be bogus, the character having actually been a guard. These programmes the family had failed to halt, although they did have more success with *Maxwell: The Musical*, a satire about him which had been due to open in London's West End during mid-1994. In the public domain, however, there were still many illustrations of what it had been like to work with, live with, or be related to Robert Maxwell, with the result that Kevin did not have to lay it on too thick. It was well known, for example, that Maxwell senior disapproved of Kevin's marriage to Pandora, and to show his displeasure he sacked his son, though he later reinstated him. (He did the same to Ian Maxwell, when the latter failed to pick him up off a flight from Paris.) Throughout the trial there were constant references to Kevin's unseen co-defendant, whose invisible presence dominated proceedings. The court was told that he could be brutal one minute, kind the next. At a board meeting he would slam his fists on the table and accuse fellow directors of being 'disloyal bastards' if they disagreed with him. He was described as the 'commanding presence' who dominated every meeting he attended; the mogul for whom the law was there to be stretched. And though examples of his generosity were known, they were not specified in court – he once paid for a secretary to spend several months in India convalescing, and for the child of an acquaintance to have a life-saving operation. Rather, it was the mundane side of Maxwell that jolted the casual listener: the millionaire who asked his wife for a separation but spent Christmas with her just the same; the yacht owner who regularly relieved himself over the side of his boat (the family's theory of his death was that he blacked out whilst doing so), when he was not snoring so loudly that his wife was driven to seek a cabin of her own. This was the same man about whom his daughter-in-law, Pandora, could say, 'I didn't have to like him ... he didn't have to like me.'

Many people did not like Robert Maxwell, but most went in awe of him, and found that they were unable to oppose him. The two children who stayed in the family business, Kevin and Ian, were often treated much worse than the other executives of Maxwell's whom he constantly subjected to ritual humiliation. Kevin Maxwell did not blame his father for his upbringing — though he accepted that he had been 'bloody arrogant', and admitted having lied to one bank. He did, however, blame him specifically for what had happened, and told the court that in two late-night meetings his father had told him that the legal ownership of both the Scitex and Teva shares had been transferred from the pension funds to the Robert Maxwell Group. At both meetings, he said, they had been alone; the only documentary evidence, he continued, was a fax relating to the first meeting, but this had never been found. The prosecution poured scorn on the suggestion that these meetings had ever taken place. However, Kevin Maxwell insisted that they had, and that the fact that they had showed that he had acted honestly when pledging the shares as security for loans. To support its case against him, the prosecution called in witness a long series of bankers, and others, who complained that he had lied to them. It was all the jury could do to keep awake during this dull procession of evidence, while the defendant in question simply dismissed the views of these witnesses as irrelevant to the charges against him.

The second part of Kevin Maxwell's defence was aimed at widening the responsibility for what had happened, insisting that bankers, accountants, and lawyers should bear their share of the blame. In trying to spread blame throughout the financial heart of London, the City, he said banks such as NatWest, accountants such as Coopers & Lybrand, and lawyers such as Nicholson Graham & Jones, had for years accepted the way in which the Maxwell empire finances had been conducted. To observers of the trial, his defence was helped by the many who gave evidence, as witness after witness told how Robert Maxwell had run his business: only he appeared to know the whole picture, he bullied his staff, the paperwork was chaotic, there was deliberate and secretive 'compartmentalization' of activities.

This attempt to spread the blame more widely included telling the jury of the 'global settlement' that Sir John Cuckney had brokered, under the terms of which Coopers & Lybrand, along with the US investment banks Lehman Brothers and Goldman Sachs, had contributed millions of pounds towards repayment of the pension funds. The prosecution argued that such factors were no defence to the charges of criminal behaviour which the two brothers faced, but their relevance to the Maxwell saga was there for everyone to see. The ghost of Robert Maxwell and his relationships with the other key players in the drama presented the prosecution with substantial problems. Even before the trial began, the scale of the task before Kevin Maxwell, that of convincing the jury of his innocence, had already been considerably lessened. He had faced a total of eight charges involving some £300 million and alleging frauds against the Maxwell pension funds, Mirror Group Newspapers, and banks such as Crédit Suisse and the Swiss Volksbank; Larry Trachtenberg faced four charges, and Ian Maxwell two. During pre-trial hearings an agreement was reached whereby, in order to keep the trial manageable, the jury would consider only two charges involving the alleged frauds against the main Maxwell pension funds.

Though the prosecuting authority, the Serious Fraud Office, had been under pressure for some time to make complex fraud trials simpler, there was little evidence in this case of their having tried to do so. Jurors were directed to a mind-numbing array of documents and 'bundles', all of them bearing catalogue numbers as soporific as the droning voices of many of the lawyers. There was also a clear difference in style between prosecution and defence counsel. Appearing for Kevin Maxwell was the well-known – and jury-friendly – Alun Jones, QC, who combined an aggressive championing of his clients with a dry sense of humour. By contrast, the style of Alan Suckling, QC, who led for the prosecution, was solid but unspectacular. The trial judge did his best to blank out the torrent of pre-trial publicity from the minds of the jury: 'The collapse of the Maxwell group ... received unprecedented publicity,' he declared on day one, 'much was ... unfair.' He went on to highlight one of the issues raised by the media: '[There] have been suggestions that Mr Kevin Maxwell and Mr Ian Maxwell should not be receiving legal aid. The cost of this trial will be very high, but that is not the defendants' fault.' They had demonstrated that they could not pay for their own defence.

Needless to say, all the defendants were cleared of all charges. The verdict was seen as yet another setback for the Serious Fraud Office and for the prospects of pursuing complex financial cases to a successful conclusion. Some commentators said that if the trial had served any useful purpose, it had been to shrink Robert Maxwell down to life size: an overconfident 1980s tycoon with insufficient respect for the law or other people's property. Rather strangely, writers on the *Guardian* newspaper put this idea in rather a different way: 'As testimony took the court back to the recessionary days of 1991, Maxwell's behaviour seemed uncomfortably close to that of millions across the country, albeit on a larger scale. As householders were raiding children's piggy banks and surrendering assurance policies in a frantic attempt to pay mortgages and avoid repossession, so Maxwell was scooping up cash from any source to keep his empire afloat.' This was a strange about-face for a newspaper which had appeared to be as concerned as any over the plight of the pensioners left high and dry by Maxwell's tactics. The difference bewteen the tycoon and the average householder with financial troubles was clear

– he stole someone else's money to keep his companies going, they robbed their own savings to keep their families in their homes. In any event, it would be interesting to know how the Maxwell pensioners responded not only to the *Guardian*'s comparison, but also the trial of the Maxwell brothers. Clearly, the court case to an extent opened up old wounds, and its result left the victims wondering once again just who stole the pensions. It comes as little comfort to the 32,000 Maxwell pensioners to look back on the years since 1991 and reflect that, in the end, most of the pensions continue to be paid. Not all the missing money has been recovered, but there has been sufficient, with the contributions from banks, finance houses and other professional bodies paid under the Cuckney deal, for those who are already receiving retirement benefits to continue to be paid. Thousands of pensioners have missed out, however, on discretionary increases, and there have been rows over lump sums and additional voluntary contributions. But the spectre of tens of thousands of pensions simply vanishing, thus reducing to poverty retired people who had contributed to schemes for twenty years, never materialized. On the other hand, those coming up to retirement whose schemes were robbed have found their options severely limited, since lack of funds forced trustees to take a harsh view of applications for early retirement or sickness pensions, although payments have been met for those retiring normally.

Those who fought for justice for the pensioners have also paid a heavy price. Seventy-year-old Ivy Needham, who was appointed MBE by the Queen for her campaigning efforts on behalf of the Maxwell pensioners, is convinced that, in the Leeds area alone, at least a hundred of the pensioners have died prematurely as a result of the strain and uncertainty arising from what Robert Maxwell did. Indeed, this woman who once chained herself to the railings outside Parliament in a fruitless effort to speak to the Prime Minister or the Social Security Secretary, is now blind herself. One of her lieutenants who helped organize that particular lobbying trip to London died of a heart attack, and another of a stroke, on the eve of the visit. Both deaths, she says, were brought on by stress and worry.

Meanwhile, what has become, or will become, of the Maxwell brothers? When, in February 1996, the verdict was read out, Ian Maxwell wept, while his brother went over to shake the hands of each and every member of the jury. Of the two, Ian had always been the more relaxed character, and also the more emotional. Former colleagues described Kevin, on the other hand, as the 'typical buttoned-up product of a public school'. Ian was always well liked; affable by nature, he was once even described by his father as a 'natural PR man'. Kevin, it appears, has few friends, though those he does have, mainly dating from his university days (he went to Balliol, Oxford, as did Ian), have remained loyal to him throughout the ordeal, and he enjoys a strong relationship with his wife, Pandora. True, the couple were forced to sell their £1 million-plus neo-Georgian home in Chelsea and a converted barn near Ipsden, in Oxfordshire, after his father's death. His wife's family, however, have helped Kevin and his dependants to maintain an upper-middle-class lifestyle, buying them the sixteen-bedroom Moulsford Manor, a sixteenth-century manor house set in some ten acres on the Berkshire-Oxfordshire border. Relatives and godparents have chipped in to pay fees for those of the couple's children (there are now six) attending school. It is not a bad lifestyle for the man who had built up £406.5 million in debts when he was made Britain's biggest ever bankrupt in 1992. Pandora was not in court to see the brothers cleared. Interviewed outside her home, she said, 'It's been a difficult time but now it's over.'

Although Ian nominally enjoyed equal seniority with Kevin in the Maxwell empire, their father having made a point of jointly promoting both sons, his only expertise was in marketing and he found it difficult to cope with the intricate financial dealing. At one time a director of 200 companies, Ian Maxwell now seems far more comfortable as a consultant at Westbourne Communications, a business consultancy started by

Jean Baddeley, his father's former personal assistant, and who worked with the man for thirty years. Kevin works there too; both receive a modest £20,000 a year. Ian's lifestyle did not suffer unduly, either, during the long wait for his case to come to court. He managed to avoid bankruptcy by raising £500,000 demanded by the liquidators. Nevertheless, he and his American-born wife, Laura, were forced to sell their luxurious Belgravia flat and rent a house in slightly less fashionable Eaton Terrace (which is also in Belgravia). They then moved to the considerably less chic London Borough of Hackney, in a three-bedroom home before splitting up.

It might have been thought that, with the case over, the protagonists would now live happily ever after. At the time, however, that was by no means certain, for it seems that what their father did continues to haunt his sons. A few days after the not guilty verdicts had been recorded, the Serious Fraud Office announced that it intended to go ahead with another trial. This was always going to be a controversial decision in view of the long, complex, extremely costly, and ultimately failed prosecution that had preceded it. Kevin Maxwell (this time, Ian was not to be prosecuted) condemned the decision as a political move in the run-up to a general election – a view rejected by both the Attorney-General, Sir Nicholas Lyell, and by Opposition (principally Labour) politicians. The SFO insisted that its decision had been taken on purely legal grounds, having considered many factors including the burden of future proceedings on the defendants. Richard Lissack, QC, who had taken over as lead prosecution for the SFO, told the Old Bailey that the decision had been reached only after 'careful and painstaking' consideration of many competing factors. The truth was, however, that the SFO found itself in a no-win situation. If it went ahead with more trials, it would be accused of being an oppressive prosecutor and a bad loser after the not guilty verdicts in the first trial; if it dropped the outstanding charges it might face accusations of weakness. Explaining the SFO's decision in greater detail, Lissack said that the jury in the earlier proceedings had considered only two of the ten charges variously brought against the six defendants, and that only a fifth of the evidence in the case had been heard. The SFO would therefore proceed on five charges, he stated. Three of those were concerned with alleged frauds against banks involving the use of shares in Berlitz, the language publisher formerly owned by Maxwell Communication Corporation. The other two charges concerned a £50 million loan obtained by Mirror Group Newspapers.

Those to be prosecuted were Kevin Maxwell, Larry Trachtenberg and two former Maxwell directors, Albert Fuller and Michael Stoney. The charges involved £100 million and, according to Lissack, 'represented a most serious course of dishonest conduct by those at the heart of the Maxwell group'. However, he added that the SFO 'did not consider it right to continue prosecuting Mr Ian Maxwell, whose role in the alleged frauds had never been regarded as central,' and the latter was therefore acquitted of the one outstanding charge against him. The SFO confirmed, too, that it was dropping, on health grounds, its prosecution of Robert Bunn, the former finance director of the Robert Maxwell Group, following the heart attack which had led to his being discharged from the first trial, although 'But for his health problems we would most certainly take a different course,' Lissack told the court. However, Bunn remained on the indictment, accused of being a co-conspirator in the alleged Berlitz fraud. The SFO's announcement was denounced as 'oppressive' by defence lawyers. Alun Jones, QC, for Kevin Maxwell, said the decision to bring a second prosecution was 'nothing less than an outrage'. In addition, a new judge might have to be appointed – Lord Justice Phillips, who was promoted to the Court of Appeal in 1995, had been asked only to take charge of the first trial.

Needless to say, the cost to the SFO of bringing more trials was likely to add up to £2 million to the tally for the Maxwell trials already, costs which would have pushed Britain's costliest trial even further from the realm of ordinary court proceedings. With the defendants once again having to claim legal aid from the state, it was thought that the total cost of bringing all the Maxwell-related cases would have moved upwards from £25 million to £30 million. Robert Maxwell would once again have featured heavily in a new trial, and he remained a named co-conspirator on the two indictments for two of the charges. The media tycoon – noted for his heavily litigious nature, whereby he used his power and wealth, via the courts, to shield his business affairs from prying eyes – was now truly *ex parte* from beyond the grave. There is a rich irony in that, which perhaps only he would have appreciated.

The Maxwell story hardly needed another dramatic twist, but as is the way when life imitates art, the fact turned out to be less fantastic than the fiction. So at the end of September 1996, Mr Justice Buckley called off a second trial saying it would not be in the public interest. To pursue the defendants, Kevin Maxwell, Larry Trachtenberg and Albert Fuller, 'in the face of the jury's unanimous verdict in the first trial would test both the public's confidence and the integrity of the system,' he said.

In making his decision, the judge said he'd decided that to put the defendants through the stress of another long trial after what they and their families had already had to endure would be unfair and oppressive and would run the risk of suggesting to the public that the authorities did not accept the jury's verdict.

His decision once again threw the spotlight on trial by jury in the case of complex fraud cases. The Serious Fraud Office has no official policy on the issue of ending trial by jury in such cases but behind the scenes many of its prosecutors now believe that the time has come for such reform. One source said that Mr Justice Buckley's ruling would send the 'horrendous' message to fraudsters that they can make their crime as large as they like, confident that the bulk of it could never be tried in a criminal court.

Mr Richard Lissack QC for the prosecution put these arguments to the judge at the hearing. Mr Justice Buckley, however, rejected that argument. 'To accept Mr Lissack's submission is to accept that in a serious and complex fraud, the limitations of jury trial prevent the prosecution from presenting a case which fairly and adequately represents the fraud alleged. If that is so, then jury trial is unfair and inappropriate. Since we have a jury system we should all accept their verdicts. In the Maxwell case that is long overdue. I accept the jury's verdict. These proceedings are stayed,' he said.

So ended the Maxwell saga – in a most unsatisfactory way for the prosecuting authorities. In such high-profile fraud cases there is always the feeling that the public thirsts for blood – someone must be guilty and they must be made to pay. But not in this case. So what was the cost? As we have seen, the failure to convict in the Maxwell case led to renewed calls for jury trials to be dropped in complex fraud cases. The global cost of the criminal proceedings is said to be between £20 million and £30 million. The cost of legal aid – from the public purse – for the six defendants, was nearly £9 million and the average administrative cost of a Crown Court jury trial was £2100 for each of the 131 days.

18

BCCI –
The bank of crack, cocaine and ice

From its very inception, the Bank of Credit and Commerce International had high ideals to live up to. The bank's founder had sold the idea of a Muslim bank to an Arab world rich on petro-dollars but sick of being treated as second-class citizens by Western countries. The bank was founded in 1972 by Agha Hassan Abedi, a Pakistani businessman and a Shi'ite Muslim, and from the word go the idea of having their own international bank which could compete with the best in the West was attractive to modern Muslims. One of the major supporters of BCCI in the early days was the ruler of Abu Dhabi and President of the United Arab Emirates, Sheikh Zayed bin Sultan Al Nahyan. His involvement was to cost him a great deal of money when the bank finally collapsed in 1991.

At the outset, BCCI and its philosophical founder decided that the bank would be run upon a strange mix of scripture and stricture; indeed, the business even employed a team of management consultants whose task was to blend traditional Muslim thought into the operations of a major finance house. Thus the topic for the BCCI annual conference held in Geneva in February 1982 was 'Submission to God, Service to Humanity, Giving and Success'. So successful was the discussion in Switzerland that it was followed up in March of 1983 with another gathering at the Inn on the Park in London. Less than two weeks later Abedi wrote to all his staff:

> As BCCI has always endeavoured to care for your spiritual and psychological needs, no less than your material requirements, it has been decided to implement the theme of '82 by initiating the process of giving. You will be paid $2\frac{1}{2}$% of your present salary for the year on 8 April for giving to any individual or cause in fulfilment of your instinct and good judgement.

Nor was this a single, isolated example. Abedi continued the theme by writing again to what he described as 'all members of the BCCI family', and saying that: 'It is in the medium of Giving that life flows into life, and God's divinity in all its embracing fullness, shines and rains softly, smoothly and blissfully on His creation.'

BCCI was to some extent run like a cult. At gatherings of top executives, Abedi would do most of the talking whilst his staff listened in spellbound silence. All the key players in the BCCI story spoke with a religious fervour about such weighty matters as the psyche and spirit of the bank, and the moral and philosophical dimensions of management. Often people would be invited to speak from the floor when the spirit moved them, and would not infrequently dissolve in floods of tears while proclaiming their gratitude to Abedi for allowing them to be involved with BCCI. Abedi himself would thank the Abu Dhabi shareholders for 'their financial support and, more than that, for the support they have provided through their kindness and by lending us all their influence and prestige ...'

So how did it come about that a bank which, having been set up with $2.5 million in 1972, became a worldwide operation in 70 countries, with 400 branches and a capital base of $23 billion, could be allowed to fail? There are two very different answers. The conventional wisdom in the West is that BCCI was corrupt from the start, and that, as Robert Morgenthau, Manhattan's District Attorney, told the world on

Monday, 29 July 1991, its operations constituted 'the largest bank fraud in world financial history'. He went on to accuse 'the bank, its founder Abedi and former chief executive Swaleh Naqvi, of swindling up to $20 billion from depositors around the world'. 'The essence of the scheme,' Morgenthau told pressmen, 'was to convince depositors and other banking and financial institutions, by means of false pretences, representations and promises, that the BCCI group was a safe financial repository and institution for funds.' He spoke of bribery, theft and false accounting – and he added that the intention, from the start, had been to deceive. 'The corporate structure of BCCI was set up to evade international and national banking laws so that its corrupt practices would be unsupervised and remain undiscovered.' Certain bank employees, he went on, 'systematically falsified the capital structure of BCCI to make it appear as though it was a solvent, profitable bank secured by the backing of wealthy businessmen from the Middle East. In fact, much of the bank's capitalization and assets were fictitious and its banking illusory.' An appearance of respectability was created by 'persuading world leaders to appear with them whilst defrauding their thousands of depositors, both small and large, who relied on the appearance of respectability'.

This sort of public pronouncement, however, deeply offended, and still offends, the rich Arab supporters of the bank, who to this day believe that the authorities were wrong to close the bank down. Their views form the second opinion as to how and why BCCI came to collapse. The members of this group, almost all of them experienced and influential people from the world of finance, believe that they were not adequately consulted, and that if they had been kept fully informed a formula could have been worked out that would have kept the bank afloat. To some extent they see the collapse of BCCI as yet another Western conspiracy. Typical of this view are remarks made by Sheikh Khalid bin Mahfouz, whose family are bankers to the Saudi royal house. Sheikh Khalid was chief operating officer of the National Commercial Bank, the largest finance house of its kind in Saudi Arabia, and in the mid-1980s decided that, given NCB's ambitious plans for international expansion, a link-up with BCCI would be a move in the right direction. In 1986, therefore, NCB purchased a 30 per cent stake in BCCI, and Sheikh Khalid joined the latter's board as a non-executive director. He also acquired a substantial stake in First American Bank (which had secretly been bought by BCCI) and at the time of BCCI's closure had more than $200 million on deposit there. He has recently settled with BCCI's liquidators, the accountants Touche Ross, paying them $245 million for oustanding claims against him and NCB. For a time Sheikh Khalid faced charges in New York and civil action in five countries because he had been a board member of BCCI; claims against him totalled $30 billion.

In an interview in the *Financial Times*, Sheikh Khalid said that he had known nothing of the fraud within the bank, but that he had realized that changes had been necessary in order to upgrade the skill levels of executives. He went on to recall that 'the quality of discussion' at board meetings had been low, with some directors falling asleep and others discussing topics which included miniskirts. During his time on the BCCI board he had called for cost cutting, the appointment to the board of directors of internationally recognized bankers, and the shifting of the regulation of the bank to the UK or the US. Publicly, however, Sheikh Khalid does not criticize the bank's founder, Agha Hassan Abedi, being quoted in that same interview as saying that, 'if he [Abedi] had not become sick I believe what happened would not have happened. We should not judge a person just by one aspect of his life.' Like many businessmen and commentators from the Middle East, Sheikh Khalid believes that the regulators should not have closed down BCCI: 'It was a great mistake. They could have helped the bank without closing it.' Even now, therefore, the BCCI case manages to arouse strong passions in those involved, convictions which clash across the cultural divide.

The BCCI fraud, like many others I have examined or reported, is both simple and complex. Often in fraud cases a network of organizations or transactions – or both – is found to have been put in place in order deliberately to obscure the true nature of the financial movement. This is undoubtedly true in the case of BCCI. There are, however, and again as in many fraud cases, certain identifiable traits, certain landmark events in the genesis of the fraud, which stand out. It was no coincidence that, year after year, Agha Hassan Abedi would trumpet his bank's rising profits. BCCI was a huge success story, a rapidly growing and highly profitable Third World enterprise that had succeeded in breaking down the barriers of, and moving in on, the traditional Western sources of finance. Abedi's comments on the group's 1980 results were typical: announcing an 84 per cent increase in profits, he said that this 'increasing return on earlier investments' showed that BCCI's 'policy for establishing a global network within a reasonably short passage of time' was, of course, the right strategy. Swaleh Naqvi echoed his boss's view: 'The balance sheet is the proof of the reality of our vision.' But the balance sheet masked a totally different reality. From the very beginning, BCCI had ignored every principle of sound banking. The result, not surprisingly, was that the group soon had a huge volume of high-risk loans which had been made to a small number of clients. The most notable example was to the Gulf Group – a collection of shipping and commodity companies run by the Gokal family of Pakistan. Abedi had lent hundreds of millions of dollars to the Gokals, thereby helping to turn the company into an international business empire. In so doing, however, he had tied the fate of the Gulf Group and the bank inextricably together. The Gulf Group owed BCCI so much money that a failure of the former would have been a disaster for the latter. It is difficult to assess what role the Gokals' debts played in bringing down BCCI – but according to a survey by Price Waterhouse, BCCI's auditors, in 1991, over the fifteen years during which the Gokals banked with BCCI they had 750 accounts and total turnover was $15 billion. Moreover, loans to the Gulf Group were made in an extremely relaxed, even cosy manner; if the Gokals required a loan, rather than approaching the credit officer, they went directly to Abedi himself. He would then instruct

Naqvi to draw the funds, paying little attention to such formalities as loan documents, statistical reviews of credit worthiness, or the volume of debt already owing to BCCI. One story tells of a company official signing for a large sum of money on tissue paper with the name 'Mickey Mouse' – the bank official simply screwed up the paper and threw it away. This casual approach to business became most dangerous in the late 1970s, when the international shipping market contracted sharply. As early as 1978, according to Price Waterhouse, the Gulf Group companies were running into difficulties, with the result that their BCCI accounts needed some massaging. In their 1991 report, the accountants stated that: 'It appears that account manipulation began at this stage, and to this end a "special duties" department was set up to oversee these accounts.' This was a full-time occupation which involved the manufacture of documentation, inflation of account turnover and concealment of fund flows, amongst other 'duties'. The Gulf managers themselves knew only too well what the situation was. In 1979 a meeting of all the managers of the Gulf Group shipbroking offices was convened in Monte Carlo. It lasted two days, and everyone who attended thought that there would be widespread redundancies. At the end of the second day the Gulf Group boss, Abbas Gokal, delivered his closing speech. To everyone's surprise he announced, not a shrinking of the business, but a plan to set up a large number of offices in the areas bordering the Persian Gulf and the Red Sea. The suggestion is that, some days before the meeting, Abbas Gokal had left for Kuwait. He had returned two days later with a cheque in his pocket reputed to have been for $1.4 billion – the money is said to have come from BCCI.

Abedi also engaged in other reckless practices, which included making large loans to 'insiders' – a specialist term for shareholders, directors and officers of the bank. When, for example, the First American takeover battle began in 1978, lawyers for the US bank discovered that a number of BCCI shareholders were also borrowers. The Gokals, of course, may also have been insiders, since it is believed that they provided some of BCCI's start-up capital. The ruler of Abu Dhabi, Sheikh Zayed, the most important shareholder, was either unaware of these practices or did nothing to stop them, while the other founding shareholder, Bank of America, soon discovered that things were far from being right. In late 1977, Bank of America cut its stake in BCCI from 30 per cent to 24 per cent, and in 1980 it pulled out entirely; indeed, so eager was it to withdraw that it lent money to a BCCI-linked unit in the Cayman Islands, ICIC Overseas Limited, so that the latter could buy the shares on BCCI's behalf. The bank regulators, too, were largely ignorant of the malpractice. Abedi had organized BCCI in such a way that no single regulatory authority had a worldwide view of its activities. During its early years the only regulatory setback had come in 1978, when the Bank of England, concerned about too rapid expansion, had frozen the bank's British branches at a total of forty-five.

The first regulator to take a serious look at BCCI was an American bank examiner, Robert Bench, deputy controller for international banking at the Office of the Comptroller of the Currency, the US Government's regulatory agency whose primary responsibility is for nationally chartered banks. In early 1978 an investigation was ordered into BCCI. The man who had the task of trying to keep track of the Middle Eastern bank and its activities was Joseph Vaez, who worked from the Comptroller of the Currency's office in London, and whose main job was to monitor the British operations of US banks, including, naturally, Bank of America. The report Vaez submitted noted that BCCI was an 'extremely complex conglomerate', that complexity making it very difficult to understand how the pieces fitted together. He went on to say that it was impossible to calculate how much money had been borrowed by BCCI or companies associated with it, including the Cayman Islands firms grouped under the name ICIC, themselves major shareholders in the bank. When dealing with a financial institution, it is important to be able to access details of all the parts of the group simultaneously, since nowadays money can be moved from one unit to another extremely quickly. But although it was difficult for Vaez to comprehend fully what was happening, he was able to detect certain worrying trends. One warning could be discerned in the bank's phenomenal growth rate. Rapid growth in loans can mean that the bank making those loans is not paying enough attention to the risk associated with its borrowers, or that it is concentrating its loans in the hands of a small number of individuals. From early 1976 to September 1977, BCCI's loans had almost doubled – from $511 million to $1.08 billion. Moreover, the way in which this lending was being funded was also unusual. Most foreign banks with a base in London funded a large part of their US dollar lending by tapping into the inter-bank market, in which banks deposit money with each other. But not BCCI – most of its $2 billion in deposits came, according to Vaez, from 'wealthy Arabian sources', and was 'mainly generated in the United Arab Emirates'. Vaez also had doubts about BCCI's lending procedures. His report referred to the bank's 'highly personal relationships with major clients', as well as to delays in reporting loans to its own board and its weak credit analysis and loan documentation.

Sizeable loans to insiders, which would become a BCCI trademark in later years, also served as a warning of too heavy a risk burden. Some of BCCI's biggest borrowers were members of the ruling families of the United Arab Emirates (UAE), and many of those states were also shareholders. The emirate of Sharjah had borrowed more than $75 million, while in the UAE as a whole there was a total of $203 million of property loans, about half of which were guaranteed by the states' ruling families. As will be seen later, the buck stopped at the door of the richest UAE ruler, and the benefactor not only of BCCI but also of the other sheikhdoms, Sheikh Zayed of Abu Dhabi.

One of Vaez's most telling findings showed that BCCI imposed no internal maximum lending limit; in Western banks, a rule of thumb applied which limited to 10 per cent of its capital the amount any bank should lend to any one borrower.

At the time of the Vaez report, BCCI's total capital was $63 million, which meant that (in theory, at least) the bank might have been unwise to have lent more than around $6 million to any individual client. However, loans to the Gokals' Gulf group totalled $185 million – three times the bank's capital and thirty times the amount indicated by the accepted ratio. Nor was this just a matter of academic theory, for if the Gokals failed to repay just a third of their loans then the bank's capital would have been wiped out and it would have gone out of business. Furthermore, BCCI also had many questionable loans for which repayment was not assured. Between June 1976 and September 1977, loans of this type had risen from $27 million to $226 million. Again, the biggest problem area here by far was the Gulf Group, for which more than $120 million in loans, out of the total of $185 million, were categorized as substandard. As a result, BCCI was confronted with a dilemma – it could either cut down its loans to the Gulf Group, and thereby risk the collapse of the group which would probably bring down the bank as well, or it could cover up the true situation in order to deceive regulators and auditors about the level of bad debt.

Abedi and Naqvi took the latter course. What they did was to offload bad loans to accounts in the Cayman Islands, where banking supervision was virtually non-existent. To oversee all this they set up the 'special duties' department, already mentioned, which was based at BCCI's Leadenhall Street headquarters in the City of London, only a few hundred yards away from the British banking regulatory authority, the Bank of England. All of this department's staff were Pakistani in origin, most of them Shi'ites whose families came from around Lucknow, and all were deeply loyal to Abedi and Naqvi. Typical of those employed was Hasan Mahmood Kazmi. His ties with Abedi were ancestral, and went back centuries to the days of the rajahs of Mahmudabad, near Lucknow – Kazmi's forebears had been servants, whilst Abedi's were courtiers. Apart from such historical and familial links, Abedi provided first-rate terms for these staff. They were not encouraged to mix with other BCCI employees, but their financial rewards more than made up for their isolation. Often brought over directly from Pakistan, the special duties staff were paid well; in addition, BCCI granted nearly all of them sizeable loans which the bank knew would probably never be repaid. And if any of these trusted clerks actually decided to leave a handsome cheque was often enclosed with the leaving card. Jamshid Khan, who handled the accounts of Kamal Adham, received $300,000 when he left (Adham was a former head of Saudi intelligence, a major BCCI investor, and a brother-in-law of King Faisal, who had ruled Saudi Arabia from 1964 until his death in 1975). Another employee, Hashem Sheikh, walked away with $1.7 million from Naqvi under similar circumstances.

These were large sums by any standards, but for people essentially engaged in clerical work such payments were staggering. But, of course, it was not just clerical work they were doing – and they were also being rewarded for their discretion, since the whole setup was highly confidential. In addition, it was not enough for BCCI simply to move its bad loans to the Cayman Islands – bank officials also used a series of dummy companies to shift loans from one place to another. As soon as the Gokal accounts were moved to the Caymans, Naqvi and Hashem Sheikh began to manipulate them, moving the money about to make it look as though regular interest payments on the loans were being made.

At the same time the bank moved its depositors' money into many of those Cayman Islands accounts which had been set up to disguise the level of debt. By booking excessive interest payments and other charges against the Gokal loans, for example, BCCI could even boast that it too was making a profit! Once this mechanism for moving money about had been established it became easy for those in charge to take money directly from depositors. As the looting gathered pace transfers were made to less regulated companies like ICIC, Capcom and other BCCI satellites, as well as to senior BCCI officials. For example, in March 1985 ICIC approved an interest-free loan to Swaleh Naqvi of £325,000. Abedi clearly thought that the loan should not be paid back; indeed, he later asked that the debt be written off and that Naqvi be paid £3,000 a month. This was the ultimate abuse of trust. Abedi and his associates had turned a Third World institution into a mechanism for robbing depositors, who by and large came from the developing world themselves. The beneficiaries of the scam were the rich sheikhs from the Middle East; more directly, though, the people who profited most were BCCI's associates around the world and the bank's management.

What the top management at BCCI were doing was akin to the fraud immortalized by the Italian-American swindler, Charles Ponzi, during the 1920s, and after whom such scams are named. Ponzi offered returns well above market expectations, and to make them he dipped into the money sent to him by other investors. This fraud works well whilst the money keeps pouring in, but eventually it produces an ever-widening hole in the accounts which simply cannot be plugged. In Ponzi's case he collected more than $15 million in less than a year by offering to double depositors' money within six months; for a while he himself prospered, and was able to move from a shabby top-floor apartment to a twenty-acre estate with a heated swimming pool.

As the fraud at BCCI grew, so too grew the need for cash – and the bank's management took to 'gambling' with depositors' money in an ever more desperate attempt to keep the holes in the balance sheets covered up. If a bank needs additional deposits then its treasury department raises the money in the inter-bank market, or issues certificates of deposit to investors. If the bank has surplus cash, the treasury department places it in the inter-bank market or invests in short-term instruments such as US Treasury bills and certificates of deposit. The treasury department is also responsible for dealing in foreign exchange markets. At conservative banks, the treasury department tries to raise money cheaply and avoid losses. More aggressive banks regard their treasury departments as potential profit centres, hoping that its traders can make money by moving more skilfully than other players in the market. BCCI's treasury department quite literally bet the bank in an attempt to cover up the fraud.

The chief trader at BCCI was Syed Ziauddin Ali Akbar who, when he left the bank in 1986, gave Naqvi a detailed summary of just how badly his department had done. Akbar's most spectacular losses came in the years between 1983 and 1985, during which he had betted on the prospective course of US interest rates by investing in options to buy US Treasury bonds at a particular yield on a particular date in the future. He was not lucky – between 1982 and 1986 he accumulated losses of $849 million. At the time time, however, he had inflated profits by more than $100 million in 1982, $136 million in 1983 and $234 million in 1984. To cover up the losses, Akbar used $400 million from deposits that were not even recorded in BCCI's books, $250 million of money managed by ICIC, as well as bogus loans, deposits from the bank's Abu Dhabi subsidiary, and funds from other sources. More than $60 million of the unrecorded deposits belonged to the government of Cameroon, in West Africa, but the biggest loser here was the Feisal Islamic Bank, based in Cairo and controlled by the Saudi ruling family.

BCCI's reckless lending and trading – and the looting of deposits to cover up losses – left Abedi, Naqvi and their associates little choice but to continue to steal ever more money in order to cover up what was happening and thus prevent the whole edifice from crashing down. Huge sums were plundered from depositors and routed through various accounts to make it appear that loans were being serviced in a timely fashion. In 1986 alone the special duties department moved $1.6 billion through a maze of accounts, many through BCCI's Swiss unit, Banque de Commerce de Placements. The major task that the top management of BCCI faced by the mid-1980s, therefore, was to keep the bank afloat without fraud being detected. It was a task that demanded a continued and massive influx of funds. When they found that legitimate deposits were drying up they turned to depositors who might be more concerned about secrecy than security – the drug barons of Latin America.

To international bankers one of the mystifying facts about BCCI was that it seemed able to thrive in markets in which other foreign banks found it difficult, if not impossible, to make a profit. Nigeria, Hong Kong and the UAE were three examples – and, of course, there was also Panama. Indeed, it was to Panama that BCCI turned when considering its first investment in Latin America – the last part of the Third World to have the dubious pleasure of being placed on the BCCI global map. The bank opened its Panama office in 1979. Throughout the early 1980s other banks were expanding their network across the continent in a mad scramble to lend money to the governments of Latin America, but this all came to an end in the debt crisis of 1983. BCCI's expansion, however, actually dates from that time because what its management was interested in was not lending money, but taking it in. Panama became a regional centre for the laundering of drugs money (that is, turn it from 'dirty' drugs money into legitimate money – so called because the cash goes in dirty and comes out clean) – and the Panamanian head of state, General Manuel Noriega, took a cut of the funds going through his country. Noriega had accounts with BCCI, as did many drugs traders from the United States, Colombia, and other regional drugs centres like Jamaica.

The BCCI networks in the UAE and in Hong Kong also thrived on drugs money – both are major centres for laundering the proceeds of heroin sales. Banks in the UAE catered to traffickers from the 'Golden Crescent' countries like Pakistan, Iran and Afghanistan. Hong Kong branches received huge sums from the world's leading opium-producing region, the 'Golden Triangle', which comprises parts of Burma, Thailand and Laos. One of BCCI's customers in Hong Kong was General Khun Sa, a Burmese warlord who was said to control up to 80 per cent of the region's opium trade; in mid-1991, it was estimated that he had deposited at least $300 million with BCCI. There were BCCI drugs accounts in the United States, too. One client of the bank's Miami branch was a Nigerian, Oluntende ('Steve') Fafowora – in 1987, a federal jury in Washington, DC, convicted him of racketeering and conspiracy to distribute heroin. Fafowora deposited money with BCCI in the name of a company called Afro-Caribbean Connections, which the US Government prosecutors described as 'a sham corporation through which Fafowora invested his drugs proceeds'. Internal records from BCCI show that the financial transactions of Fafowora's company were indeed consistent with money laundering, because all of the deposits were in cash and cashier's cheques.

But it was in Panama that BCCI enjoyed, at least for a time, its greatest success in attracting drugs money. The man responsible for this impressive track record, if it can be called that, was Amjad Awan. In many ways he was a typical BCCI senior manager. Born in Kashmir in 1947, into an elite Pakistani family, he was the son of Ayub Awan, one of the country's highest-ranking police and intelligence officials. Amjad Awan graduated from Punjab University with a degree in economics and went to work for an investment bank in Pakistan, later joining United Bank, which was then being run by Abedi. Awan moved to Britain in 1971, where he continued to work for United Bank for five more years, after which he joined a subsidiary of the Bank of Montreal and worked in Canada, London and Dubai. Along the way he became a British citizen and married the daughter of one of Pakistan's most prominent politicians – Asghar Khan, later an unsuccessful candidate for the post of Prime Minister following General Zia's death in 1988. In December 1978 Awan was hired by BCCI as marketing manager for its City of London branch. At the time his immediate superior, Allaudiln Shaik, was involved in negotiations to open a BCCI branch in Panama. One of the Panamanians cultivated by officials of the bank was the country's Ambassador to Britain, Guillermo Vega, who was very close to Noriega, then a high-ranking intelligence officer. Shaik and Awan met with the Ambassador and with Panamanian officials who visited London, including Noriega, and Awan asked the latter for help in obtaining a licence to establish a branch in Panama. A short time later the application was granted and in 1979 the bank duly opened an office on via España in Panama City. The following year Awan was offered a choice of jobs in Britain, Zambia or Panama; he chose to become BCCI's country manager in Panama, and left Britain early in 1981. One of his first phone calls on arrival in Panama City was to Noriega.

At that time General Noriega was head of G2, the intelligence branch of the Panamanian National Guard, but in 1981, when President Torrijos was killed in a plane crash, he effectively became head of state. At some time during the next year Noriega told Awan that he wanted to open an account with BCCI, which he described as a secret service account. Noriega said that he required total secrecy about this account, and Awan assured him of that. During the next few years the General moved tens of millions of dollars through BCCI – the highest bank balance was said to be in the region of $25 million. His wife, Felicidad, also put money into the account – sometimes up to $500,000 in cash at a time.

In 1983, Noriega transferred his account from Panama City to London because he felt it would be more secure there. As he became more and more powerful in Panama, so he received increasing amounts of money from drugs traffickers anxious to buy his approval for the transit of their wares through the country. Some of Noriega's cronies who were involved in the drugs trade were also BCCI customers, including Enrique ('Kiki') Pretelt and Cesar Rodriguez; both men were partners of the General in a variety of businesses, including drug trafficking. Their banker, like Noriega's, was Amjad Awan.

In 1983 Pretelt and Rodriguez brought an American, Steven Michael Kalish, to Noriega. Kalish began selling drugs at high school in Texas during the 1960s. He dropped out of school in the 1970s and became a full-time marijuana importer, but after a conviction in Texas he moved to Florida and took on a business partner, Leigh Bruce Ritch. Based in Tampa, the two of them operated a sophisticated smuggling and distribution network. They had computers, private planes, money-counting machines – and lots and lots of money to feed into those machines. Between 1981 and 1985 they imported 500,000 pounds of marijuana and 3,000 pounds of cocaine into the United States. The marijuana alone was worth hundreds of millions of dollars, and at one point the cash they had collected actually filled rooms. Needing to find someone to handle the mountain of cash their business was generating, they made contact with Cesar Rodriguez. For months following the initial contact in September 1983 Kalish spent millions of dollars getting to know Noriega, even allowing the General free use of his LearJet to fly to and from the US. Kalish was later to say that eventually Noriega became a co-conspirator in the drug operations. Rodriguez took responsibility for the money laundering, moving millions of dollars from the Kalish-Ritch organization into bank accounts in Panama – much of it into BCCI accounts, where it was managed by Amjad Awan.

But although Awan's money-laundering credentials were second to none, he was not as efficient as a conventional banker. In 1984 he cleared $3.7 million in cheques which turned out to be forged, with the result that he was transferred out of Panama and appointed to BCCI's representative office in Washington, DC. Even though he had left Panama, however, he continued in his role as Noriega's personal banker. Then, in August 1987, he was again transferred, this time to Miami.

In Miami, Amjad Awan began doing business with a professional money launderer from Tampa, a man who claimed to have access to vast sums from the biggest names amongst the drug barons of Colombia. Awan soon began socializing with him, just as he had done with Noriega. His new friend's name, or so he said, was Robert Musella, and he proved to be a client Awan should have avoided. Musella had earlier opened an account with BCCI in Miami, and another with the bank's branch in Panama. He began depositing cheques, one of which contained a mistake; on it he had written $110,000, but in words he had put $110,300. In late November 1987, a BCCI officer in Panama, Synod Afar Hussain, telephoned Musella about the discrepancy and suggested that they meet to discuss the latter's business and the services the bank could provide. They met the following month in Miami, and in the course of the meeting Hussain told Musella that if he was trying to hide money he was going about it the wrong way because cheques could be traced. Musella bluntly replied that he was laundering drugs money, and that he was working for the biggest names among Colombia's drugs barons. Eager to help, Hussain introduced Musella to some of his BCCI colleagues, including Amjad Awan. Over the next few months they helped him launder $14 million through banks accounts in the United States, Latin America and Europe. This was, for them at least, a mistake of catastrophic proportions, because Robert Musella didn't exist – his real name was Robert Mazur, and he was an undercover agent for the US Customs Service. Mazur's dealings with BCCI were part of an elaborate sting operation aimed at catching drug traffickers and the crooked bankers who assisted them. As the BCCI men plotted with Mazur, a tape recorder concealed in his briefcase whirred away, capturing their incriminating conversations.

Robert Mazur, alias Musella, was one of two leading undercover agents in the largest exercise of its kind ever undertaken by US Customs – Operation C-Chase, so named after the apartment block in Tampa, Florida, which housed the customs agents. The agents' job was, as we have seen, to set themselves up as representatives of the Colombian drug dealers who were looking for sympathetic banks through which to launder money. Musella's colleague was Emilio Gomez. Together they first made contact with the Medellin drugs groups in December 1986 – named after Medellin, an industrial city at the foot of the Colombian Andes which became the centre of this illicit trade. In that month they met Gonzalo Mora, an exporter of lentils who told them that, under that apparently legitimate cover, he had been exporting drugs money to the United States for years; he added, however, that the people he worked with had been unable to find enough banks to take the money. Musella said that this was where he could fit in, and later took Mora to New York to introduce him to his 'distribution network'. In fact he introduced the Colombian to more undercover customs officials. Mora was sold on the idea and decided to put business Musella's way, offering him a 7 per cent cut. A short time later Mora introduced Musella to what in the drugs world is known as a 'VIP' – a major player. His name was Roberto Baez Alcaino, and he was the owner of Tiffany's jewellery shops in Los Angeles, as well as being a major dealer in Colombian cocaine. The two met in style, with Musella playing his part by flying into Panama with a beautiful Scandinavian woman on his arm. She was introduced as his associate and fiancée, but in fact Kathleen Erickson was also an undercover agent. Next day Mora took Musella and Erickson to a BCCI branch, where he told the agents that the bank had offices all around the world and had no objection to taking in large cash sums. An account was therefore opened with BCCI in the name of IDC International, and Musella made his purpose quite clear to the bank's officials, telling the manager that he represented an international operation whose sole purpose was to launder money produced by drugs trading.

During 1987, the IDC operation grew apace. Money was collected from cities in the US and sent by cable to the IDC International account in Panama; at the same time, signed cheques drawn on this account, but with the amounts left blank, were sent by Musella to Mora in Medellin before being negotiated in a sympathetic foreign exchange house, suitable amounts having been written in. While Panama's drugs money trade was being closely monitored, Noriega was living it up on the proceeds – he and Awan even went on a trip to the gambling dens of Las Vegas in March of that year.

In order to look deeper into the Medellin organization – or 'cartel', as it become known – Musella told Mora that he wanted to do some bigger deals. The latter admitted that he could not make that sort of decision himself but would have to contact his two immediate superiors, Genado Moncada, known as 'Don Chepe', and Rudolph Armbrech. Bigger deals meant more elaborate laundering, and in November 1987

Musella therefore set up a meeting with BCCI's Amjad Awan. The two men met at the Grove Restaurant in Miami, and there Musella explained to Awan that these new clients would be 'as important to Awan's bank as Lee Iacocca was to Chrysler, the only difference being that Iacocca sold cars and his clients sold cocaine'. Awan, by now more than interested, countered by saying that he had thought of a better, safer method of laundering the money. Under this system, cash would be collected from the US and transferred via cable to London or Paris, where it would be used to issue fixed-term deposits. These certificates would then be used as collateral to obtain loans, which would in turn be transferred to Panama and credited to a current account. Funds could then be taken from that account, much as was already being done with the IDC International account.

In March of the next year Musella met representatives of the Medellin cartel at the Hotel Cariari in San José, Costa Rica. The cartel boss Pablo Escobar was not there, but his aide, Javier Ospina, was among others who did attend. When they met Musella explained the money-laundering techniques to Ospina and told him of BCCI's role, adding that his contact in the bank, Awan, had many years' experience of dealing with VIPs and was General Noriega's personal banker. Ospina pledged between $12 million and $20 million which he wanted laundered. Since the plan for laundering this money aimed to make use of BCCI branches in London and Paris, Ospina and Mora were told that Armbrech and Moncada would need to go to those cities and open accounts there. In May the cartel bosses had a last meeting with Awan and Akbar Bilgrami, BCCI's Latin American manager, to discuss final details and obtain letters of introduction. The Colombian group which arrived in Paris later in May included frontman Mora and his wife, Rudolph Armbrech, who ran Escobar's finances and who also had the power to make decisions in the cartel boss's absence, and Javier Ospina, who worked for Moncada and Escobar. On touchdown, the 'tourists' were met by Nazir Chinoy, the Paris manager for BCCI, and two of his colleagues, who explained how the system was to work. Couriers would bring suitcases of dirty money to BCCI branches around America at prearranged times and swap them with identical empty suitcases brought by bank officials. The money would then be transferred by cable to BCCI in London with instructions to credit the Paris branch. Fixed-term certificates would then be issued in the name of Rudolph Armbrech, who had opened three accounts at that branch; the drugs cartel had also opened accounts with BCCI in London. BCCI in Grand Cayman and Nassau, in the Bahamas, would create a loan guaranteed by these certificates, and that loan would then be transferred by cable to Panama and credited to Moncada and IDC International. Musella would send signed cheques but with details of payee and amount left blank, against these accounts to Mora.

A complex system was devised to make it very difficult for the authorities to trace the drugs money. All the funds collected in America were to go to Tampa, Florida, from where they would be telexed to BCCI in Luxembourg, through a New York bank. From Luxembourg the funds went to London, where fixed-term certificates of deposit would be issued, which in turn were used to guarantee loans made to different companies controlled by the cartels. The cartels would in turn move their loans to their current accounts in Tampa, from where they would be sent to BCCI in Uruguay. At this point the cartels in South America were then able to gain access to the money either by going to the bank directly or by taking out a cheque which they could negotiate on the Colombian black market through foreign-exchange dealers. The organization used for the laundering operation in London was called Capcom Financial Services, whose director was Syed Ziauddin Ali Akbar, the former treasury manager at BCCI in London. In early July of 1988 a scheme involving Capcom was devised for linking up BCCI offices in London with those in Nassau. The funds for this operation by Capcom were to come from General Noriega, who by then was facing drugs charges, and as a result wanted to move his money out of Panama.

In February 1988, at a court in Florida, Noriega had faced charges connected with drugs and money-laundering offences, having been indicted by a US grand jury despite his friendly standing with the US Government, which had even tried to involve him in CIA operations. One of the accusations was that he had conspired to import into the United States, and then distribute, more than a million tons of marijuana. The chief witness in the case stated that he had passed on to Noriega almost $1 million in bribes between 1983 and 1984 in return for a diplomatic passport, a multi-million-dollar letter of credit, and safe passage for large quantities of drugs. The General was also charged with accepting $4.6 million in return for allowing Colombian ships, bearing between them more than 4,000 pounds of cocaine, to pass through Panama on their way to the United States. In addition, it was also claimed that he had permitted the Colombians to establish a cocaine processing plant on Panamanian soil.

The scene was not set for the finale, at least so far as the US Customs operation was concerned. The drugs-money-laundering operation had been brilliantly executed; and all the information was at hand – the names of the people involved, methods, routes, and so on. All that was now required was to bring together the suppliers of the drugs and the launderers of the money – and the excuse for that meeting was a wedding. The villains were told that their 'friend' and business associate, Musella, was marrying his girlfriend, Kathleen Erickson. The date and venue were set – 10 am on 9 October 1988 at the Innisbrook Golf Club and Hotel in Tarpon Springs, Florida – and everyone was invited. The ever-watchful Naqvi, however, made sure that the event would not be a complete success, from the Customs agents' point of view when he stopped the BCCI general manager from attending, on the grounds that senior people should not be too obviously linked with this sort of business.

To make the arrests even easier, the men were separated from the women by the simple expedient of holding stag and hen parties on the night before. The men were taken in limousines driven by undercover agents to the NCNB Bank building in the centre of town. They had been told that the party was to be held in the penthouse, but the lift stopped on the second floor where federal agents were waiting for them. They were then driven in the same cars to the county prison.

The news was then released to the press. A formal statement announced that eighty-five suspects had been arrested, and that some had been charged with conspiring to import illegal drugs into the United States, and others with laundering money from the sale of illegal drugs. BCCI was charged with laundering $18.8 million worth of the proceeds of the illegal drugs traffic. Nine officers of the bank were charged by name, among them Akbar Bilgrami, manager of the Latin American organization; Amjad Awan, his number two; Aftaab Usaidn, operations manager for Panama; Nazir Chinoy, Sibte Hassan and Ian Howard from the Paris operation; Asif Baakza from the corporate unit in London; the two others named were officers of BCCI in Los Angeles.

After plea bargaining, the bank was fined $14.8 million, and four of its employees received prison sentences. Though the BCCI struggled on, in a sense the case marked the beginning of the end. The small businessmen in the wider Muslim world continued to use the bank, perhaps unaware of the fine for laundering drugs money imposed in the United States. But over the next two or three years, before the final collapse, its image as a Third World success story – the charitable, moral, giving bank built by Muslims for Muslims – gave way to that of a hulk riddled with corruption. Little by little, other unpalatable facts emerged: BCCI had been actively involved in shady weapons deals, and had offered accounts to some of the world's most notorious terrorist organizations. Its customers had included Mossad, the Israeli security service; the international terrorist, Abu Nidal; the CIA – which had used the bank for Irangate payments organized by Colonel Oliver North to the Nicaraguan Contras; both the Iranian and the Iraqi governments, which had processed payments for arms through BCCI; and the secret services of Britain, France and

Switzerland. Arab terrorists had bought weapons in deals run by a BCCI manager and which had used BCCI finance, with Mossad acting as middleman. BCCI staff had also assisted Arab terrorists to smuggle arms between the US and the Communist Eastern Bloc, not only by providing the money but by assisting with fraudulent documentation. Perhaps most surprisingly of all, Arab terrorists had bought Israeli-made weapons using BCCI finance – though there are suggestions that these weapons had been sabotaged or electronically bugged before being shipped out.

BCCI was a bank that never said no – a bank that, if it had wanted to (though of course it never would do such a thing), would have pointed out to its terrorist customers that it was well used to secrecy – after all, that had been vital in its illicit drugs-money-laundering operations. Secrecy had been crucial, too, in its other American operations, in which the bank had violated US laws on bank ownership, a violation which was eventually punished by the US Government's regulatory body, the Federal Reserve, in July 1991, when it fined BCCI $200 million. In brief, what had happened was this: back in 1977, Abedi had decided that he wanted BCCI to be a truly global player. That could not be achieved without a presence in America, and he therefore set about creating that presence. The target was a bank based in Washington called Financial General, later to become First American. This bank holding company was unique in the US banking system because it was not subject to the federal law which prohibited a bank from owning another bank outside its home state. Financial General was represented in Washington, DC, Maryland, New York, Tennessee and Virginia. The view was that BCCI's link with Bank of America precluded its buying Financial General, because of the statute forbidding the ownership of another bank outside Bank of America's home state. BCCI therefore set about using nominees – men who were apparently acting on their own in trying to buy Financial General, but were in fact working for BCCI; indeed, the latter had already used this ploy to buy the National Bank of Georgia (NBG) from Financial

General. Abedi's frontman for the NBG buyout had been Ghaith Pharaon, a Saudi Arabian who had made his home in the US and who was an important investor in BCCI. Pharaon was an ideal frontman for the bank – he had mixed in high circles since coming to America in 1969 to study mining; and in 1965 he had taken a Master's degree in business administration from Harvard. The Georgia bank deal had been his first for BCCI, but he went on to front the purchase of other financial institutions like the Central Bank of Independence in California in 1985, and CenTrust, a Savings and Loan in Miami which later went bankrupt.

Using NBG almost as a Trojan Horse, Abedi was able to get to know disgruntled shareholders in its former parent company, Financial General. Among these was the late Dr Armand Hammer, the extremely powerful and influential Chairman of Occidental Petroleum, who held 5 per cent of Financial General's stock; associates of his held another 5 per cent. In addition, there was another 10 per cent of Financial General's stock on the market, and Abedi was willing to take the lot, but ran up against US banking regulations, which held that investors were not individually allowed to own more than 5 per cent of the shares. Abedi quickly found four Arab frontmen to support BCCI, each of them taking up 5 per cent of the Financial General stock available – the 10 per cent owned or controlled by Hammer, and the 10 per cent on the market. These four were the Saudi security chief Kamal Adham, right-hand man to the late King Faisal; Faisal Saud al Fulaij; Abdullah Dharwaish, who represented Sheikh Mohammad bin-Zayed, son of Sheikh Zayed and at that time too young to conduct his own affairs, and Sheikh Sultan bin-Zayed. Abedi believed that the deal would go through without a hitch, but the incumbent Chairman of Financial General, a former Secretary to the US Navy, was willing to fight. He lodged a complaint with the Securities and Exchange Commission in March 1978 arguing that the four men were acting in concert – under American law if that were the case they would not be able to own more than 5 per cent of the bank's stock between them.

To fight these allegations, Abedi hired Clark Clifford, formerly a legal adviser to both Presidents Truman and Kennedy. Alongside Clifford was Robert Altman (the husband of actress Lynda Carter, who played Wonder Woman in the eponymous television series), a man who knew his way around Wall Street and the Securities and Exchange Commission. In the bitter battle with Financial General and the Commission that followed, the two men argued that BCCI was only participating as adviser to the Arab investors, not as principals.

There is no doubt, however, that this was far from being the case. A special company had been created in the poorly regulated Netherlands Antilles, Credit and Commerce American Holdings (CCAH), together with one in the Cayman Islands, Credit and Commerce American Investments (CCAI). The US regulators were assured by Abedi that the Arabs seeking to buy stock in Financial General, who were investors with CCAH, all had substantial funds, and that the 'funds to be used by each of them to purchase their equity interest in CCAH will be provided from their personal funds'. The regulators waved BCCI through, but in fact BCCI had controlled about a quarter of CCAH's shares from the first day. In August 1982 Financial General, now effectively in the hands of BCCI, was renamed First American Bancshares. The lawyer and political fixer Clark Clifford was made managing director of CCAH, his partner Robert Altman, as well as a former Senator and client of Clifford's, Stuart Symington, became directors. Clifford and Symington were both from Missouri, and were seen as President Carter's men; as will be seen, Carter had good reason to be friendly with BCCI.

The use of frontmen to disguise the true ownership of First American was only the beginning of the First American bank fraud. A whole merry-go-round of loans, and of share buying followed by false repayments of loans, was established. Further proof of the link between CCAH and BCCI became apparent during 1986 when the 'parent' company needed new money to supplement its capital base in the wake of its disastrous treasury operations. Recapitalization was achieved by selling both BCCI shares and the CCAH shares it controlled to the bin-Mahfouz family, whose members became owners of $250 million in CCAH shares. Finally, BCCI's ownership of CCAH didn't simply amount to buying and selling its shares, for the bank actually selected and appointed its staff. As an example, Abedi himself had asked Aijaz Afridi, First American Vice-President in New York between 1983 and 1987, and formerly a BCCI employee in Luxembourg, if he wanted the New York job, and had duly had him appointed.

The acquisition of First American using offshore, so-called 'shell', companies, to put BCCI out of reach of the regulators was not an end in itself, however. The bank wanted to flex political muscle. The BCCI satellite, National Bank of Georgia, was already the biggest single lender to President Jimmy Carter's peanut farm, and Carter and Abedi were extremely idealistic when it came to Third World charities, and BCCI and its friends made substantial donations to set up the Carter Presidential Centre and Global 2000. Other notable US political figures also benefited from BCCI's generous nature. Among these were two noted sympathizers with the Arab cause – the former US Ambassador to the United Nations, Andrew Young, and the black Presidential candidate, Jesse Jackson. Young was to admit that BCCI made a loan to his consulting firm, which it was understood did not have to be paid back. He explained the loan away as a late repayment of a retainer he had been promised.

It has been suggested that such political influence, at the very least, bought BCCI time, and that the regulatory bodies were slow in getting to grips with what has turned out to be the most serious breach of their procedures, and of criminal laws relating to those procedures, this century. It is interesting to note that as early as March 1981 a former US Comptroller of the Currency, John Heimann, wrote to the Federal Reserve calling for BCCI to be closed. However, Federal Reserve officials claim that they only learnt of the secret takeover of First American, NBG, and of another finance house, the Independence Bank of Encino, California, in a telephone call from the US Customs as late as December 1988. A year later the head of the Luxembourg regulatory authority wrote to the Federal Reserve about loans made by BCCI to CCAH, but the American authority did nothing. Eventually, in January 1990, the Federal Reserve launched its own inquiry which culminated in the charges and subsequent fines of July 1991.

Now it is a fact that twelve years before BCCI was closed, its auditors had expressed concern about being unable to gain an overall picture of the bank's financial well-being. Indeed, Whinney Murray Ernst & Ernst (now part of Ernst & Young, the international accountancy firm), had written to BCCI's founder, Agha Hassan Abedi, and demanded that it be allowed to audit more companies within the group. Of course, this was the last thing Abedi wanted – but the accountants persisted, and eventually he was forced to concede the point by making Price Waterhouse sole auditors in 1986. In October 1990, however, the latter reported that BCCI management might have 'colluded with major customers to misstate or disguise the real purpose of significant transactions'. The bank's Chief Executive, Swaleh Naqvi, stepped down and Abedi severed all formal ties with the bank. In December of that year an informant told the Bank of England that there was evidence of 'substantial unrecorded deposits'. The Bank of England ordered an investigation by Price Waterhouse in March 1991; two months later, the Abu Dhabi government took over more than 4 billion dollars' worth of bad loans from BCCI. In June of that year the Price Waterhouse report landed on desks at the Bank of England – it described 'evidence of massive and widespread fraud'.

Less than two weeks later, the Bank of England closed BCCI, in a co-ordinated action with central banks in the United States, Luxembourg, France, Spain and the Cayman Islands. The then Governor of the Bank of England, Robin Leigh-Pemberton, had acted because he had not wanted to be beaten to the punch by the courts in New York, where District Attorney Robert Morgenthau was about to launch prosecutions. The Governor had previously believed that the problems could be solved, but now said that the 'culture of the bank was criminal'. In New York, Morgenthau's words and deeds were stronger. Describing BCCI as 'the largest bank fraud in history', he accused the bank, its founder Abedi, and its former Chief Executive, Naqvi, of swindling up to $20 billion from depositors around the world. Morgenthau went on to say that he wanted Abedi and Naqvi extradited to face the charges, which could carry a twenty-five-year prison sentence, and he also called for a permanent ban on involvement in any US banks by the men who had fronted the First American takeover. Abedi and Naqvi were two; the others were Kamal Adham, Ghaith Pharaon, Hassan Kazmi (secretary of the ICIC Foundation), Faisal al-Fulaij, Abdul Raouf Khalil (a Saudi Arabian property investor), El-Sayed Jawhary (an investor in Financial General), and Khuaro Elley (a BCCI executive).

Of course, with the closure of the bank and the announcement in Britain of an inquiry headed by Lord Justice Bingham, the inevitable search for the guilty began. That search focused not just on those like Abedi and Naqvi, who had retired to safer foreign climes, but also on BCCI's accountants and the regulatory authorities themselves. The question on everyone's lips was, shouldn't something have been done sooner? This is all too large a topic to be handled in a book of this kind, but in the aftermath of the collapse there were many harrowing stories of small businessmen and women across the world whose lives were now in ruins. Companies collapsed, individuals who had retired as successful entrepreneurs and put their lifes' savings into BCCI now, in the autumn of their years, were forced back on to the labour market, often working in poorly paid menial jobs to make ends meet. The scale of the losses could be calculated, at least in part – Sheikh Zayed of Abu Dhabi was the biggest loser, down by $5 billion, but he at least could afford it. Depositors in Britain lost undisclosed millions; in Spain and Gibraltar, £83 million; in Iran, $100 million; one local authority in Britain, the Western Isles Council, lost £23 million on its own, and other councils lost £30 million between them. In January 1995, after a lengthy campaign, and three and a half years after the Bank of England had closed BCCI, depositors were offered a deal by the majority shareholder, the government of Abu Dhabi. This worldwide settlement of £1.2 billion would give back to depositors between 20 and 40 per cent of their money. For some it is too little, for many too late. The nagging doubt amongst depositors arises from a feeling that if the Bank of England had not swooped, and if the Abu Dhabi government had poured more money into BCCI, would they now be better off? It is, of course, a question that cannot be answered.

In June of 1996, an appeal court in Abu Dhabi overturned the convictions of two former BCCI executives. Nasim Hassan Sheikh, a British national, and Fakhir Hussein, a Pakistani, had been detained in 1991, and were among thirteen executives of the now-defunct BCCI convicted of fraud, misappropriation and criminal breach of trust of the bank's majority shareholders. They were also ordered to pay $9.13 billion in civil damages to the bank's majority shareholder, the Abu Dhabi government. The appeal court, however, also ruled that Fakhir Hussein and Nasim Hassan Sheikh, who have served out their three-year sentences, will not have to pay the civil fines. The court did rule, though, that eight others of the thirteen originally convicted would still have to pay the $9.13 billion ordered by the lower court in 1994, plus an additional $8.3 million in civil damages.

19

Japan –
The land of the rising share price

One day in March 1992, Masahiro Dozen, the President of Daiwa, Japan's second largest brokerage house, stood before a crowd of reporters and television cameras, bowed deeply, said that he was taking responsibility, and resigned. He was standing down after it had come out that an official of the Daiwa Securities Company had approached the Tokyu department store and proposed that the latter pay more than 90 billion yen (about $675 million) for securities whose market value was only 30 billion yen. According to Tokyu, Daiwa promised that it would repurchase the securities later, at a price that would guarantee Tokyu a small profit.

This kind of scheme is only for privileged customers of brokerage houses, but it is not unusual. Indeed, the practice is so well established that it is known in the Japanese stock market as *tobashi*, or 'flying'. A client whose securities have dropped in value is spared from having to show the losses when a broker arranges for another customer to purchase them at an unrealistically high price, a practice technically prohibited when stocks are involved. Each new purchaser is persuaded to go along with an increasingly inflated price because, though an informal trade, the broker guarantees a profit no matter what happens to share prices. The stocks 'fly' from account to account. Once the market rises enough, and the market value of the securities is finally the same as that of the last rigged trade, the game stops, with everyone having profited along the way.

In Tokyu's case, however, the problem was that the Tokyo market was going through one of its vicious downward spirals, so that the market value of the securities Tokyu had bought declined even further. Faced with a loss running into hundreds of millions of dollars, Daiwa refused to repurchase at the promised price. That refusal prompted a desperate Tokyu to go to court – something which rarely happens in a society where financial transactions are almost always kept from public scrutiny.

In its defence, Daiwa claimed that one of its officials, acting alone, had initiated the deal, but that view was received with a good deal of scepticism, particularly given Daiwa's own admission that it had been involved in six other instances of *tobashi*. In the end, Daiwa and Tokyu agreed to split the losses, but the publicity surrounding the affair forced the resignation of Daiwa's President. Masahiro Dozen's fall was the latest in a string of resignations – the seventh of a top brokerage or bank executive inside a year. Moreover, what attracted interest in this case was that the scam had taken place in August 1991; that is, at the worst moment in an earlier stock market scandal. That same month, the former top executives of Nomura Securities and Nikko Securities – the largest and third largest brokerage houses in Japan – had told the Japanese parliament that their firms had for years done business with a leading figure from the world of organized crime, helping to finance what may have been a huge stock manipulation scheme. Naturally, the industry itself had promised that it was mending its ways in the wake of this scandal, and the Finance Ministry, the financial market's watchdog, had given undertakings that it was going to police the market more intensively. At precisely that moment, however, Daiwa had been arranging the *tobashi* with Tokyu.

The outsider's view of Japan is of an industrial giant with a well-drilled workforce which outperforms the West in the production of everything from cars to videos – that it is a world where hard work and discipline are the watchwords, and where the most highly regarded, and most highly rewarded, have had to serve their companies long and faithfully in order to achieve their status. But there is another world – a country where politicians, speculators, members of organized crime syndicates, and a whole host of other players, driven by greed or by a craving for political power, can dip into a vast cash machine. That machine is known officially as the Tokyo Stock Exchange.

There is no doubt that the capital which that stock exchange created was the fuel behind the five-year economic boom which began in the mid-1980s, the longest in Japan since the Second World War. Nevertheless, the Japanese securities industry has long had a slightly disreputable air about it, akin to that of a casino which can always be manipulated by the big players. In the Japanese context, these players are the so called 'Big Four' securities firms – Nomura, Daiwa, Nikko, Yamaichi – and the Government.

During the 1980s both Wall Street and the City enjoyed tremendous runs, but these were nothing compared with the Japanese stock market. For so much wealth to be created so quickly was utterly unprecedented. From the beginning of 1985 to the market peak, on the last business day of 1989, the value of shares traded on the main section of the Tokyo Stock Exchange increased by 435.5 thousand billion yen, or roughly $3.2 thousand billion. As the stock market soared in the 1980s, Japanese companies found that they could sell unlimited amounts of new shares to raise funds at rates far cheaper than those they could get from banks. In 1989, the best year, Japanese companies raised a little more than 27 thousand billion yen (around $200 billion) from selling new share- or equity-linked bonds. This was far more than these businesses actually needed for expansion and modernization; so as much as 40 per cent of the money thus raised was simply ploughed back into the market, which pushed up prices even further.

These cash-rich Japanese companies then went on a spending

binge, investing in new equipment, new plants and new technologies. They outspent their Western competitors by tens of billions of dollars, thereby buying for themselves an important edge. Much of the money was invested overseas, as well, so that Japanese enterprises acquired a vast portfolio of assets, ranging, in the US, from the Rockefeller Center in Manhattan to the Pebble Beach Golf Club and Columbia Pictures, and, in Britain, from a stake in Rover cars to the *Financial Times* building in the heart of the City.

As the Japanese financial tidal wave swept over everyone, so the Big Four brokerage houses rode in upon its crest. At the beginning of the 1980s they had been sales machines orientated towards the domestic market, employing brokers who often went from door to door. By the end of the decade, however, the market value of the Tokyo Stock Exchange was greater than that of the New York Stock Exchange. Tokyo's equivalent of the City or Wall Street is called 'Kabutocho', a word that carries a disreputable ring to Japanese ears – after all, investment bankers and brokers there are known as *kabuya*, a disparaging term which roughly translates as 'stock pedlar'. This less than approving view of such people was probably reinforced in August 1991, when two of the 'industry's' top executives made a rare public appearance before parliament. One of them had been, until a few weeks earlier, the acknowledged ruler of the Japanese financial world, before he had resigned his position as Chairman of Nomura Securities. His name was Setsuya Tabuchi.

Shortly before Tabuchi's appearance, all of Japan's major brokerage houses had admitted to making improper payoffs to cover the stock-trading losses of favoured clients. This form of compensation, uncovered by the tax authorities, clearly discriminated against the bulk of the firms' clients, particularly individuals and foreigners, who were not offered such terms. The list of the recipients of these payoffs included such giants as Toyota Motors, Hitachi and Matsushita; and government pension funds and the family of a former deputy Prime Minister, Shin Kanemaru, also benefited.

To parliament, Tabuchi described how Nomura's board of

directors had explicitly approved the payoffs, even though the directors had known that they were improper. He also gave detailed accounts of the firm's long-standing ties to Susumu Ishii – who was, until his death in September 1991, the boss of a major *yakuza* family, or organized crime group. Tabuchi explained that Ishii had been introduced to his company by a *sokaiya* – that is, a member of the underworld who specializes in corporate extortion. The *sokaiya* generally threaten to disclose embarrassing facts about companies (financial impropriety, payoffs, or the sexual liaisons of top officers), or to disrupt their annual meetings with catcalls and endless questioning. For a payoff, however, the *sokaiya* will keep the peace. According to Tabuchi, Nomura had been on such good terms with this *sokaiya* that the latter had been able to arrange a meeting between Ishii and a member of Nomura's board of directors. The director in question had then introduced Ishii to the head of Nomura's sales department, who agreed to handle the gangster's sizeable account personally. In this way, Ishii received help in raising loans to jack up his holdings in the Tokyu Corporation (a railway, retail and property concern) to 27 million shares. There was, needless to say, a handsome profit in it.

Another victim of the scandal was the Finance Ministry, long seen as the most powerful department in government, and which was supposed to be a tough overseer of the financial markets. In fact, though, the ministry's Securities Enforcement Division has a staff of only seventeen, while about sixty more monitor the market in the Investigation Division of the Securities Bureau. By contrast, the Securities and Exchange Commission in the US has 300 enforcement staff. One of the problems raised by the exposure of the share indemnity chicanery was the fact that the public received confirmation of the cosy relationship between the brokerage houses and the Finance Ministry. Yoshihisa Tabuchi, who was Nomura's President and Chief Executive until resigning as a result of the scandal in June 1991, when on the receiving end of some sustained questioning at the company's AGM, told shareholders that everything

Nomura had done had been approved by the Ministry of Finance. The ministry, upset by such public pronouncements, decided to carry out its own investigation, which resulted in – no legal proceedings, no writs issued, no public inquiry. The worst that happened to any of those involved was that they accepted a 'voluntary' pay cut.

There is a feeling in Japan that if a business has 'Inc.' attached to its name – indeed, if the name a person trades under is in fact a company name – then that company can get away with almost anything without fear of punishment. There is no doubt that the stock market has a casino-like atmosphere. For their part, brokers in Japan say that they have found that if their customers lose money they do not demand that the system be reformed, they demand some inside information which will enable them not only to get their money back, but also to show a profit on both deals. The widespread links between the big players on the stock market and organized crime are also understandable. The *yakuza* serve a very useful purpose in resolving disputes where no other mechanism exists, something which, to some extent, legitimizes them anyway. The reason for this is because in Japan litigation is almost unheard of, since it is extremely expensive, rarely produces any results which challenge the existing social framework, and is unbelievably time-consuming – cases can take more than ten years to come to court. As a result, in order to collect an overdue loan it is much more efficient to hire a member of a *yakuza* gang to stand outside the home of the debtor and hurl obscenities and insults until the defaulter gives in. Of course, securities firms often deal with the gangsters on behalf of their clients – in a way, this is just another of the services they offer to valued customers.

But if the brokerage houses have been guilty of giving preferential treatment, however improperly, to their most favoured customers, even the big banks are not immune from becoming too cosy with their valued clients. Take the case of the Industrial Bank of Japan (IBJ) which in October 1991 was the world's sixth largest. On 22 October of that year its Chairman, Kaneo

Nakamura, resigned after taking full responsibility for the bank's dealings with a sixty-one-year-old woman who had been charged with procuring illegal loans to fund stock market investment. Nui Onoue, a former waitress and self-styled mystic, had been offered credit by the bank in 1987 when IBJ reversed its traditional long-term banking policy of lending exclusively to industrial corporations and went for riskier lending to named individuals. Mrs Onoue was, at the time, a known shares speculator on the Tokyo Stock Exchange, and had once been the largest individual holder of IBJ stock. The bank lent her large sums of money, loans which reached a peak when she was in receipt of over 240 billion yen (more than £1 billion) in loans in the autumn of 1991. At around the same time, however, Mrs Onoue was arrested for allegedly using forged deposit receipts as collateral in order fraudulently to obtain loans from several financial institutions – including the Industrial Bank of Japan.

A senior IBJ director and counsellor, Kisburo Ikekura, also resigned alongside Nakamura; the latter became the eleventh financial figurehead to resign under the shadow of scandal during 1991. The Industrial Bank of Japan has always claimed that a large part of the credit for rebuilding Japan from out of the post-war ruins was due to its work – suggesting that it was as much interested in the public good as it was in turning a profit. But in the late 1980s the bank had been squeezed by competition, and by the loss of corporate-loan customers, who had begun to raise capital themselves on the securities market. Inevitably the bank tried – indeed, was forced – to seek new customers, and it found them amongst the fast-multiplying but ill-reputed stock and land speculators. The Onoue scandal revealed that IBJ had become just as greedy for profit as had other Japanese banks – of all the major city banks, Mitsubishi Bank alone escaped without having to make a public admission of involvement in scandals. Ironically, in that same year, 1991, Mitsubishi Bank found itself being branded by Tokyo's financiers as a dinosaur because it was failing to explore some of the more risky business prospects.

20

Sagawa Kyubin – The wheels come off the Japanese trucking scandal

In February 1992 police staged fourteen separate raids throughout the Japanese capital, Tokyo, in connection with shady loans and bribes allegedly paid by Sagawa Kyubin, a delivery company, to politicians, private companies and a major organized crime syndicate. The sums of money, and the number of politicians, involved were said to overshadow the Recruit affair which had toppled the government of Noboru Takeshita in 1989 – the Prime Minister in February 1992 was Kiichi Miyazawa, who had been forced to resign as Finance Minister in Takeshita's government after making conflicting statements about his role in the Recruit affair. The police also raided the headquarters of the Inagawa-kai, Japan's second biggest *yakuza* syndicate. (The *yakuza* have often been described as Japan's answer to the Mafia, and despite the simplistic analogy they are, at the very least, gangster organizations.) The homes of two former executives of Sagawa Kyubin and of the officers of companies with close ties to the delivery company were also raided. In a television interview the sixty-nine-year-old Chairman of Sagawa Kyubin, Kiyoshi Sagawa, admitted that his company had given money to politicians – for 'hiring secretaries'.

Although the scandal had been brewing for months, the investigators now had the task of unravelling the financial manipulations, kickbacks and loan guarantees allegedly undertaken by Sagawa from around 1987. The Sagawa story quickly overshadowed another political corruption case in which Fumio Abe, a former head of Miyazawa's ruling Liberal Democratic Party (LDP), had been arrested and charged with taking 80 million yen (£350,000) in bribes from Kyowa, a company which manufactured steel frames. In the Kyowa case the allegation against Abe was that when he had been Director-General of the Hokkaido Development Agency he had had passed on information about the route of a proposed motorway, so that the steel company was able to make a killing by buying property in the vicinity. Kyowa's interest in property was typical of a great many Japanese companies at the time. A long-established maker of steel frames for the construction industry, it had embraced property development after a change of management in the 1980s. Kyowa had collapsed in November 1990, however, with outstanding debts of around 200 billion yen, after an increase in interest rates and a decline in the property market had undermined its ambitious resort and golf course projects.

It is interesting to reflect here that corruption, fraud – scandal, if you like – know no ideological barriers. In America, with its open-market economy and deregulation, serious fraud raises its head from time to time; and precisely the same is true in the highly regulated Japanese economy. In Japan, the old established companies hold all the trump cards. They have the political connections, the contacts amongst the civil servants in government ministries, and they receive the lion's share of government business. New, aggressively hungry companies often feel shut out, and doors in Japan all too frequently need a little oiling if they are to open properly. What has so often happened in the past, therefore, is that bribes and kickbacks have become institutionalized amongst those new companies seeking to establish themselves in the marketplace.

By April 1992, the talk in Japan was of the Sagawa Kyubin affair, and how the company was being investigated by the Public Prosecutor's office for alleged breach of trust offences involving 528 billion yen (£2.2 billion), an amount which dwarfed the stocks-for-favours scandal and the Lockheed bribery affair of the 1970s. What seemed to shock the public the most was the upfront involvement of the *yakuza*. What the affair showed, though, was just how easily a rapidly growing, cash-rich company can attract the attention of both politician and gangster alike. In the tightly regulated trucking business, companies often called on politicians to help them cut through the red tape – and Sagawa Kyubin was a delivery business. The gangsters, however, hover around the periphery, hoping to extract money for 'settling' disputes arising from traffic accidents, and are thus an ever-present factor in the business.

At the top of his career, the group's founder, Kiyoshi Sagawa, a former building-site foreman, had dined with prime ministers and even written an autobiography, rather grandly titled: *The Penniless Emperor*. As the scandal broke around him, he became too ill to give evidence. His two most powerful executives, the fifty-seven-year-old Hiroyasu Watanabe, and Watanabe's lieutenant, Jun Saotome, were both charged with embezzling Sagawa Kyubin funds.

Kiyoshi Sagawa's business had begun in Kyowa and had expanded across Japan, mainly through acquisition, since in that way he was able to circumvent the trucking regulations. Until 1990, when a change of rules was brought in, companies needed two kinds of licences: one allowed long-haul operations on a set route; the other permitted deliveries within a region. The Transport Ministry took up to twelve months to process licence applications, but a company that had taken over another's operations could also take over its licences. The most impotant deal for the company came when Sagawa reached agreement with Watanabe, then head of a large Tokyo trucking company; in 1974 the two businesses merged, with Watanabe retaining control of the Tokyo operations, which remained a separate company and which contributed around 25 per cent of the group's profits. Sagawa Kyubin grew into Japan's second biggest delivery group, but as it did so Watanabe began to resent playing second fiddle to his brash boss. After all, it was he that was the skilful negotiator for the company, steering a course between banks, financial companies, gangsters and politicians.

In 1986 the company fell foul of the authorities. The Transport Ministry had warned it repeatedly about drivers' hours, because of the increased risk of traffic accidents, and Sagawa Kyubin was banned from trucking for twenty-five days after its practices had been criticized by a parliamentary transport committee. The company tried to improve its record, cutting drivers' hours and increasing the time allowed for holidays. But, like many Japanese companies, it began increasingly to rely on helpful politicians to smooth relations with officialdom. Again like other Japanese groups, Sagawa Kyubin rewarded its friends with political donations. Kyoshi Sagawa's political links dated back to the 1960s, when he had hired the Speaker of the upper house of the Diet (parliament) as an adviser. By the mid-1970s, and with Watanabe's aid, he had taken on Kakuei Tanaka, then Prime Minister, as a consultant to the Sagawa Kyubin group. The group, according to Japanese newspapers, paid up to 80 billion yen to more than 100 politicians, including Tanaka and other ministers.

The company's links with the *yakuza* originated, as I have mentioned, in the practice of employing gangsters to settle disputes over traffic accidents. In Japan, a person who has caused an accident is expected to pay compensation to a victim, separately from any insurance payment; *yakuza* often act on behalf of victims, taking a cut of the compensation payment for their services. The allegation against Sagawa Kyubin was that it had bought off the *yakuza en bloc* by making payments to their national bosses – more particularly, to Susumu Ishii, a former head of Inagawakai, the country's second largest crime syndicate. As the fortunes of Sagawa Kyubin prospered, so did those of Ishii. Using dummy companies, Watanabe channelled a total of 528 billion yen in loans and loan guarantees out of the company for speculative property and stock market investments. The biggest share of that money – around 114 billion yen – went to Inagawakai. According to the Public Prosecutor's office, a further 59 billion yen went to companies in which Watanabe had a personal interest, 85.7 billion yen to companies linked to his assistant, Saotome.

These links came to light in the wake of the 1990 crash in Japanese stock prices for, with the value of their assets plunging, recipients of Watanabe's largesse could no longer repay their debts. Then, too, there appears to have been a row between Watanabe and Sagawa. The latter said that he was shocked by the extent of his top executive's financial operations, and he postponed his planned retirement in order to ensure that the group did not fall into Mr Watanabe's hands. Watanabe and Saotome resigned in the summer and were arrested. As for the company, it was left facing the very real threat that a majority of its loans might never be returned. In order to spread the financial burden, it therefore planned to merge Tokyo Sagawa Kyubin with other group companies.

Of course, the political party bosses quickly found alternative funds – a by no means difficult task in a society where it is not unusual for MPs to spend the equivalent of £500,000 a year on presents and other sweeteners for their constituents and supporters, a sum which might treble or quadruple for Cabinet ministers. Japan's system of what is described as 'money politics' is so pervasive that businessmen, local councillors and a whole range of officials and special interest groups are often enmeshed in complex, but mutually beneficial, financial back-scratching. Despite reports at the time that the Sagawa Kyubin affair was 'rocking' Japan's political world, little changed – largely because all too often the high cost of being in politics leads politicians to accept payment from many different sources. After all, neither the Lockheed bribery-for-orders scandal of the 1970s nor the more recent Recruit affair had produced any very marked effect, at least in terms of stamping out corruption in business and political life. The ruling LDP party had vowed to purge itself of 'money politics' after Recruit, but even so several prominent political figures were implicated in the Sagawa Kyubin scandal. The affair did, however, bring about the resignation of the most powerful politician within the ruling Liberal Democratic Party, Shin Kanemaru, and Kiyowshi Kaneko, the influential Governor of the prefecture of Nigatea, in western Japan, was questioned on suspicion of having received 300 million yen (£1.2 million) from Sagawa Kyubin. The prosecutors were looking to charge Kaneko with violating the Political Fund Control Law – if they succeed, he will be the first politician indicted under the law since 1954. The feeling among those in the know, however, was that Kaneko was being set up as the political fallguy.

21

Asil Nadir –
'An Island, entire of itself'

In early May 1993 a private jet took off from an airfield in Hertfordshire. On board was a former investors' darling – a man who had taken a penny share company that boxed fruit in Cyprus and turned it into a conglomerate which spanned the world. At the height of its success, the business was valued in billions of pounds, making him one of Britain's richest men. His name was Asil Nadir.

This was no ordinary flight, and not least because the details of the aircraft's destination had been hidden from prying officialdom. Nadir – whose personal fortune had once been estimated at £400 million – was jumping bail set at £3.5 million, four months before he was due to appear at the Old Bailey in London on thirteen charges of theft and false accounting; he was also being sued in the civil courts by the administrators for his collapsed Polly Peck business empire for £371 million. And while, in Britain, he no longer commanded the respect he once had, that was far from the case in his homeland – Turkish-occupied northern Cyprus – where the plane eventually touched down. Here Nadir's wealth was largely intact; here, among much else, he owned newspapers, hotels, three homes, orchards and packing companies. In all, he was said to employ locally around 9,000 people, and to be responsible for four-fifths of the Turkish sector's economy. Turkish Cyprus is the only country in which his Polly Peck companies continue to operate, and Asil Nadir is a hero in his homeland.

Though Nadir left Britain suddenly on a Tuesday, on the previous Friday he had sent his maid to pay the newspaper bill. On Monday he had checked into West End Central police station as a condition of his bail, and he had last been seen by the caretaker at his Eaton Square flat that evening. According to neighbours there, he had recently been living in the place as a virtual recluse, though with a secretary and the domestic staff coming in daily; it was also a condition of his bail that he slept there. Nadir's flight left his younger son, Serhan, aged seventeen, to face the publicity from the exclusive grounds of Britain's premier public school, Eton College, where he was studying for his A levels – a spokesman for the school confirmed that Serhan was still there.

When Nadir's plane touched down he was met by his sister Bilge – for all the world as if he had arrived on a holiday charter – and was driven to one of his homes. In an interview with a local paper, which he owns, he said that he had 'come back to my people', adding that 'Of course, there are many things I would say about what happened in the past three years in Britain.' Indeed, over the next three years he did say many things about his failed businesses, most notably, that bringing about the fall of his empire had all been a plot by Greek interests which wanted to see the Turkish-Cypriot republic fail. (In July 1974, after a coup in Cyprus staged by supporters of the military junta then ruling Greece had forced the President, Archbishop Makarios, to flee, Turkish troops invaded the island, eventually occupying the northern part, about one-third of the total. Repeated UN resolutions calling for the withdrawal of all foreign troops have consistently failed, and Cyprus remains partitioned, the north being effectively a province of Turkey, and going by the name, unofficial so far as the UN is concerned, of the 'Turkish Republic of Northern Cyprus'.) Nadir had always been a strong supporter of Turkish-Cypriot independence, for although the republic has a government, a parliament and an airline, it is, in effect, a colony of Turkey. In order to fly there, ordinary travellers have to stop in the Turkish city of Istanbul, and without aid from Turkey, the economy of Northern Cyprus would collapse. After the intervention of 1974 Nadir was asked by the Turkish government to help revive the economy of the north, and this he did, campaigning along the way for formal recognition of the republic, and investing millions of pounds of his own money there. In return, the Turkish Cypriots loyally protected his assets from the British courts – and, of course, since few countries recognize the republic, and Britain is not among those that do, there is no extradition treaty. So the British High Commissioner in Nicosia, the capital of Cyprus which *is* recognized, had to cross the UN-patrolled 'Green Line' between Greek and Turkish territory in order to meet the Turkish-Cypriot leader, Rauf Denktash, and formally ask for Nadir's return to Britain. Denktash, a London-trained lawyer, replied that it would be 'legally impossible' to 'respond positively' to the request; 'Even if there were an extradition treaty between Northern Cyprus and Britain we would not be able to hand him over. The matter must be settled in court.' The view from London was that if Nadir failed to return to stand trial he would be in breach of the most expensive bail conditions in British legal history, and that this, therefore, was likely to induce him to come back and face the charges. But although he has always claimed – like Harry Houdini – that he would come back when the time was right, so far he has not appeared.

Asil Nadir, it almost goes without saying, had come quite a long way in his business career. He had started modestly enough, selling newspapers on the streets of Famagusta (now Ammókhostos in Northern Cyprus), but from an early age he had devoted his life to getting rich. With the rise in Polly Peck's fortunes, Nadir tried to become an English country gentleman – he was never really accepted by the members of the society he sought to join, however. He bought a stately home, Burley on the Hill in Leicestershire, for £7 million; however, investigators swiftly discovered that the house had been on credit. His company's offices were in prestigious Berkeley Square, but for all the trappings of wealth and success, many in the City of London never really trusted him. There always seemed to be some question mark over the incredible profits he was apparently able to make, and since a great many of his business interests lay behind a curtain in Turkish Cyprus, no one was every really quite sure what he was up to. Over the years Asil Nadir came to resent this lack of recognition for his business achievements, and in the end would blame an undermining of confidence in him and his companies for the eventual collapse.

Nadir's business background in Britain was in the rag trade. He was first noticed in the City through his chairmanship of a company called Wearwell, which had been started by his father in the early 1960s. He took it to the stock market in 1973, and branched out into the cash-and-carry business. Nadir based that early success, which twice won him the Queen's Award for Export Achievement, on his ability to exploit markets that others had ignored, exporting to countries like Iraq and Libya, but always being quick enough to get out when those markets became unstable. As he began to expand he moved away from textiles, which he understood, into new businesses, about which he knew nothing but in which he felt there were markets to exploit. His group's rapid expansion began with television assembly in Turkey; he then spent £537 million buying Del Monte's fresh fruit business (not to be confused with the canned fruit company of the same name). In the 1980s, however, Nadir began to make the mistakes that many entrepreneurs did – he began to think that anything he did could be turned to gold. For instance, he paid over the odds for fruit distribution businesses in Europe, which he acquired as a means of increasing sales of his company's output in Turkey and Cyprus. Another notable failure was the Russell Hobbs Tower electrical appliance business which he bought from TI Group. Polly Peck sank £60 million into the business, yet there was never any benefit to the rest of Nadir's electronic interests, and it never made a profit under the Polly Peck banner. Taking a generous view of the outstanding assets of Nadir's empire, which included the Sansui electrical goods company, they were probably worth around £840 million in 1993, but not as much as that if they had to be disposed of quickly. That was less than half of the group's outstanding debts.

What prompted the collapse of Nadir's empire, apart from the huge borrowing, was a series of events that began in the summer of 1989. A well-known stockbroking house had become suspicious of share transactions being carried out by Jason Davies, a twenty-seven-year-old stockbroker – the firm simply did not believe that Davies was acting alone in his purchases of vast quantities of Polly Peck shares. Payments for the shares were often late in arriving, and the firm's compliance office (the person who has responsibility for making sure that deals are being done according to Stock Exchange rules) was told by Elizabeth Forsyth, Asil Nadir's personal assistant, that Polly Peck funds were behind the purchases. The compliance officer reported this to the Stock Exchange – potentially it was in breach of their regulations – and was told, 'The matter is now with a higher authority.' He heard nothing more until he was visited by Richard Cook, an investigation officer from the Inland Revenue Special Office 2, responsible for cases where large-scale tax evasion, or even fraud, are suspected. Cook said that he was investigating the tax status of the owners of the Swiss-based companies for which Davies had been dealing, and added that he believed that millions of pounds of capital gains tax were due. Cook was then allowed access to the Stock Exchange's database records, which showed all the transactions for the Swiss-based companies. In February 1990, in a separate development, Kroll Associates, the New York corporate investigation firm, began looking at Nadir's affairs – Kroll had been retained by a group of foreign investors. In June Cook had enough evidence to interview Nadir, but when challenged by the *Sunday Times* the latter said he was not aware of any Inland Revenue investigation and forecast record profits for Polly Peck of £240 million for 1990.

The month after the appearance of the *Sunday Times* piece, which had confirmed to a great extent the Inland Revenue's suspicions, and detailed its interest in Nadir and his companies, a former senior Polly Peck executive, Tim Wood, walked into the Serious Fraud Office in London's Elm Street to say that when he had left at the beginning of the year he had been growing increasingly worried about the activities of Nadir. It was an open secret that he was looking to break up the conglomerate that he had created. Analysts were talking gleefully of a fine break-up value of 680–850p. a share, well above the current trading value. On Sunday, 12 August 1990, the same day on which the Inland Revenue's investigation became a matter of public record, Nadir announced to bemused fellow directors at a specially convened board meeting that he would be buying out the company. Briefly the share price of Polly Peck soared to 417p. It was not to last, however. By the end of the week Nadir had confirmed what most serious analysts had already assumed: there would be no buyout. Institutions desperately tried to offload millions of shares, and within minutes Polly Peck's share value had slumped by 78p. to 324p. The final straw came when the Serious Fraud Office raided the premises of South Audley Management (SAM), a company run by Elizabeth Forsyth with the sole purpose of looking after Nadir's personal finances, and which was apparently linked to a number of the offshore companies that had been dealing heavily in Polly Peck shares. Nadir and his family had been behind the surges in the price of Polly Peck shares. The stock market heard of the raid the following day, and in frantic selling Polly Peck shares halved in value to 108p. before dealing was suspended.

Former associates of Nadir's are in no doubt about what brought about Polly Peck's collapse: 'This was not created by rumour and sensationalism in the press,' the *Sunday Times* was told, by one of them, as it reported in an article published on 28 October 1990, 'but by him making a bid for the company. When he made the bid he might have thought that he could raise the £1.5 billion it would have cost to take out shareholders. But he also needed to pay off all the creditors and bondholders as well. That totalled at least another £1.5

billion and the interest on that would have been £600 million a year. Nobody would ever have lent him that sort of money.'

Asil Nadir stepped down as Chairman of Polly Peck in mid-October 1990. At one time, the former boss of the fruit, electronic and manufacturing conglomerate faced sixty fraud charges involving more than £150 million, putting him into the record books as one of the largest alleged fraudsters in British criminal history. By the time he jumped bail the indictment had been slimmed down to just thirteen allegations of theft involving more than £30 million, spanning the period from August 1987 to August 1990. Lawyers have repeatedly said that a trial in Nadir's absence is inconceivable. Without a doubt, Nadir is a charismatic man who inspires tremendous loyalty in people who knew him, and especially those who worked or work for him. In his home state, he is virtually worshipped, and he could probably become Prime Minister of the 'Republic of Northern Cyprus' if he so wished. Ayesha Nadir, his ex-wife, has twice married and divorced him, but remains totally loyal to the man she first met in Istanbul when she was sixteen and he was an economics student.

Some of Nadir's close business colleagues have also been loyal, as have some of his political contacts too – and a number have paid a heavy price. Asil Nadir had at one time been a generous contributor of funds to the Conservative Party. Almost because of that, the Conservative Government wanted, and still wants, the public to appreciate that everything will be done to bring him to trial. However, links to Nadir cost one minister his job. Back in 1991, Michael Mates, MP, then the Northern Ireland Minister, was approached by Christopher Morgan, a public-relations consultant whose firm, Morgan Rogerson, represented Nadir, after the businessman had been charged with theft and false accounting. Mates became convinced that Nadir was being pursued unfairly, and wrote to the Attorney-General, Sir Nicholas Lyell, to raise his concerns. The letter closely resembled a draft which had been drawn up for Nadir. In 1993 Mates wrote again to Lyell, saying, 'My concerns about the injustice of this case continue to grow.' The letter was actually dated 17 May 1993 – six weeks before Nadir jumped bail. Some time after the letter was sent, but before Nadir skipped the country, the latter's trustees in bankruptcy (the court-appointed officials who are responsible for getting as much back for creditors as possible) raided his London home and took the Swiss watch off his wrist, on the grounds that it was a valuable item which could be sold to raise money towards his debts. Michael Mates heard about this and, thinking it a childish and unnecessary humiliation, send Nadir a watch on which he had had inscribed 'Don't let the buggers get you down!' It was the disclosure of this act which set in motion the events which finally led to Mates's resignation. At first he rode the storm. He stayed silent. The Prime Minister, John Major, said that while Mates had made a misjudgement, it was not a hanging offence, and added: 'I am assured by Mr Mates that he had had no financial involvement with Mr Nadir, nor with any of his companies or his advisers, either before he became a minister or since.' Though there were calls from the back benches for Mates to resign, Major, rather in the style of the chairman of a football club saying that the team's manager has his full support, continued to back his minister. But then came the fatal blow. It seemed that Mates had accepted the loan of car for his estranged wife from one of Asil Nadir's PR advisers, who was also one of the MP's constituents, Mark Rogerson. This, taken with the watch incident, was too much. Michael Mates finally bowed to the pressure to spare the Government further embarrassment, although in his resignation letter to the Prime Minister he wrote, 'In retrospect, I rather wish I had sent the watch with its now famous message to you.'

The Tory Party itself was not to be let off so easily, however, and questions were asked, and continued to be asked, about £400,000 in donations which had been sent by Nadir from an account in Jersey – through which it was known stolen money was also channelled. There were constant calls for the money to be repaid. Meanwhile, Nadir's most loyal employee, Elizabeth Forsyth, for thirty years an active Conservative Party member, and the former Chairman of South Audley Management, had since the collapse of her boss's empire been living in Turkish Cyprus as one of his guests. The fifty-nine-year-old grandmother was paid £70,000 a year to manage Nadir's private tax affairs. Before the crash she had had two houses – one in Chelsea, and one in Grantham in Lincolnshire. When the raid on SAM occurred she was in Switzerland on a skiing holiday, but she returned in January of 1991 to be questioned by the Serious Fraud Office. Her income had gone, however, and both her houses had been repossessed, and Nadir therefore suggested that she go to Cyprus – he, of course, later joined her there after jumping bail. There has never been any suggestion of an affair between the two, although, again, there is great affection between Forsyth and her former boss. Nadir had wanted her to stay in Cyprus, saying when she decided to return to face the music in September 1994: 'I love Elizabeth and it's her decision. But I fear in order to gain more time for themselves, the SFO might find some charge.' But Forsyth had been in Cyprus for 956 days by then. She missed her daughter and granddaughter, she was bored, and she wanted to return. As she said: 'It would be impossible to stay out there. I want to get my own life back on track. There is no way they can charge me: they have no evidence because I have done nothing wrong.' Four years to the day after the SFO raid on her offices she presented herself at Holborn police station in Central London and gave herself up.

Elizabeth Forsyth was wrong, however, and she was duly charged. At the end of April 1995 she was sentenced to five years in prison for handling £400,000 of stolen money. Her eighty-nine-year-old mother was in court to hear her sentenced, and there were cries of anguish from her supporters as she was gaoled. Her lawyer said that she had been made a scapegoat, but the court had heard how she had 'cleaned' cash stolen from Polly Peck by feeding it from a Swiss bank to London, although she did not herself profit from the fraud. The judge told her: 'The sum of £400,000 may not have been regarded in the circles you were working in as particularly large, but to most people it represents a substantial amount. Those who deal dishonestly with such sums must expect to also deal with corresponding punishment.' Forsyth was said to be devastated by the verdict. As for Nadir, he had been furious when she was charged because if the case against her had failed, he had been planning to return to Britain to sue the Serious Fraud Office. Now, almost certainly convinced he will not get a fair trial, he is stuck in Northern Cyprus, unable to pursue the globetrotting he so loves. After the verdict he said: 'It is a most unfair sentence. She should never have been tried because Mrs Forsyth was innocent. She went to Britain voluntarily with a view to having this whole thing cleared up.' He had also offered to give evidence in her behalf via a video link from Northern Cyprus.

Throughout her trial, Elizabeth Forsyth was composed, chatty, and beautifully made-up, giving the impression of being the very epitome of middle-class respectability. Nothing in her character seemed to offer any hint that she would find herself behind bars. The daughter of an accountant, she had been educated privately before training as an opera singer. But after working for a time as a secretary she 'fell into banking', as she said. Twice divorced, there had been only one past indication that Mrs Forsyth might not have been the pillar of respectability that she seemed. In 1987 her second husband, Hamish Forsyth, a City financier, had been gaoled for eighteen months for swindling elderly relatives out of £23,000. In court, he said that he had done it to finance his wife's £1,500 a week spending sprees, and his barrister told the Old Bailey that she 'spent money like water'. Forsyth had met Asil Nadir in 1984, while she had been working for Citibank. At the time she specialized in schemes to limit the tax liability of foreign nationals living in Britain; Nadir had been so impressed by her that he had asked her to take charge of his personal tax affairs. Forsyth's barrister, Geoffrey Robertson, QC, said during the trial that 'she has lost everything she has worked for in life.' She is, however, thought to have returned to England as a 'stalking horse' in order to test the Crown's case against her former boss;

indeed, she had told friends she believed the charges would be dropped, as they had been in the case of another Polly Peck employee.

Despite her sentence Elizabeth Forsyth said she retained her faith in British justice. On 30 January it was vindicated when three High Court judges freed her after ten months in prison pending a full appeal. Lord Justice Beldam said that her five-year sentence had been 'disproportionate' for the offence. On 17 March the same judges cleared her completely.

In ruling that her conviction was unsafe Lord Justice Beldam said the trial judge, Mr Justice Tucker, had misdirected the jury on two 'crucial' issues: whether Miss Forsyth knew or believed that the money she was handling was stolen; and why a stockbroker, Jason Davies, had not been called as a witness. Lord Justice Beldam said Miss Forsyth's position was that she completely trusted Mr Nadir and, having regard to his immense wealth and enormous income, it did not occur to her to question this particular transaction. The judge's direction could have led the jury to find her guilty without finding that she actually believed the money was stolen. The trial judge's misdirection also made it almost certain that the jury would decide that the defence had not called Mr Davies from choice – because they knew his evidence would not support Miss Forsyth, said Lord Justice Beldam.

Outside the High Court Miss Forsyth said: 'I have never lost my faith in British justice. Today's decision will, I hope, restore the faith of others who have fled from it and encourage them to return to face trial or judicial inquiry to clear their names.' When asked if she was still in touch with her former employer, Asil Nadir, she said that she was and that she 'had always believed in his integrity'. Would he return to the UK to face the charges against him? Miss Forsyth said: 'That's a question you should ask him.'

22

The Case of New Era Philanthropy – Or, just how easy it is to get the rich to part with their money when you're talking millions

It is a strange name – but then, New Era Philanthropy was a strange organization. The idea behind it was a simple one. New Era was a charity, and it operated by telling its prospective clients that many rich and famous philanthropists did not have time to figure out where their charitable donations should be made. So New Era did it for them. Moreover, the charity offered to a variety of organizations – churches, museums, universities and other charities – the opportunity to benefit themselves by helping to benefit others. This was the lure – and it was an age-old one, at that: give us your money today, and in six months' time we will double it. In operation, this was a classic Ponzi, or pyramid-selling scheme, in which victims are enticed with promises of huge returns and paid off using other victims' money. Of course, in order for the lure to work there have to be successful examples. The story of the University of Pennsylvania is typical. Scott Lederman is the university's treasurer, it is in the nature of his job to be sceptical, even suspicious, of everyone. As he was when a charity based in Radnor, Pennsylvania, called New Era, first approached him

The Case of New Era Philanthropy 289

with the idea that he could double any contribution he cared to make within six months, provided he put his money into an account operated by New Era. But despite his scepticism, he and other officials at the University of Pennsylvania were tempted. Lederman says that the charity intimated that it was backed by wealthy people who did not have the time themselves to find worthy causes for their money, and therefore relied on New Era to do it for them. Being cautious, the University tried to check out the story – sure enough, two Philadelphia museums told Lederman that they had received double their money back from New Era. So in 1993 he decided to take a chance and signed a cheque for $600,000. He admitted that he 'sweated a lot', but he felt vindicated when New Era came through. As a result, the University invested more money with the charity.

Early in May 1995, however, the scheme began to unravel. America's most important regulatory federal agencies, the Securities and Exchange Commission, began investigating whether or not New Era had broken any federal securities laws. Auditors and accountants began to tell important local clients to be wary. On 12 May, Prudential Securities Inc. sued New Era and its chief executive for $44.9 million – money the securities company claimed the charity had borrowed and failed to repay. The collateral for the loan was the account into which the University of Pennsylvania and other clients had turned over their money in the expectation of doubling it; furthermore, Prudential also maintained that New Era had been unable to explain where the funds in that account had gone. Prudential Securities therefore claimed title to a New Era brokerage account containing US Treasury bills, in lieu of the funds which the company said New Era owed it. Suddenly the suspicion began to grow that the anonymous philanthropists didn't exist. Consequently, New Era hired a public-relations man in an attempt to quell the rumours, after the charity's founder and chief executive, John G. Bennett Jr, had said, 'Financially, everything is in order in this organization.' The PR man told the press that he would set up interviews with anonymous donors over a weekend, but on the Saturday he announced that he had been unable to arrange any such meetings, and as a result was severing all ties with New Era. The writing was on the wall.

In the second week of May, New Era filed for protection under US bankruptcy law, Chapter 11, which allows a company to declare itself bankrupt while at the same time continuing its reparations in order to give it breathing space and protection from creditors for a specified period of time whilst attempts are made to sort out the mess. In the case of New Era, though, the mess was a big one. The charity claimed assets worth $80 million and liabilities totalling $551 million. Shortly afterwards the FBI swooped to search Bennett's $600,000 home, the agents taking away with them six boxes of undisclosed papers. Earlier in the day, the Securities and Exchange Commission had filed a lawsuit against Bennett alleging that he had diverted $4.2 million of New Era funds for his own private use. In the US Bankruptcy Court, Judge Bruce Fox received notice of a list of creditors who had placed millions of dollars with New Era Philanthropy. The victims included some of America's richest givers: the philanthropist Laurance Rockefeller was out $11.3 million; the entrepreneur Jim Herr, $10.8 million; the insurance magnate Hugh MacLellan, $9.9 million; and William Simon, a former US Treasury Secretary, $6.5 million. Other victims included the global investor John Templeton, and a former Goldman Sachs partner, John Whitehead; the latter lost more than $2 million. Apart from rich individuals, there were groups of victims across the United States, among them other charities, as well as museums, universities and churches. While many expressed regret at having bought into the scheme, others began to come forward saying that though they had been beneficiaries, and had indeed doubled their money as New Era had promised, they felt that morally they should not profit from such a scheme, and offered to pay their profits back. Still more said that though they too had doubled their money, they had used their returns for buildings or other capital outlay, or had dispensed it in charitable donations; obviously, in these cases giving the money back was not an option.

As in most such frauds, what was created was a very large mess, which, even now, it will take years to sort out. Bennett at least made a start when, through lawyers acting for what was left of New Era, he admitted that there were no anonymous donors. The court released two lists, one naming the 20 charities and 20 individuals who had lost the most money, the other detailing all 315 creditors. On the shorter list, losses for the charities were estimated at $136.9 million, whilst the individuals, it was thought, had lost a total of $136.2 million. Top of the individual creditors list was the Reverend Glenn Blossom of the Chelten Baptist Church in Dresher, who was out $27.5 million. The top creditor amongst the charities was the Lancaster Bible College, at $16.9 million.

In the course of its legal action, the Securities and Exchange Commission said that New Era had run 'a massive fraudulent scheme'. The state government of Pennsylvania won a court order freezing all of New Era's assets in that state, while the Museum of American Jewish History, based in Philadelphia, which claimed to have lost $100,000, also took legal action. In addition, the foundation also faced scrutiny by the US Attorney, the FBI, and the Internal Revenue Service. The problem facing all these claimants, however, is to find out where all the money went. In the first four months of 1995 alone New Era, which also had offices in London and Hong Kong, took in $100 million in donations. Of course, the charity's founder, John Bennett, had bought his house in Philadelphia, reportedly with $600,000 in cash, and investigators are looking into allegations that the heads of other charitable organizations were paid commissions to bring in investors – these sums, however, are likely to be only a very small proportion of the total liabilities of $551 million. At least a hundred religious bodies and some two hundred other groups and individuals invested money with New Era. Officials from the evangelical relief organization, World Vision, and from the InterVarsity Christian Fellowship, said that their organizations had initially made substantial investments in New Era, and had received the promised returns. Encouraged by their success, both had invested another

$1 million or more. Neither World Vision nor the InterVarsity Christian Fellowship knows whether it will ever see any of that money again. William McConnell shed some light on just why it was that the charities seemed to get sucked in, when he said of New Era's founder: 'He was subtly persuasive ... his reputation preceded him. Everyone we consulted with vouched for the guy as being deeply religious and genuinely kindhearted. A family man.' The latter part of the statement is certainly true, for Bennett had several of his family members working for New Era. These included his wife, Joyce; Dave Edwards, the fiancé of his daughter Keri; another daughter, Kristin; and Mark Staples, believed to be Kristin's boyfriend. Other close associates were Bill Bennington, Richard Ohman and Mary Sinclair, all of whom served on the board of directors of New Era. Ohman was the president of Multi Media Communications Inc., one of the two companies to which, according to the Securities and Exchange Commission, Bennett funnelled New Era money. Both Bennington and Ohman acted as consultants to the charity.

Accountants investigating New Era are surprised at the poor level of accounting for an organization dealing in hundreds of millions of dollars. Much of the record-keeping was done using personal finance software on a personal computer. George L. Miller, an accountant with Miller Tate in Philadelphia, gave it as his view that, 'New Era grew too quickly and Bennett simply had difficulty keeping up with his promises.' Amongst those organizations which have had to pay dearly for Bennett's learning curve, the Fuller Theological Seminary in Pasadena stands to lose $1 million, a deposit it made in April, only a few weeks before the scandal broke. However, an anonymous donor has said that if the seminary cannot get the money back he will cover the loss in full. Meanwhile, some of the other creditors also may not end up as out of pocket as was at first thought. Biola University, based in La Miranda, is not alone in deciding that the gains it made as a result of giving money to New Era were probably achieved at the expense of some other charities. So, although the university

The Case of New Era Philanthropy   293

deposited $500,000 in October 1994 and received $1 million in return in May, it has decided to return the money to benefit other creditors. Its spokesman, Chi-Chung Keung, said that Biola had 'A moral obligation to other organizations that may have lost funds.' He went on to explain that university finance officers had insisted before depositing their money that New Era keep it in a separate account – 'As a result no Biola donations were at risk and not a penny was lost.'

Biola was, however, something of an exception among investors, most of whom simply left the charity to do as it wished with their funds. In the main, though, it is hard to believe that so many sophisticated people failed to scrutinize New Era more carefully before giving it their money. John Craig, treasurer of the charity the Commonwealth Fund, runs a session on wise investing at the Council on Foundations. The key to New Era's appeal, he suspects, was that investors 'thought these anonymous donors would step up, people who didn't know how to give away their money and relied on Bennett for guidance.'

Bennett's background had not singled him out for the challenge of running a multi-million-dollar charity. He had held several posts as a substance abuse counsellor, including a stint in the early 1970s as assistant administrator in charge of a suburban county's addiction programmes, and he had also served as a consultant to the National Institute of Drug Abuse. In the 1980s he became head of a programme called Bell Institutes, which trained non-profit-making organizations in management. In 1993 he and his family moved to Philadelphia's well-to-do suburb, Devon, paying $620,000 in cash for their new home – he had sold the house they had been living in for fifteen years before that, in Merion Station, for $211,000. Neighbours there remember him as a good Christian: 'I felt you could trust him with anything,' said one. 'He has a way of making you feel like you have known him for ever. Jack's a real charmer.'

Bennett founded New Era in 1989, and built it into a charity which donated more than $100 million in 1993, according to forms filed with the Internal Revenue Service. Nearly 1,100 gifts, ranging in value from $10 to $2.1 million, were awarded to a varied group of 840 organizations. Grant recipients included Billy Graham's Evangelistic Association, the Boy Scouts of America, Planned Parenthood, and Jews for Jesus. Pat Robertson's Christian Broadcasting Network is listed as having received $100,000 – though a CBN spokesman, Gene Kapp, said the network's records showed that it never received a penny from Bennett's organization. When CBN had been approached to invest in New Era, it had declined: 'I guess you could say we don't make investments ... that fall into the it-seems-to-be-too-good-to-be-true category,' said Kapp. And the Prison Fellowship, run by the former Watergate felon, Charles Colson, turned down an offer from New Era to participate in its regular matching fund programme because the money to be matched had to be placed in an escrow account under New Era's control.

It is clear, therefore, that not everyone suffered at Bennett's hands, and some even profited. Moreover, Bob Smucker of Independent Sector, America's major association of charitable groups, says the New Era scandal will not be as damaging to charities as it might at first appear: 'People generally give to charities they know. They are going to continue to give. It's not like the charities – who may have made a mistake in putting their money in New Era – absconded with the funds.' But the board members of the various charities that approved investments in New Era may face legal action from donors to those charities. That, however, is unlikely to happen until a better assessment of the state of New Era's finances can be made, and some idea of how much, if anything, creditors can expect to receive back is forthcoming. Through the uncertainty two facts emerge with striking clarity – it is going to take a long time to sort the New Era mess out; and the only beneficiaries are going to be the lawyers and accountants who will be paid to do that sorting.

In November 1996 Prudential Securities agreed to pay out $18 million to settle claims against it as New Era's broker. The scale of the deal was such that the charities that lost money when New Era went under would recoup around 85 per cent of their potential losses. More than six hundred religious groups, colleges, museums and philanthropists had claimed major losses when New Era went under in 1995. There were reports that the charities lost the opportunity to make up to $500 million on their investments, making the New Era collapse the largest bankruptcy in the US history for a non-profitmaking organization.

A preliminary hearing was held in October 1996 and John G. Bennett Jr. was charged with 82 counts of fraud and money laundering before a federal grand jury in Philadelphia. He pleaded not guilty. The authorities are suggesting he may claim insanity. According to Richard Goldberg, a federal attorney prosecuting the case, the government believes Bennett hatched the plan in 1989 after he was caught floating bad cheques between several bank accounts. The indictment alleges that Bennett used the first contributions to pay off his debts – yet the court documents point out that he took a relatively small percentage for himself: $3.5 million, about 1 per cent of the $354 million total he collected through New Era.

Observers say that complicates things. 'He was the nicest man. Not a flashy figure, very humble,' said the Rev. Gordon Adams, head of the Vision Foundation and a member of the Christian Businessmen's Committee, which together claims a loss of more than $500,000.

'He was very believable and very well connected,' Adams recalled. 'If you went to his office, you could see a picture of him with Billy Graham, who called him a "friend in the crusade".'

When New Era went bankrupt, Bennett sent groups a videotaped apology. The groups said he explained, with tears in his eyes, how he never meant to hurt anyone. The charitable organizations and church groups say the video made them wonder why such a man would coldly scam thousands of charities and non-profit organizations, as prosecutors contend.

23

Daiwa – Not noticing an elephant in the living room?

The Japanese bank, Daiwa, is one of the world's leading financial institutions. Based in Osaka, it ranks nineteenth in the global league table. It is Japan's tenth largest bank. The group's total assets are a staggering £125 billion, so that losing some £700 million ($1.1 billion), less than 1 per cent of available funds, is not as dire a disaster as it might be for smaller banks. Yet for one trader in New York to run up those kind of losses in 30,000 unauthorized deals over an eleven-year period, without anyone knowing what was going on, is, as one Wall Street insider put it, 'Like not noticing there is an elephant in the living room.'

Toshihide Iguchi, a native of Kobe, near Osaka, came to the United States in the early 1970s and studied psychology at Southeast Missouri State University; faculty staff members say that he was shy and courteous. He worked as a car salesman for two years before joining Daiwa in 1976. Highly rated by his superiors, he quickly earned a reputation as a hotshot in the trading of US Government bonds. In 1979 he was given responsibility for both trading and accounting (just the duties Nick Leeson had had with Barings in Singapore). In 1986, ten years after joining the bank, Iguchi was made head of its government-bond trading operations in New York, one of the bank's most prestigious and profitable departments. He was known to colleagues as 'Tosh', an apparently able and affable man, so fond of his job that he never took a holiday – though by 1994 he had become very intolerant at work and had begun to shout at people. Perhaps he needed a break? And perhaps not, for we now know that it was probably the strain caused by eleven years of lying, and by his knowledge of the financial scandal that was about to break, that was playing on Iguchi's temper.

Forty-four years old in 1994, Toshihide Iguchi had two sons but was separated from his wife, and lived in a $400,000 colonial-style house in the wooded commuter settlement of Kinnelon, in New Jersey – about an hour and a half's journey from his office in Manhattan. I have seen his house, an average American home – front lawn, basketball hoop, even a plastic model of a deer. His neighbours say they nodded to him but had never spoken, and that the family members kept themselves to themselves. On the day the story broke no one was answering the phone and cigarette butts were spilled out on the driveway, as if the occupants had departed in a hurry.

What apparently happened in Iguchi's case was that in 1983 he made a loss of $200,000 trading US Treasury bonds. Rather than report it, he tried to cover it up – gambling to win the money back. He kept losing, however, and in eleven years ran up those staggering debts. To conceal his illicit transactions he hid records and forged trading documents to make it appear that the bank still owned securities which he had sold. In a statement, the bank said that Iguchi had 'concealed false transactions, exceeded his trading limits, hid[den] trade-confirmation documents and forged statements that enabled him to sell securities without authorization or detection'. Though there was no evidence that he benefited personally from his deals, if convicted Iguchi faces up to thirty years in prison and a fine of $1 million. The scale of his deception even dwarfs the $300 million of fictitious profits Wall Street firm Kidder Peabody & Company claim their head of bond trading, Joseph Jett, entered into the computers over a two-year period.

Iguchi's illicit trading came to light in a bizarre way, when, in July 1994, he wrote a thirty-page confession to the President of Daiwa, Akira Fujita. In it he detailed his losses, informing the bank that for eleven years he had lost an average of $400,000 every working day. It seems that the strain of keeping all this a secret had finally proved too much for him.

When news of the losses finally became public – three months later – the bank, clearly mortified by the fraud, was apologetic. The New York branch's general manager, Masahiro Tsuda, said: 'We are deeply embarrassed that our internal controls and procedures were not sufficient to prevent this fraudulent action.' When asked how it had been possible to hide such huge losses for so long, Daiwa Bank's senior managing director, Kazuya Sunahara, told a press conference in Osaka: 'We're not exactly sure how he did it, but he might have been using duplicate order forms.'

Whilst the investigations continued, so did the apologies. Fujita and his Chairman, Sumio Abekawa, declared that they would take a pay cut of 30 per cent over the next six months as a sign of penance. Other directors would have their salaries reduced by between 10 and 30 per cent. Top managers would not receive their bonuses. It is a strangely Japanese custom – one which Western businessmen might perhaps take on board – that when a company is suffering, for whatever reason, top management takes a cut in pay. These sacrifices by Daiwa's senior men followed those of the Chairman and President of Japan Airlines, executives of Nippon Steel, the President of Nippon Telegraph and Telephone, the Finance Ministry's top bureaucrat, and even the Finance Minister, Masayoshi Takemura, all of whom had recently voluntarily taken cuts in salary or benefits after some perceived failure or another. Further, Daiwa said that it would write off what amounted to the biggest single trading setback ever suffered by a Japanese financial institution, against its profits for the first half of 1995, and went on to declare that no customers would suffer as a result of Iguchi's activities. So that when Toshihide Iguchi appeared in Manhattan's Federal District Court charged with forgery and falsifying records, an observer might have been forgiven for thinking that, apart from his prosecution, there the matter rested.

That, however, was very far from being the case, and not

least because the regulatory authorities in the United States were deeply upset about what had happened. There were three main reasons for their annoyance. Firstly, they liked to think that the financial sector in America is the best-supervised, most strictly regulated in the world, and the Daiwa scandal was a blow to that image. Secondly, they had actually warned Daiwa in New York on more than one occasion that there was a potential problem, specifically concerning Iguchi's doing both the job of trading and auditing, which meant that potentially he could hide losses. Thirdly, Daiwa's head office had known of Iguchi's alleged crimes months earlier, and had not notified the US authorities then. For all these reasons, officials at the Federal Reserve Bank, the authority in America for regulating foreign banks, were seething. They moved swiftly, too. Only five days after the news broke investigators in the United States expanded their inquiry to determine whether a conspiracy to deceive regulators and investors had been involved. For though it had taken the bank two months to notify US authorities, Daiwa had launched a $500 million issue of its stocks only days after hearing of the huge losses in New York. One US federal agent said: 'Daiwa could face federal prosecution for hiding the losses for so long, and investors could sue for fraud if they lose money as a result of buying the stock offered.' Daiwa shares fell by 7 per cent the day after the Iguchi affair became public.

The spotlight then turned on to the question of who had known what. One official told me that Daiwa had claimed that it simply had not known that it had a statutory duty to inform the US authorities of the losses. The more cynical view, however, was that the bank did not want anything to interfere with the $500 million share issue, a belief shared by Yoshi Tsurumi, Professor of International Business at Baruch College, New York. He appeared on television in Japan, where he claimed that the Japanese Government, through the Ministry of Finance, had been tipped off about Daiwa's losses two months before the news became public. 'Obviously the MoF is claiming it did not know anything, but I am sure Daiwa gave some hint before it issued the stock,' he said. 'It has a cosy, collusive relationship with MoF.' American regulators began investigating this idea too. Daiwa officials claim that it took them seven weeks to wade through thirty boxes of false receipts before they could confirm Iguchi's story and tell the authorities. The Japanese Ministry of Finance, as the local regulatory body, admitted that it had known about the losses a week before its American counterparts; it had, however, used that time to take steps to ensure that the loss, once made public, did not rock Japan's already unsteady financial system – which had been shaken by very high levels of bad debt over recent months.

A few days later, in the middle of the first week of October, the Japanese Finance Minister, Masayoshi Takemura, declared that 'management must take proper responsibility' for what had happened at Daiwa. His meaning was clear, and three days later both the President of the bank, Akira Fujita, and the Chairman, Sumio Abekawa, announced their decisions to resign. One reason behind the Finance Ministry's declaration was that international lenders had become concerned about the Japanese banking system as a whole, and were now demanding a 'Japanese premium' – an extra quarter to three-quarters of a per cent for lending to Japan. As a further exercise in damage control, the Ministry of Finance and the Bank of Japan jointly launched an investigation into Daiwa's systems for managing the sort of crisis thrown up by Iguchi's unauthorized trading.

But whatever their findings, it is clear that there was a culture of complicity. The Minister of Finance – like the American authorities – believes that Daiwa withheld information on the fraud for two months after becoming aware of it. In the process, the bank was able to earn large profits from the sale of stockholdings, at a time when the Tokyo Stock Exchange's Index was 2,000 points higher than it was after the fraud became public knowledge. There were, too, a number of other anomalies surrounding Daiwa's actions, including the share issue. Furthermore, at around this time concerns began to be expressed that perhaps Iguchi had not acted alone. Although he had sold bonds himself to hide the losses, he had entrusted the proceeds of such sales to associates. The regulatory authorities became particularly interested to know whether senior branch officials received reports from Iguchi's assistants on the difference between the real transactions and the fictitious ones. These sentiments were expressed more powerfully a few weeks later when the central character of the drama, Toshihide Iguchi himself appeared again in court. This time he pleaded guilty to charges of fraud, but in entering his plea he made a long statement that contained damning allegations against the bank and its senior management. The statement claimed that Daiwa's management entered into a pact with the trader to hide the losses from the US authorities. According to Iguchi, after he had informed the bank of his disastrous losses on 24 July, a member of the senior management had told him to continue to cover up the deficit. Management, he said, had filed a false report with the regulatory authority, the Federal Reserve, on 31 July which stated that it still held $600 million in US Government securities that Iguchi had in fact sold. Again, at the direction of senior management, he had then sold other securities to cover interest payments, and had continued to falsify the bank's records, all with the management's approval. This deception, he claimed, had continued until September. 'On three occasions I sold securities with the knowledge of the management to pay interest, and I produced two fictitious safekeeping statements, also with the knowledge of senior management,' he said.

The bank's version of events is, not surprisingly, somewhat different. It admits asking Iguchi to continue to make payments, but says that the action was taken to enable customers to continue to be paid. But in any event, it was clear that the bank had obviously been in no hurry to inform the US authorities, as it was required to do under US law. Then, on 3 November – on what was a public holiday in Japan – the management of Daiwa and the Japanese regulators woke up to what was probably their worst nightmare come true – the US regulatory authorities had decided to shut down Daiwa's entire

American operations, and had issued an order to that effect. Not since the Second World War had foreign authorities closed a Japanese bank's operations overseas. In a statement, the US Federal Reserve, the Federal Deposit Insurance Corporation, and the New York State Banking Department, said that the action had been taken 'on the basis of information indicating that Daiwa ... and their officials engaged in a pattern of unsafe and unsound banking practices and violations of law over an extended period of time that are most serious in nature.' The statement went on to dwell on the cover-up of Iguchi's activities in New York during the two-month period after he had informed the President of the bank about his activities. It also mentioned that in 1992, and again in 1993, the bank regulators had been assured by Daiwa that its New York branch had separated its trading and accounting procedures, and that these were no longer in the care of one man, Toshihide Iguchi; indeed, the branch even said as much to the Federal Reserve in writing. In fact, however, nothing had been done. As a side effect of the scandal, the regulatory authorities also recommend that traders take at least one week's annual holiday per year – as Iguchi had singularly failed to do. This is so that whilst a trader is away, his or her job is done by someone else, the view being that any discrepancies would be likely to surface within a week. In all the time that he worked for Daiwa, Iguchi never took more than two consecutive days off. This should have sounded the alarm bells. But again nothing had been done.

The effect of the US regulatory order – in which were included the banking departments (and thus the financial regulators) of the states of California, Illinois, Massachusetts, Florida and Georgia – was to close Daiwa's offices in eleven states by 2 February 1995. At the same time, federal prosecutors in New York released a sweeping criminal indictment listing twenty-four counts against Daiwa Bank, including conspiracy to defraud the Federal Reserve. The bank and a senior manager were accused of directing a $1.1 billion scheme to cover up the New York bond-trading losses. If convicted of criminal charges to defraud the US Federal Reserve, prosecutors said that Daiwa could be fined more than $1 billion. The indictment, filed by US Attorney Mary Jo White, named for the first time Masahiro Tsuda, the manager of Daiwa's New York branch, as a defendant. He was relieved of his duties on 9 October, and subsequently resigned as a director of the bank.

Daiwa described the indictment as 'regrettable and unfortunate', and said that it planned to fight the criminal charges. The bank added: 'We deeply regret the decision to proceed with these charges. The bank was motivated by our desire to investigate thoroughly the unauthorized activities by which it was victimized, to take all necessary action to protect our customers and to act in a way that was not harmful to the international banking system.' Since the discovery of Iguchi's activities, the statement continued, controls and procedures had been tightened up. In future, it said, overseas branches would not trade on their own account, and Daiwa would focus its attention less globally and more upon its core areas of Japan and South-East Asia. As a direct result of the shutdown in America, it would reduce its international staff from 9,600 to 7,000.

Just before Christmas 1995, Masahiro Tsuda appeared in court, charged with conspiracy to defraud the US Federal Reserve by allegedly helping to conceal $1.1 billion in trading losses. The indictment described how the manager had postponed an audit and hidden records at his home, and also alleged that he and other managers had taken steps to conceal losses rather than report them. As a result, Tsuda is also charged with failing to prevent a crime. In his defence, Tsuda's lawyer said that he had followed 'What his employer and the Japanese Ministry of Finance determined was the only appropriate course here: that a thorough investigation of Iguchi's extraordinary trading loss be conducted before a report was filed with US regulators. What happened was a good-faith misunderstanding, not a crime.'

Still more information was to seep out, however. It now appeared that Iguchi had filled the gap his disastrous trading had produced by selling securities held by Daiwa and then forging bank statements to make it appear that the securities were still there. The bank's securities were lodged with Bankers Trust, the US investment bank, which acted as custodian for the securities, and sent regular statements of Daiwa's account, number 053110, addressed to Iguchi. He, however, would hide these, and then forge statements on Bankers Trust headed paper for Daiwa's files. The FBI released the bank statements that revealed the extent of the forgery. The account balance for 31 July 1995 on the authentic Bankers Trust statement came to $3,490,031,902, while that on the forged statement was $4,599,850,902 – a difference of $1,109,819,000.

As is clear from the Barings case, as well as from that of Daiwa, one reason why it was so easy for Iguchi to cover his tracks was that for a time he was in charge of both the bond-trading operations and the settlements departments, which reconciled transactions. After warnings from the Federal Reserve, however, Daiwa did eventually take action before Iguchi's dealings had been revealed. In theory, therefore, management should have been able to detect what had happened – but it did not. As if the failure to spot the looming catastrophe were not bad enough, the Daiwa management's behaviour after they did learn about it was inexplicable. The exact chronology of events was this. The letter from Iguchi, dated 13 July, was sent through the company's internal mail and read by Fujita on 24 July. Head office then dispatched the boss of its international division, Hriroyuki Yamaji, to New York to interview Iguchi. Yamaji found the story to be 'largely true'. As we have seen, however, two days later the bank went ahead with a planned share issue in an affiliated company. The bank might have been expected at least to delay the placement because the losses would have been likely to affect investors' views of the company. But it went ahead, later saying that the decision to issue the shares had been taken at the end of June, and that since it would take time to check Iguchi's story, there was no justification for delay. Even then, the bank did not tell Japanese authorities until mid-September – seven weeks after the share issue and Yamaji's trip to New York. As if all this were not enough, details of attempts to cover up the problem have emerged. According to Iguchi, the bank tried to erase from the computer the letter he had written to the Daiwa President, in which he had revealed the losses. The bank also held secret meetings in hotel rooms to discuss shifting the losses to the Cayman Islands, away from the gaze of the US regulators, and there were, too, other schemes to deceive the authorities by falsifying the books of the branches. All were eventually abandoned, apparently because the size of the scandal made it impossible to hide it.

In January 1996, Daiwa Bank sold its US assets for a meagre $65 million to its larger Japanese rival, Sumitomo Bank. At the same time, the former indicated that it would plea bargain with the federal authorities over the twenty-four fraud charges filed against it. The bank wanted to bring the case to a settlement by the end of March, when it was to close its books for the 1995 financial year. Daiwa wanted to put the whole affair behind it, for there was no doubt that it had seriously shaken its standing in the world; in addition, if the scandal were to drag on, then it would also hold up talks with Sumitomo over a planned merger. At the end of February, therefore, Daiwa agreed to plead guilty to sixteen criminal charges stemming from the Iguchi cover-up. The Japanese bank also agreed to pay a fine of $340 million – the largest ever levied against a financial institution in the United States. As the US Attorney-General, Janet Reno, said, 'This record fine demonstrates that we take the rules seriously.' The financial markets, however, thought differently, and Daiwa's share price increased by 18 yen to 710 yen on the Tokyo Stock Exchange following the announcement of the agreement. Since it halted a potentially long and costly trial in which, if convicted, Daiwa faced a $1.3 billion fine, the deal with the US courts was seen as a good one. The general view was that the smaller than expected fine might also help to keep the bank independent, and thereby scupper a possible merger with Sumitomo.

With the criminal proceedings now behind Daiwa, there were only two matters outstanding. Eventually, Masahiro Tsuda agreed to plead guilty to one count of conspiracy to defraud the Federal Reserve Board, but stuck to his story that he had been following orders from his supervisors and from the Japanese Ministry of Finance in concealing the losses the bank had sustained. Tsuda, who had worked for Daiwa for thirty years, faces a maximum five years in prison and a fine when he is sentenced. The man who started the scandal with one bad deal all those years ago, Toshihide Iguchi, has also negotiated a plea. He was sentenced in December 1996.

Iguchi didn't deny his role in developing one of the biggest trading losses on record – confessing to hundreds of unauthorised trades which took place over more than a decade. He was sentenced to four years in prison.

Once there he lost no time in putting his account of events down on paper. His book, *The Confession*, was published in January 1997. In the book he claims that the losses would have come to light much earlier but for carelessness by investigators from the Japanese Finance Ministry and the US Federal Reserve. He also accuses his former employers, Daiwa, of trying to cover up the losses and other regulatory transgressions in its New York office. He describes how the New York office was filled with cardboard boxes back in 1992 to fool Fed officials into thinking it was a storeroom not a trading room. The Fed examination which was supposed to take two days lasted a meagre 15 minutes and the examiners didn't spot the ruse.

The Federal Reserve later found out it failed to discover Iguchi's mounting losses. When Daiwa reported to Japan's Ministry of Finance that it was having problems with the Fed, the ministry sent officials on what was supposed to be a weeklong investigation. Iguchi feared that the game was up. But the officials spent just an hour at Daiwa's offices in mid-town Manhattan chatting with top executives and failed to visit the Wall Street office at all. Instead they went to Las Vegas! The rest, as they say, is now history.

24

Sumitomo Corporation – Copper-bottom investments?

With a 154 offices on 5 continents, the Sumitomo Corporation has assets of about $50 billion. So losing $3 billion would not bring the house down, though it might make the boss a little edgy. In June of 1996 the President of Sumitomo, Tomiichi Akiyama, found out that the head of his copper-trading department in Tokyo had lost nearly $2 billion (a sum later revised upwards) in unauthorized copper trades over a ten-year period. In a statement issued through the firm's New York lawyers, Akiyama said: 'We deeply regret – and are profoundly embarrassed by – these severe violations of our Company's business policies and our long-standing and clear standards of ethical and professional behaviour. Management at all levels of this Company, together with the employees in our trading operations, are completely committed to working with regulatory officials to identify the causes of these extraordinary violations.'

At the centre of the storm was Yasuo Hamanaka, the world's most famous copper trader, and an employee of Sumitomo. Hamanaka was known as 'Mr Five Per Cent' because, together with his team, he was said to control 5 per cent of the world's copper trade; indeed, when rumours began to circulate at his base in Tokyo that he had resigned from Sumitomo, copper prices fell by 25 per cent, such was his influence.

Japan is the world's largest market for copper, taking in 13 per cent of global supply. As the Japanese economy began to recover from the recession of the 1980s, so copper and other metal commodities began to move up in value. The view was that copper would be needed for renewed activity – everything from construction to car production – and that the prices would therefore move up. And they did, with copper being traded at a price 75 per cent above that of twelve months earlier. Early in 1996, however, prices crashed. This prompted an investigation by regulatory authorities in Britain and the United States (most of the world's commodities are traded in New York and London). Sumitomo was co-operating with investigations by the US Commodities Futures Trading Commission and Britain's Securities and Investment Board when Yasuo Hamanaka's misdemeanours were discovered.

Clearly the two regulatory bodies were concerned that someone had been manipulating prices. According to the Sumitomo Corporation, Yasuo Hamanaka had been relieved of his trading duties in May, and 'assigned exclusively to supporting the Company's undertaking to co-operate fully with the pending CFTC and SIB investigation.' During this inquiry, however, a bank statement was unearthed which showed that Sumitomo had been credited with funds from a transaction that the company's accounts department knew nothing about. When this became known, Hamanaka went to his bosses and confessed. He told them that over a ten-year period he had engaged in a series of unauthorized transactions which 'resulted in substantial losses that he intentionally concealed by means of falsifying the books and records of the Sumitomo Corporation.' Further inquiries revealed that in the early stages of his deception, Hamanaka had had help. Someone else knew what was going on, though the company says that the person in question left eight years ago, at which time the losses were still small.

Once again a picture began to emerge of a man with too much power, and who could account for his own trades. Yasuo Hamanaka's reputation amongst copper traders was such that his bosses had not questioned what he was doing. His losses completely overshadowed those of Nick Leeson at Barings and of Daiwa's Toshihide Iguchi, bringing Hamanaka the unenviable accolade of being the world's biggest loser. The Sumitomo Corporation, anxious that their operations in both London and New York should continue unaffected by the scandal, moved quickly to contain the damage. Their New York law firm of Paul, Weiss, Rifkind, Wharton & Garrison was instructed to employ an independent accounting firm whose task was to advise senior management about all aspects of the problem, including the conducting of an exhaustive examination of trading operations and control systems. Sumitomo wanted to make the changes necessary to ensure that such a thing never happened again. 'We are determined that our actions will demonstrate this Company's unwavering commitment to ethical and responsible conduct in the copper markets and in all of our business operations,' Akiyama declared. A part of that will mean continuing to co-operate with the regulatory investigations. The company says that it learnt of Hamanaka's fraud just a week before making it public – and the consequences of not keeping the regulatory authorities informed will be all too clear to them. Daiwa was forced to close its American operations following the losses in New York, and was fined $340 million. Ironically, its entire US operation was sold to the Sumitomo Bank, which itself has a 5 per cent holding in the Sumitomo Corporation.

At the end of February 1997, Tomiichi Akiyama resigned to become a special adviser to the Sumitomo Corporation. Since the copper scandal struck he'd taken up a long-standing promotion and moved from company president to chairman, so that in the light of the $2.6 billion in unauthorized deals by Yasuo Hamanaka, he had even further to fall from grace. The move was seen as a symbolic gesture – the trading equivalent of falling on his sword – and is something that Japanese bosses often do when their companies become scandal-tainted. Two other members of Sumitomo's board of directors also offered to resign, but the company reiterated that its management knew nothing of the deals by former copper trading chief Yasuo Hamanaka that generated the largest losses ever in a financial market.

In a resignation letter sent to the company's New York lawyers, Tomiichi Akiyama said that: "While I knew nothing about Mr Hamanaka's hidden trading, I was the president of the corporation when much of the trading occurred." He said he had considered resigning immediately after the announcement, but remained in office to help deal with the aftermath of the scandal. At a press conference to announce the resignation Sumitomo President, Kenji Miyahara, said that the company's probe of Hamanaka's trading would take several more months, delayed by the limited information available from internal Sumitomo documents alone. He said, for example, that the company learned some facts on Hamanaka's activities for the first time from a *Panorama* documentary programme, the news and current affairs flagship broadcast by the British Broadcasting Corporation in the second week of February. He added that, prodded by the scandal, Sumitomo plans to set up an office of market risk management for all commodities in April. Sumitomo's system of checks and controls is a central part of Hamanaka's legal argument – his lawyers claim that Sumitomo contributed to the losses because of their lax system of controls. Hamanaka himself pleaded guilty in a Tokyo court to charges of fraud and forgery in connection with the losses in the week before his former boss resigned. Since the scandal, Sumitomo has cut back its copper trading activity, although the company says it has no intention of withdrawing from the copper market altogether.

The Sumitomo Corporation is a company with a history even richer than that of Barings Bank. The House of Sumitomo was founded in the sixteenth century by Masatomo Sumitomo; interestingly, he once advertised the firm, now the world's biggest buyer and seller of copper, as the world's largest copper exporter. The merchant family prospered, chiefly by its purchase of the Besshi copper mine on the southern Japanese island of Shikoku, and it became the official copper trader to the Tokugawa shogunate, Japan's ruling family from 1603 to 1868. As Japan opened itself to the West in the mid-1800s, Sumitomo involved itself in copper rolling, steel manufacture and other fields. By the early 1900s the family had risen to become the country's third most powerful financial conglomerate or *zaibatsu*. These politically influential concerns were the backbone of Japan's military-industrial complex during the 1930s and on through the Second World War. Sumitomo was known at the time to be much more centralized than other business clans, with power concentrated in the hands of a single family. In 1937, the head of the family, the sixteenth in line since the company's founding, held 90 per cent of the total shares. After the Japanese defeat in 1945 the Allied powers dismantled the *zaibatsu* and Sumitomo reconstituted itself as a group of affiliated companies. Today, the family no longer exerts the influence it once did, though the remains of the original copper refinery can still be seen, and the glory of the clan's wealth imagined, in the grounds of their mansion in Osaka.

The Sumitomo Corporation is now one of Japan's four leading trading houses. Its business activities span the globe, dealing in a wide range of goods including metals, machinery, chemicals, fuels, food and textiles. In 1995 the company had worldwide sales of more than 16 trillion yen (nearly $150 billion), from its operations in a total of ninety countries.

25

Miscellaneous Mischief

In this chapter I have decided to add a short rogues' gallery of some of the minor players on the stage of financial wrongdoing. These people are drawn largely from the past, and though they may have been notorious in their own time, they are hardly known today. Even so, in their characters, and in the manner in which they got away with what they did, however briefly, they exhibit all the arts of the successful fraudster. Whilst some of the financial scandals I have described in other chapters may have been sophisticated, complex, wide ranging – perhaps even hard to follow through minefields of figures – in these examples the various scams were often simply executed; straightforward theft, for example, features prominently. But each villain has been selected as presenting a cameo of his own criminal art-form, so I make no excuses for their presence.

George Hudson – also known as 'King' Hudson. There was much speculation during the boom years of railway building in Britain. It was not only in Britain, however, that this speculation took place, for it occurred sooner or later in all the countries where railways were built. The railway age certainly altered the way capital was raised, since the projects were just so huge that the capital markets had to be altered in order to respond to them. George Hudson, the York-born railway promoter, seemed to epitomize the railway age. He made his fortune originally as a draper, before turning to the railways; at the height of his fame he controlled a vast network of enterprises. His mansion in Kensington was the haunt of the great and the good. Like Mr Merdle, the swindling financier in Dickens's *Little Dorrit*, it appeared that all he invested in turned to gold. He was MP for his native York, having also been the city's Mayor, and in 1844 he told a House of Commons Committee that his basic aim was the establishment of a controlled monopoly of the railways through amalgamations, leases and purchases. To achieve his goal, and achieve it quickly, he too used the tricks of the trade employed to great effect by many driven entrepreneurs – he manipulated the share prices of the many companies in which he was interested.

The political history of the time gives an idea of just how big the railway business was. In 1845 Parliament passed 225 Railway Bills, and there were a further 270 in the following sessions, providing 4,450 miles of track at a cost of nearly £100 million. And many MPs were not exactly impartial – 157 of them had their names on the registers of new railway companies, while one such company boasted of being able to command 100 votes in the House of Commons when it needed to. Railway mania gripped the country, fuelled by stories of ordinary men and women who had made vast fortunes by investing in the right stocks. Even Anne Brontë invested, though she had been warned off by her sister, Charlotte. When, in 1847, the crash came it was severe, with thousands of investors up and down the country suffering losses. Hudson survived in business for a further two years, but his downfall was sparked by a crisis in the affairs of the Eastern Counties Railway, which fell under suspicion of fraud. The chairman of the investigating committee – a Quaker – added drama to the proceedings when he asked Hudson: 'Didst thou, after the accountant had made up the yearly accounts, alter any of the figures? ... Wilt thou give the committee an answer, yea or nay?' The answer, of course, was 'Yea', though Hudson did not quite put it that way. With his questionable business practices exposed, his fall was inevitable; in 1854 he resigned his chairmanships of several railway companies and retired to the Continent.

At the time of his fall, Hudson controlled 1,450 miles out of the 5,000 miles of railway in Britain. But a part of his ploy to maximize profits had been to make the routes less than direct, and his doom was therefore sealed once a direct line from London to York was established!

In October 1837, one of England's greatest novelists, Charles Dickens, had satirized the railway speculation in an essay for *Bentley's Miscellany*. His main aim in the piece was to mock scientists, whom he thought arrogant, particularly those meeting at the time of writing in York as members of the British Association for the Advancement of Science. In his essay, Dickens attacks both them and railway owners like Hudson by describing a discussion of the latest scientific gadget displayed during a meeting of the Mudfog Association:

> Mr Jobba produced a forcing machine on a novel plan, for bringing joint-stock railway shares prematurely to premium. The instrument was in the form of an elegant gilt weather-glass, of most dazzling appearance, and was worked behind, by strings, after the manner of a pantomime trick, the strings being always pulled by the directors of the company to which the machine belonged. The quicksilver was so ingeniously placed, that when the acting directors held shares in their pockets, figures denoting very small expenses and very large returns appeared upon the glass; but the moment the directors parted with these pieces of paper, the estimate of needful expenditure suddenly increased itself to an immense extent, while the statements of certain profits became reduced in the same proportion. Mr Jobba stated that the machine had been in constant requisition for some months past, and he had never once known it to fail.
>
> A member expressed his opinion that it was extremely neat and pretty. He wished to know whether it was not

liable to accidental derangement? Mr Jobba said that the whole machine was undoubtedly liable to be blown up, but that was the only objection to it.

William George Pullinger. Pullinger's name came to the fore in April 1860, at which time he was chief cashier at the Union Bank of London. He was a tall, imposing man known for never taking a holiday; however, he became notorious for taking something rather more valuable. Only because of his unavoidable absence at a funeral did the dastardly deed come to light: namely, that the bank was suffering a deficiency of £260,000 (a staggering sum by the standards of 1860). When Pullinger returned from doing his solemn duty, he again did his solemn duty and confessed to his crime. He had, he said, been siphoning off money for five years – ever since he had become chief cashier at the bank. He also said that because of disastrous speculation on the Stock Exchange, most of the money had been lost.

The bank passed on to the Stock Exchange the names of the brokers who had acted for Pullinger, and there followed a Stock Exchange inquiry, since it was against the rules for a member to do speculative bargains on behalf of a mere bank clerk. The brokers in question claimed that Pullinger had said that he was acting on behalf of another – a Mr Wessell, who had indeed been a clerk at the Union Bank but who had left after marrying a rich widow, and who, of course, knew nothing of the scam.

Pullinger duly appeared at the Old Bailey, and pleaded guilty. He told the court that he had co-operated fully once his misdemeanour had come to light, and that he and his wife had turned over everything they owned to make good as much of the losses as possible. He blamed his recently deceased broker for the fact that he could not give back more, the broker having lost money on his speculations in the stock market. He then told the judge that if he felt, like the bank, that he could not show mercy, then he, Pullinger, would quite understand. However, when the judge sentenced him to transportation and servitude for twenty years the prisoner, by all contemporary accounts, appeared to be overwhelmed. The following year Pullinger left Chatham on the *Lincelles*, bound for Western Australia to serve his term of transportation. According to official reports he is said to have died en route, but it was generally assumed that, like Robert Maxwell, he had fallen overboard.

Jabez Spencer Balfour, MP. In December 1892 Jabez Spencer Balfour, the MP for Burnley and the man who ran the Liberator Building Society, Britain's biggest at the time, disappeared. His magic vanishing act followed the arrest of two of his associates in a scandal that was to change the way building societies were regulated. Balfour was implicated in a series of frauds which first estimates suggested had cost shareholders and depositors of the Liberator and seven associated companies, all of which collapsed, more than £8 million. He was – like many conmen before and since – an apparent pillar of the community. He had just been re-elected as a Liberal Member of Parliament, and served on the boards of many City companies. He owned an estate in Oxfordshire and had been associated with the building of some of London's most notable landmarks – the Hyde Park Hotel and the Liberal Club, to name but two. In addition, he had strong nonconformist and Temperance Society connections, and the early success of the Liberator owed a great deal not only to his qualities of leadership but also to those connections. The society made loans available not only for homes but also for the building of chapels. He even established an agency amongst nonconformist ministers who, for a small fee, would encourage their flocks to deposit savings with the Liberator.

The pattern of the financial débâcle to come is, by now, an all too familiar one. Founded in 1868, the Liberator's early years were characterized by rapid growth. At first it operated just as any other building society might have done, but in the 1880s Balfour established or bought a number of construction, property development, and surveying businesses. The Liberator became the main source of finance for this expansion. At the time of the building society's collapse nearly all its assets had been advanced to Balfour's own companies with little or no security; indeed, one of his money-making methods might well have been studied in this century by Robert Maxwell. Balfour would obtain an option on an estate, then sell it to one of the four connected companies at an inflated price, with the full purchase money being advanced by the Liberator. Balfour would then pocket the profit.

As was the case with Maxwell, Balfour's business colleagues said that he had a forceful personality and an aggressive style. Deals were done at breakneck speed, and he would hold no truck with people who disagreed with him. Furthermore, a resolution agreed by the board of one of his companies gave him unlimited power to invest wherever he chose. And, in yet another echo of Maxwell, he survived on very little sleep – it was said that he slept for only four hours a night.

The result of the Liberator scandal was the Building Societies Act of 1894, which sought to prevent the sort of abuses perpetrated by Balfour and his like. The 3,000 depositors who lost money as a result of the collapse of the Liberator and its associated companies were compensated over the following two decades, after a relief fund was established. As for Balfour himself, he fled to Argentina, but was extradited in 1895. Sentenced to a total of fourteen years' imprisonment, he became a model inmate at Parkhurst, where he served as both librarian and organist. Released in 1906, he died ten years later.

DISCARDED

JUN 2 2025